Mykhailo Minakov

From Servant to Leader
Chronicles of Ukraine under the Zelensky Presidency, 2019–2024

With a foreword by John Lloyd

UKRAINIAN VOICES

Collected by Andreas Umland

77   Viktoriia Grivina
     Kharkiv—A War City
     A Collection of Essays from 2022–23
     ISBN 978-3-8382-1988-2

78   Hjørdis Clemmensen, Viktoriia Grivina,
     Vasylysa Shchogoleva
     Kharkiv Is a Dream
     Public Art and Activism 2013–2023
     With a foreword by Bohdan Volynskyi
     ISBN 978-3-8382-2005-5

79   Olga Khomenko
     The Faraway Sky of Kyiv
     Ukrainians in the War
     With a foreword by Hiroaki Kuromiya
     ISBN 978-3-8382-2006-2

80   Daria Mattingly, Jonathon Vsetecka (eds.)
     The Holodomor in Global Perspective
     How the Famine in Ukraine Shaped the World
     With a foreword by Anne Applebaum
     ISBN 978-3-8382-1953-0

81   Olga Khomenko
     Ukrainians beyond Borders
     Nine Life Journeys Through the History of Eastern Europe
     With a foreword by Zbigniew Wojnowski
     ISBN 978-3-8382-2007-9

The book series "Ukrainian Voices" publishes English- and German-language monographs, edited volumes, document collections, and anthologies of articles authored and composed by Ukrainian politicians, intellectuals, activists, officials, researchers, and diplomats. The series' aim is to introduce Western and other audiences to Ukrainian explorations, deliberations and interpretations of historic and current, domestic, and international affairs. The purpose of these books is to make non-Ukrainian readers familiar with how some prominent Ukrainians approach, view and assess their country's development and position in the world. The series was founded, and the volumes are collected by Andreas Umland, Dr. phil. (FU Berlin), Ph. D. (Cambridge), Associate Professor of Politics at the Kyiv-Mohyla Academy and an Analyst in the Stockholm Centre for Eastern European Studies at the Swedish Institute of International Affairs.

Mykhailo Minakov

FROM SERVANT TO LEADER
Chronicles of Ukraine under the Zelensky Presidency, 2019–2024

With a foreword by John Lloyd

Bibliografische Information der Deutschen Nationalbibliothek
Die Deutsche Nationalbibliothek verzeichnet diese Publikation in der Deutschen Nationalbibliografie; detaillierte bibliografische Daten sind im Internet über http://dnb.d-nb.de abrufbar.

Bibliographic information published by the Deutsche Nationalbibliothek
The Deutsche Nationalbibliothek lists this publication in the Deutsche Nationalbibliografie; detailed bibliographic data are available on the Internet at http://dnb.d-nb.de.

ISBN (Print): 978-3-8382-2002-4
ISBN (E-Book [PDF]): 978-3-8382-8002-8
© *ibidem*-Verlag, Hannover • Stuttgart 2025

Alle Rechte vorbehalten

Leuschnerstraße 40
30457 Hannover
info@ibidem.eu

Das Werk einschließlich aller seiner Teile ist urheberrechtlich geschützt. Jede Verwertung außerhalb der engen Grenzen des Urheberrechtsgesetzes ist ohne Zustimmung des Verlages unzulässig und strafbar. Dies gilt insbesondere für Vervielfältigungen, Übersetzungen, Mikroverfilmungen und elektronische Speicherformen sowie die Einspeicherung und Verarbeitung in elektronischen Systemen.

All rights reserved. No part of this publication may be reproduced, stored in or introduced into a retrieval system, or transmitted, in any form, or by any means (electronic, mechanical, photocopying, recording or otherwise) without the prior written permission of the publisher. Any person who commits any unauthorized act in relation to this publication may be liable to criminal prosecution and civil claims for damages.

Printed in the EU

Annotation

President Zelensky is not only a showman and politician. He is also a political phenomenon through which history revealed something very important about Ukrainian society. This book is dedicated to Ukraine under the presidency of Volodymyr Zelensky. It consists of columns, originally written for the expert blog *Focus Ukraine* and the *Kennan Cable* publication series of Wilson Centre's Kennan Institute. Put together, these columns constitute a chronicle of a society surviving oligarchy, pandemic, and war with dignity and resilience — in spite of all the challenges of recent and current history.

Contents

Acknowledgments 11

Foreword: The Good Servant. By *John Lloyd* 13

Introduction 19

I. 1. Servant 23
    The start of the presidential electoral campaign in 2019 23
    Debates on war and peace in the presidential elections of
    2019 27
    Results of the first round of Ukraine's presidential
    elections 32
    Expectations from the newly elected President Zelensky 35

I. 2. Winner 41
    Delayed start of Zelensky's presidency 41
    Parliamentary elections and political cleavages in Ukraine
    of the 2019 summer 45
    President Zelensky establishes one-party majority 49

I. 3. Reformer 53
    The first Zelensky's reforms and challenge for checks and
    balances 53
    Zelensky's Achievements after the first six months in power . 57
    Zelensky meets Putin in Paris 64
    Political struggle and media wars in the winter of
    2019–2020 68

II. Master 73
    New Zelensky's administration: arrival of Yermak and
    Shmyhal 73
    Zelensky's version of *perestroika* and the oligarchs 78

Ukraine's politics in the fall of 2020 82
President Zelensky's personnel problem 87
Ukraine's politics in the first half of 2021 90
Zelensky's presidency at the two-year mark 96
Zelensky starts the fight against oligarchs 103
Waiting for the storm? Ukraine's political situation before the autumn of 2021 108
Three decades of Ukraine's independence: outcomes so far 113
The Afghanistan Syndrome and US–Ukraine Relations 118
Growing disenchantment with President Zelensky 124
Expectations from Ukraine's political processes in the beginning of 2022 129
Separatists threaten Ukrainian sovereignty 135

III. Leader 139
The start of the Russian war on Ukraine 139
First attempts of Ukraine-Russia talks 143
Zelensky versus Putin: the personality factor in Russia's war on Ukraine 149
The Kremlin's secessionist plans put Ukrainian statehood at risk 152
The first two months of the big war in Ukraine 156
Ukraine's government tries to balance military and socioeconomic needs 159
Ukraine becomes EU member candidate 165
Ukraine's wartime political struggle continues with a new twist 169
The Russian annexation of Southeastern Ukraine 172
The war changes the Ukrainian oligarchy 176
Violent referendum in occupied territories of Southeastern Ukraine 181

Ukraine in center of the militarist remapping of Europe and Northern Eurasia 185

Further problems for Ukrainian oligarchs 189

Fighting corruption in wartime Ukraine 192

Further steps with Ukraine's EU membership goals in 2023 198

Ukraine's historical moment a year after the start of the war 203

The wartime constitutional process 207

Political struggle in the first half of 2023 212

The paradox of deoligarchization in post-Soviet Ukraine ... 216

Ukraine and the rise of the middle powers in the global interstate system 220

Russian local "elections" in the occupied Ukrainian territories 224

Pros and cons of elections in wartime Ukraine 228

Ukrainian society on the anniversary of twin tragedies 240

The Ukrainian military assistance is finally approved by the US Congress 245

Five years of Zelensky's presidency 248

Ukrainian politics reacts to the US electoral drama 253

Zelensky's six Independence Day speeches as milestones of his presidency 258

Epilogue: The Three Ages of Zelensky's Presidency 265

Key Literature and Sources 271

Acknowledgments

This book is based on the analytical papers written for the expert blog *Focus Ukraine* and the *Kennan Cable* publication series of Wilson Centre's Kennan Institute. I am sincerely grateful to my colleagues F. Joseph Dresen, Sabrina W. Detlef, Marjorie Pannell, William E. Pomeranz, Izabella Tabarovsky, and Jennifer Wistrand for their encouragement, review, and editorial advice.

For our rewarding cooperation, I owe Iliya Kusa, Andrian Prokip, and Matthew Rojansky, my coauthors of several analytical papers published in this book.

I am much indebted to Andreas Umland, a dear colleague and an editor of the ibidem Verlag's series "Ukrainian Voices," for the idea of collecting my papers in a volume and his constant support of many other projects of mine.

Foreword
The Good Servant

John Lloyd

In an essay written while sheltering from Covid in 2020–2021, Russian President Vladimir Putin wrote an essay — *On the Historical Unity of Russians and Ukrainians* — published on July 12, 2021. Much of it sought to prove that Ukraine and Russia had grown together — linguistically, religiously, culturally — throughout the centuries, until, in the 2000s, malign actors, who included radicals and neo-Nazis, encouraged by Western forces which turned the new leadership into "willing hostages," began to tear Ukraine away from Russia, discriminating against the many Russians living in Ukraine, forcing them into a narrow Ukrainian nationalism in which Russian speakers were suspect. Putin wrote, "It would not be an exaggeration to say that the path of forced assimilation, the formation of an ethnically pure Ukrainian state, aggressive towards Russia, is *comparable in its consequences to the use of mass destruction against us*" (my italics).[1]

    This was a huge inflation in the danger the Russian President claimed to see in Ukraine's efforts to deal with him as one sovereign state to another. His description of the threat in such a manner makes it clear, in retrospect, that he posed this as the most extreme danger an attack would bring — and thus raised the need to defend Russia militarily against it. The invasion, when it came a little over eight months from the essay's publication, could thus be framed as a necessary defense against a regime led by Nazis (their leader in the cunning disguise of a Jewish comedian) which had committed itself to a war against Russia which threatened its extinction. The attack against such a foe was his essay 'proved,' a necessary defense. That attack came on February 24th, 2022.

---

[1]   Putin, V. (2021). On the Historical Unity of Russians and Ukrainians. *President of Russia Official Website*, July 12, http://en.kremlin.ru/events/president/news/66181.

Putin had seen the Jewish comedian—Volodymyr Zelensky, President of Ukraine for the past five and a half years—as one he could brush aside, probably kill, in the first days of a strike on Kyiv. He was elected in the largest vote any President of Ukraine had achieved because he was not a creature of the old system: the fact that he was a favorite figure on television—playing, in a series called "Servant of the People," the part of a teacher suddenly elevated into the presidency—also helped. In office, with a new party calling itself by the name of his show, he lived up to the ideal of service by his efforts to reduce both an all-pervasive corruption and the immense power of the billionaire oligarchs. On the day of the attack, several Western ambassadors offered him a swift passage out: he refused at once.

Mikhail Minakov, in this collage of reports and reflections written for the Wilson Centre's Kennan Institute through the years of Zelensky's rule, illuminates with great clarity the passage of the Ukrainian president—nervous novice leader in 2019, weary and burdened in 2024, yet always giving heart to a country trapped in a flesh-grinding war, holding out the promise of freedom in the midst of ruins and death.

Freedom, and with it an attachment to democracy and a strong civil society, plays well to a country which, unlike most of the other former Soviet states (the small Baltic countries, now in the European Union and NATO, the main exception), has resisted the attempts by various leaders to return to autocracy. Minakov makes clear that Zelensky and the group around him—many former colleagues from his TV career—were the bringers of a new form of politics. He also knows it to be a partial new-ness, with corruption, oligarchic pressure and jockeying for power within the governing apparatus and around it still much in evidence.

Former leaders, such as Petro Poroshenko (president, 2014-2019), support the war effort—but contribute to the criticism of Zelensky, which has seen his ratings—still the highest of any major figure—decline. Social media, fake news, and leaks to journalists give critics weapons to use against a leadership that increasingly worries that the Western allies—without whose support and weaponry the war would be lost—are themselves under increasing pressure to force Ukraine to make a deal with Putin. The fault lines in Ukrainian society have been blurred by a common determination to confront the invaders: corruption has been tackled; the oligarchs are less powerful, in part because of the damage the war has brought to their possessions. But a fundamental transformation takes time.

The winter of 2024-2025 will be a hard one. The Russian forces have targeted power supplies: peak power may now be only one-third of what would be needed in winter. Putin, now with some confidence that a long-drawn-out war will play to his ability to draw on a population four to five times larger than that of Ukraine and the fruits of a massive investment in the creation of a full war economy. Its losses have been huge: Russia 600,000 of the mainly young men pressed into military service over the past four years, and one estimate shows that 540 Russian tanks have been destroyed. But it can still ensure an adequate supply of manpower and weaponry to continue the struggle as far ahead as plans can realistically be made.

Volodymyr Zelensky also has a plan—which he presented to the main Western leaders in mid-October.[2] It includes more weapons, especially the latest rocket technology; the lifting of restrictions on long-range strikes inside Russia, an agreement that Ukrainian forces can continue to strike inside Russia, and a formal invitation to join NATO. The Ukrainian president believes he could defeat the Russians over the next year, if the allies endorse the plan. Inevitably, it assumes that the West, especially the US, will continue its support.

Yet as a commentary by the Atlantic Council made clear after the Western leaders' meeting, they "consistently voice their support for Zelenskyy's goals, (but) some remain preoccupied by fears of escalation and appear deeply reluctant to do anything that might risk provoking Putin... there was no progress on Ukraine's request

---

2   Bortoletto, F. (2024). Here Is The "Plan for Victory" That Zelensky Will Present to EU Leaders' Summit. *The EU News*, October 16, https://www.eunews.it/en/2024/10/16/here-is-the-plan-for-victory-that-zelensky-will-present-to-eu-leaders-summit/.

to allow air strikes against Russian targets using Western weapons. The United States, France, and the United Kingdom have all provided Ukraine with long-range missiles, but Kyiv has yet to receive the green light for long-range attacks inside Russia."[3] President Biden spoke of "total unanimity" at the meeting: but that is a post-meeting press release, not a true indication of the present western mood. Germany, in the summer of 2024, announced it would cut its aid to Ukraine in half in 2025: that says much more.

The fallback position for the West is to bring the two sides together in a negotiation: we are constantly reminded that "wars end with an agreement." Yet now, as Russian confidence rises, the conditions for such talks remain, for the Ukrainians, impossibly harsh. They demand that, *before* a negotiation can begin, Ukraine must agree that Russia retains all the Ukrainian land it presently controls; that it proclaims neutrality; and that it must not join NATO. As the scholar of military strategy, Sir Laurence Friedman, said in a lecture to the Bearr Trust, "Ukraine has no choice but to continue the struggle."

Putin received a further boost in late October. He had called together the BRICS countries — the group so called because it was originally composed of Brazil, Russia, India, China, and (later) South Africa — for a conference in the ancient Russian city of Kazan. The membership grows: the United Arab Emirates, Ethiopia, Iran, and Egypt have all joined, while Armenia, Kazakhstan, Mongolia, Bolivia, Congo, and Laos, not yet members, will attend. Most of these have been, in the 19th and early 20th centuries, colonial possessions of Western states: the anti-colonial nature of the group is heavily stressed, with fingers pointed at the West. No one, of course, would point out that Russia's attack on Ukraine is the contemporary world's most striking example of murderous imperialism. Ukraine's foreign ministry released a statement during the mission, protesting the presence of Antonio Guterres, the UN

---

3   Cwalina, A. (2024). Western Leaders Offer Underwhelming Response to Zelenskyy's Victory Plan. *Atlantic Council*, October 22, https://www.atlanticcouncil.org/blogs/ukrainealert/western-leaders-offer-underwhelming-response-to-zelenskyys-victory-plan/.

Secretary-General, at the BRICS summit in Kazan in 2024, at the invitation of "war criminal Putin."[4]

What had been a designation to describe the growing economic strength of these states—especially of China—has begun to turn into a more explicit counterweight to the West. The BRICS has no formal leader, but by far, the most significant member in China, with some 70 percent of the group's total GDP. A representative of the Chinese foreign ministry, Mao Ning, said that "China is ready to work with all parties to strengthen BRICS cooperation, ushering in a new era of unity and self-reliance in the Global South, and jointly promoting peace and development worldwide."[5] The sub text of the statement is that the era of Western hegemony is ending—yet Ukraine is wholly dependent on support from that quarter.

President Zelensky argued, in the presentation of his plan to the Ukrainian parliament, that his country and its allies must re-dedicate themselves to achieve victory over the invaders.[6] He came to power, almost light-heartedly, as a servant of the people—a joke turned into a political party turned into a titanic struggle. In the nearly five years of office, he has become, as Mikhail Minakov has illuminated, a courageous and inspiring leader. In 2025, he and the people he serves will need all the courage and inspiration—and support—they can muster.

---

4   Ukraine Blasts U.N.'s Guterres over Invitation to BRICS Summit in Russia. *Reuters*, October 22, 2024, https://www.reuters.com/world/ukraine-blasts-uns-guterres-over-invitation-brics-summit-russia-2024-10-22/.
5   China's President Xi to Attend BRICS Summit in Russia. *SwissInfo*, October 18, 2024, https://www.swissinfo.ch/eng/china%27s-president-xi-to-attend-brics-summit-in-russia/87754122.
6   Waterhouse, J., Gozzi, L. (2024). Zelensky Presents 'Victory Plan' to Ukrainian Parliament. *BBC*, October 16, https://www.bbc.com/news/articles/cd0z8gg5v14o.

Introduction

Kyiv has a tradition of chronicling that is over a thousand years long. I resolved to continue this tradition: between 2019 and 2024, I published many columns and articles on the Wilson Center's platforms, *Focus Ukraine* and *Kennan Cable*, about Ukraine—its politics, society, and leaders. Now, some of these papers are brought together into a book, *From Servant to Leader: Chronicles of Ukraine under the Zelensky Presidency, 2019-2024*.

As the ancient tradition shows, a chronicle measures history in terms of rulers of territories. This book gives the history of Ukraine during Volodymyr Zelensky's presidency. This blindingly flashy, extraordinarily optimistic, and abysmally tragic period will be long remembered by Ukrainians and their neighbors. Historians will also discuss it, attempting to squeeze the chaotic events, inconsistent processes, and ambiguous perceptions of its participants and witnesses into a single structured narrative.

Historians, political scholars, and journalists in the United States, Britain, and Europe have already published books about Zelensky and Ukraine under his presidency, ranging from the scholarly *The Zelensky Effect* by Olga Onuch and Henry E. Hale (Hurst, 2022) to the non-fiction bestseller *The Showman* by Simon Shuster (HarperCollins, 2024) and to the children's book *Brave Volodymyr* by Linda Elovitz Marshall (HarperCollins, 2023). This line of publications constitutes a new subgenre, the "Zelensky legend." This subgenre may soon overshadow the "young Mazeppa legend," which was so popular in Europe and Northern America in the times of Romanticism.[7] Some of these books on Zelensky and Ukraine will be read and reread by future generations. Others will be soon forgotten, as too emotionally involved or as having misread the facts. But together, they have laid the narrative foundation for Zelensky's Ukraine imagery.

---

[7] On that legend see: Babiński, H. F. (1974). *The Mazeppa Legend in European Romanticism*. New York: Columbia University Press; Voss, T. (1997). Wild and Free: Byron's Mazeppa. *The Byron Journal*, (25), 71-82; Lansdown, R. (2020). The Riddles of Mazeppa, April 1817-September 1818. *Romanticism* 26(3), 267-279.

I joined these narrative constructions not without hesitation. My chronicle was written when President Zelensky still ruled, so this is an open-ended story of an unfinished presidency. How do we write about a period whose outcomes are still uncertain? But this was exactly the reason why I overcame my doubts and accepted the offer of Andreas Umland, a longtime colleague, scholar, and editor of the ibidem Verlag series "Ukrainian Voices." A chronicle is usually a non-finalized account of ongoing occurrences. It is a series of testimonies about a series of events mixed with participants' and witnesses' first reactions, both emotional and analytical. This way, a chronicle is much closer to reality than any well-structured post-factum narrative of a scholarly, historical volume. And this quality of a chronicle was the reason why I compiled my book.

The 52 essays that comprise this chronicle were published online. This type of information- and analysis-sharing reaches out to much wider audiences and in a much faster way than any printed publication. The series also allowed me to link my factual or analytical statements to a number of online sources and in-depth materials for those who wanted to learn more about Ukraine, its people, and its culture. However, while revising the essays as this book's chapters, I realized how unreliable online resources are: about 25% of the links and references were "dead," even though they were published in just five past years. I had to find new sources and make fresher references for this printed publication.

My chronicle covers Ukraine in three different phases where Zelensky demonstrated himself very differently. The first phase was the last year of the Ukrainian "Behemoth." Thomas Hobbes used two biblical monsters—Leviathan and Behemoth—as symbols of two ideal types of political order. The first was "the peacekeeping state" under one almighty sovereign, and the second was the state of permanent civil conflict.[8] If Leviathan is a human-made "god" and a superrational political machine, Behemoth embodies emotional politics with shortsighted, conflicting parties. In

---

8   For more on this, see: Holmes, S. (1990). Political Psychology in Hobbes's Behemoth. In: Dietz, M. G. (ed.). (1990). *Thomas Hobbes and Political Theory*. Lawrence: University Press of Kansas, 120-152.

Ukraine, the Behemoth-like processes started in the wave of the post-Soviet color revolutions and evolved from 2004 through 2019. A grand master of public emotions management, Zelensky won elections with the promise to end all conflicts inherent to such an order. In this phase, Zelensky showed himself a servant (to the supportive majority of the Ukrainian people), a winner (in elections where all the established institutions were against him), and a reformer (fulfilling his electoral program).

The second phase was during the social disarray caused by the COVID-19 pandemic and the gathering threats from Putin's Russia. Here, Zelensky and his team lost their reformist zeal and encountered the brute reality of the Donbas War, socioeconomic hardships, and dysfunctional government. The Ukrainian Behemoth was not giving up, and the Russian Leviathan was getting ready to strike. Under pressure from outside and inside the country, Zelensky became a master who ruled with less and less support from the citizens and elites.

The third phase started with the major Russian invasion of Ukraine in 2022. The old quarrels among Ukrainians were forgotten, and Zelensky reinvented himself as a wartime leader who used his showmanship to build global charisma and gain unprecedented support for his country. Ukrainian state and society started a new era under the conditions of a big, unending war.

Following Zelensky's changing political roles, this chronicle is organized around five periods, as suggested in the title *From Servant to Leader*. Its chapters were written during or immediately after the events described, and they bear the opinions and perceptions of those moments. I have not corrected this in the final text of this book. Yes, looking back at them now, in the fall of 2024, many of my impressions and judgments look debatable; I could have been much more prescient, calmer, and wiser. But the fluidity of participants' and witnesses' perceptions is also a history, as is the history of events. This book, therefore, combines all the advantages and disadvantages of the chronicle. I hope that this peculiarity will be accepted with understanding by my readers.

I. 1. Servant

The start of the presidential electoral campaign in 2019

February 2019[9]

With the start of 2019, Ukraine has entered a super-election year. Presidential elections are scheduled for March 31, with an expected run-off election in April, and parliamentary elections are slated for October. These elections will test the political system established after the Euromaidan.

Ukrainians will be asked to make choices about their future in a climate of low trust in public institutions and ruling groups. According to a recent poll, only 8 percent of Ukrainians trust parliament (80 percent do not trust it), 11 percent trust the cabinet of ministers (74 percent do not trust it), and 16 percent trust the presidential institute (70 percent do not trust it). Instead, Ukrainians trust their neighbors (68 percent), volunteers (63 percent), their church (51 percent), and the army (51 percent).[10]

Another poll shows that 80 percent of Ukrainians are dissatisfied with the performance of President Poroshenko (15 percent are satisfied), 81 percent disapprove of Prime Minister Groysman's performance (12 percent approve), and 90 percent are unhappy with parliament's achievements (only 5 percent are happy). Disapproval of the political class is also evident in the lack of solid popular support for any of the current candidates: unlike in previous campaigns, the most popular candidate is preferred by fewer than 15 percent of the general population. At the same time, dissatisfaction with the current ruling groups seems to be a strong factor motivating citizens to vote: 79 percent of those polled are planning to

---

[9] A shorter version of this column has previously been published as: Minakov, M. (2019). Presidential Elections in Ukraine: Candidates and Chances. *Focus Ukraine*, February 12, https://www.wilsoncenter.org/blog-post/presidential-elections-ukraine-candidates-and-chances.

[10] Paniotto, V. (2019). Trust to Social Institutes. *Kyiv International Institute of Sociology (hereinafter KIIS)*, January 21, https://www.kiis.com.ua/?lang=eng&cat=reports&id=817&page=1.

vote in the March 31 presidential election.[11] Thus the electoral contest has kicked off in the context of a highly motivated yet frustrated electorate.

Of the four basic phases in a Ukrainian election—determining the candidates, campaigning, voting, and determining the winner—the first phase for the presidential elections has just concluded. On February 8 the Central Election Commission (CEC) finished the official registration of candidates. The CEC approved the participation of forty-four candidates and denied participation to forty-seven others.[12] This is a record number of candidates for Ukrainian presidential elections. In 1991, six candidates competed in the first presidential elections in independent Ukraine. Seven candidates were registered in 1994, thirteen in 1999, twenty-four in 2004, eighteen in 2009, and twenty-one in 2014.

The registered candidates fall into two large groups. In the first group are those with a chance of meaningful participation in the campaign. According to a January poll by the Sociological Group "Rating," only six of them are supported by 5 percent or more of the electorate.[13] Volodymyr Zelensky has the support of 14.1 percent, followed by Yulia Tymoshenko, at 13.1 percent, the current president Petro Poroshenko, at 10.8 percent, Yuri Boyko, at 7.5 percent, Anatoliy Hrytsenko, at 6.1 percent, and Oleh Lyashko, at 5.2 percent. It is quite probable that support for Zelensky and Poroshenko will grow even bigger in February. Others, like Dmytro Hnap, a pro-Maidan investigative journalist, or Yevheniy Muraiev, an anti-Maidan politician and MP, though having no serious

---

11 Monitoring of Electoral Moods of Ukrainians: January 2019. *Social Group "Rating" (hereinafter SGR)*, January 31, 2019, https://ratinggroup.ua/en/research/ukraine/monitoring_elektoralnyh_nastroeniy_ukraincev_yanvar_2019.html.
12 All-Time Record: 44 Candidates Registered to Run for President in Ukraine (Full list). *UNIAN*, February 2, 2019, https://2cm.es/LR-g; ЦВК відмовила у реєстрації майже півсотні «кандидатів» у президенти (from Ukrainian: Central Electoral Committee Denies Registration to Almost Fifty "Presidential Candidates"). *Ukrainska Pravda*, February 8, 2019, https://www.pravda.com.ua/news/2019/02/8/7206166/.
13 Monitoring of Electoral Moods of Ukrainians: January 2019. *SGR*, January 31, 2019, https://ratinggroup.ua/en/research/ukraine/monitoring_elektoralnyh_nastroeniy_ukraincev_yanvar_2019.html.

electoral support, inject into the public debate sound and competing ideological positions.

In the second group are candidates who, in the post-Soviet political culture, are called "technical candidates." These candidates serve the purposes of their patron candidates. They bring into the public debate messages intended to compromise their patron's competitors, manipulate public opinion, and get their patron's representatives on local election commissions. This last function is decisive during ballot tabulation, where the potential for election fraud is high.

Another function of technical candidates is to confuse voters. For example, the presidential ballot will include two candidates whose names are written as "Yu. Tymoshenko" — Yulia and Yuriy Tymoshenko. Some inattentive supporters of Ms. Tymoshenko may inadvertently vote for an unknown Mr. Tymoshenko in an endless list of forty-four candidates.

The vast majority of those who tried but failed to be registered as candidates did not meet the legal requirements to do so. They did not submit the necessary documents, or they could not afford the registration fee (2.5 million UAH, or approximately US $100,000). However, according to CEC chair Tetyana Slipachuk, six candidates were denied whose programs included statements aimed at changing the constitution; also, Petro Symonenko, who was nominated by the Communist Party, was denied on the ground that symbols of that party contradict Ukraine's decommunizations laws.[14]

Campaigning is now peaking, with the relative rankings of the leading candidates changing rapidly. So far the success of Volodymyr Zelensky, who recently became the leading candidate, is the biggest news.[15] A showman, comic and successful businessman who is allegedly connected to an oligarch, Ihor Kolomoisky, Zelensky is supported by people who are tired of the pro-/anti-Maidan

---

14 Українська Правда (8 лютого 2019), Op. cit.
15 This Comedy Star Wants to Be Ukraine's Donald Trump. *Bloomberg*, January 10, 2019, https://shorturl.at/5ilr9.

debates.[16] Usually these frustrated individuals, mainly young people living in the eastern, southern, and north-central regions, do not actively participate in elections. Zelensky's campaign aims to motivate those supporting him to actually vote.

From November 2018 to January 2019, Yulia Tymoshenko's ratings stagnated.[17] She and her team had focused too much on preparatory work, and lost momentum in the public debate over issues connected to the Orthodox Church autocephaly and the imposition of martial law in response to Russian aggression in the Sea of Azov. However, Tymoshenko, along with Zelensky, remains at the front of voters' sympathies. And unlike Zelensky, she has a developed party network able to deliver her messages around Ukrainian regions and defend her votes during the tabulation process.

President Poroshenko gained several points during the thirty-day period of martial law in November–December 2018 and as a result of his campaign for a united autocephalic church, rising to 10.8 percent.[18] However, he remains in third place. After two recent forums in which he was nominated as a nonpartisan candidate, having positioned himself as the only non-Kremlin-friendly candidate, his team is directing their efforts to getting their candidate into the second round of the presidential elections.[19]

A leader among the electorate in Ukraine's South-East, Yuri Boyko faces growing rivalry from splinter groups of the Opposition Bloc (formerly the Russia-inclined Party of Regions).[20] He competes

---

16   Jarábik, B. (2019). Ukraine's Joke of An Election. *Politico*, February 5, https://www.politico.eu/article/ukraine-joke-election-vladimir-Zelensky/.
17   Gic, A. (2019). Yulia Tymoshenko: A Ghost of Ukraine's Past. *New Eastern Europe*, January 21, https://neweasterneurope.eu/2019/01/21/yulia-tymoshenko-a-ghost-of-ukraines-past/.
18   Martial Law Comes to an End in Ukraine after 30 Days. *BBC*, December 26, 2018, https://www.bbc.com/news/world-europe-46684602; Decree on Independence Handed Over to New Orthodox Church in Ukraine. *RFERL*, January 6, 2019, https://www.rferl.org/a/ukraine-bartholomew-presents-tomos-chirch-independence/29693771.html.
19   Poroshenko to Seek Re-election in Ukraine. *Deutsche Welle*, January 29, 2019, https://www.dw.com/en/ukraine-president-petro-poroshenko-to-seek-re-election/a-47279778.
20   Talant, B. (2018). Boyko, Opposition Platform Leader Tied to Yanukovych, Chosen as Candidate for Ukrainian Presidency. *Kyiv Post*, November 18, https://shorturl.at/WNvYm.

with his ex-comrades Oleksandr Vilkul and Yevheniy Muraev on basically the same set of programmatic ideas, including making peace with Russia and reviving Ukraine's industrial potential.[21]

Finally, Anatoliy Hrytsenko has managed to consolidate some of the pro-Maidan opposition leaders into one electoral team.[22] Supported by little more than 6 percent of likely voters, Hrytsenko is participating in the presidential elections to make sure he and his team get a solid representation in the future Verkhovna Rada (VRU), for which elections will be held in October.

With campaigning in an extremely active and controversial phase, the outcome of the upcoming vote is impossible to predict. Arsen Avakov, minister of interior and a member of the People's Front party, which does not participate in elections, has repeatedly said that police will make sure all candidates compete lawfully.[23] Later this month we will review the final phase of campaigning and how it ends.

Debates on war and peace in the presidential elections of 2019

March 2019[24]

As the day to elect Ukraine's next president draws near, the candidates' campaigns have become more aggressive and their positions more intransigent. The three leading candidates have entered the campaign phase in which, in addition to their official platforms, nonpolitical tools are being wielded to gain an edge on the

---

21 Vilkul Told What He Would Do in the First 100 Days as a President. *Novostnoj Portal*, January 30, 2019, https://zi.ua/en/news/vilkul-told-what-he-would-do-in-the-first-100-days-as-a-president_71179/.
22 Kuzio, T. (2019). Will Strongman Hrytsenko Appeal to Ukrainian Voters? *New Eastern Europe*, January 30, https://neweasterneurope.eu/2019/01/30/will-strongman-hrytsenko-appeal-to-ukrainian-voters/.
23 Casting Ballots Instead of Citizens Working Abroad to Be Punished by Prison Term, — Avakov. *Censor.Net*, January 29, 2019, https://shorturl.at/b80Q4.
24 A shorter version of this column has previously been published as: Minakov, M. (2019). War and Peace in Ukraine's Presidential Race. *Focus Ukraine*, March 14, https://www.wilsoncenter.org/blog-post/war-and-peace-ukraines-presidential-race.

competition. For example, Volodymyr Zelensky, whose office was allegedly wired by Ukraine's Security Service (SSU),[25] has announced that the authorities are preparing criminal charges against him for a car accident in 2002.[26] Yulia Tymoshenko has accused the incumbent's team of "systemic bribery all over Ukraine" directed toward distributing money to people in exchange for votes.[27] The SSU, for its part, has accused Tymoshenko of organizing an "electoral pyramid" to buy votes in the amount of nearly US $82 million.[28] However, all these disturbing events still afford Ukrainians, as the Parliamentary Assembly of the Council of Europe's Mission to Ukraine put it, the "general environment… [to] allow [the] holding of democratic elections."[29]

All elections produce heated accusations and denunciations, so brilliantly ridiculed by Mark Twain in his "Running for Governor" over a century ago. In today's Ukraine, however, there is an obvious and distressing lack of sensible debate on the key challenges facing a nation at war.

In fact, the issue of war and peace is the most prominent challenge, overshadowing all others. According to a recent poll, 67 percent of Ukrainians feel that what Ukraine needs the most is peace;

---

25 Губар, О. (2019). Біля офісу Зеленського виявили апаратуру для прослуховування (from Ukrainian: Wiretapping Equipment Was Found Near Zelensky's Office). *Deutsche Welle*, March 4, https://rb.gy/vxc9h0.

26 Зеленский заявил, что власть готовит против него дела и провокации в ОРЛО (from Ukrainian: Zelensky Said That the Authorities Were Preparing Cases and Provocations Against Him in ORLO). *Ukrainiska Pravda, March 7*, 2019, https://www.pravda.com.ua/rus/news/2019/03/7/7208588/.

27 Тимошенко звинуватила штаб Порошенка у підкупі виборців (from Ukrainian: Tymoshenko Accuses Poroshenko's Campaign of Bribing Voters). *TSN*, February 19, 2019, https://tsn.ua/politika/timoshenko-zvinuvatila-shtab-poroshenka-u-pidkupi-viborciv-1299801.html.

28 Васильченко, Ю. (2019). "Виборча піраміда": До чого призведе "брудна війна" Тимошенко з Порошенком (from Ukrainian: "Electoral Pyramid": What Will Tymoshenko's "Dirty War" With Poroshenko Lead To?). *Depo.ua*, February 21, https://shorturl.at/hsAwe.

29 Observation of the Presidential Election in Ukraine (31 March and 21 April 2019). *PACE Mission*, May 23, 2019, https://assembly.coe.int/nw/xml/XRef/Xref-XML2HTML-en.asp?fileid=27698&lang=en.

this figure swelled from 62 percent in just six months[30]. How do the Ukrainian presidential candidates address the military conflict with Russia and Russia-backed separatists? What are their proposed solutions?

The platforms of the three leading candidates offer some clues. Currently in the lead (with the support of 24.7 percent of likely voters),[31] Volodymyr Zelensky is openly in support of a peaceful resolution to the conflict with Russia and the reintegration of the noncontrolled lands in the Donbas.[32] In his official platform, Zelensky outlines four steps to returning Ukraine to the path of peaceful development.[33] First, he suggests organizing a conference with the participation of the 1994 Budapest Memorandum signatories (Russia, the UK, and the United States, with the addition of France and China) and the EU that would mediate an end to the war, the return of occupied lands, and Russia's reparation payments. (The original signers committed to never using weapons against each other.) Second, Zelensky proposes furthering reform of the defense sector with the creation of an efficient army staffed by professional soldiers and untainted by corruption. Third, he supports "movement toward NATO"; however, he feels membership should be decided on the basis of a national referendum. Finally, he promises to reform the SSU, which should cease being used to apply pressure on businesses and return to its nominal task of providing security for citizens. Basically, Volodymyr Zelensky is ready to talk "even with the devil" if that will deliver peace to Ukraine.[34]

Yulia Tymoshenko (supported by 18.3 percent of likely voters) identifies achieving peace and security as the first task in her "New

---

30 Moods and Assessment of Threats by Ukrainians. *SGR*, February 4, 2019, https://ratinggroup.ua/en/research/ukraine/nastroeniya_i_ocenka_ugroz_ukraincami.html.
31 Assessment of the Election Process: Intentions and Reasons for Voting, Trust and Sympathies. *SGR*, March 11, 2019, https://shorturl.at/Kproc.
32 Zelensky About War in Donbas: Negotiations with Russia Inevitable. *UNIAN*, March 1, 2019, https://t.ly/8Hb79.
33 This and other programs of the presidential candidates of the 2019 campaign are not accessible anymore on the website of the Central Electoral Commission of Ukraine.
34 Presidential election: Volodymyr Zelensky About War and Peace. *Ostrov*, January 25, 2019, https://www.ostro.info/articles/271/.

Course for Ukraine" program. She has proposed diplomacy in the Budapest Memorandum format as a tool to make Russia return the Donbas and Crimea to Ukraine. To support diplomatic steps, Tymoshenko promises to develop the Ukrainian army in accordance with NATO standards to "guarantee security to the country and to each family." She also promises to increase the current financial and material "motivational package" offered to Ukrainian soldiers and to beef up social security benefits for veterans. Tymoshenko aims at reintegrating the Donbas and Crimea by destroying "the wall of fear, non-understanding and hatred that is being artificially created between Ukraine and the occupied territories." She offers dialogue to lead millions of citizens out of a "state of stress." Finally, the leader of the Batkivshchyna party proposes forcing Russia to cover financially all the restorative processes in Ukraine. As the aggressor, Russia must pay — to each citizen, Ukrainian business, and the state — for the damage it has caused by annexing Crimea and supporting the Donbas separatists.

The current president, Petro Poroshenko (supported by 16.8 percent of Ukrainians likely to vote) aims at achieving peace as well.[35] His program defines peace as "the full restoration of the territorial integrity, sovereignty and independence of Ukraine" and "the indisputable recognition by Moscow of our right to move our own way." To achieve this peace, Poroshenko proposes continuing to build a strong army and developing closer ties with NATO allies. He also states that "only full membership in the EU and NATO would finally and irrevocably guarantee our Ukrainian independence ... and national security." Poroshenko promises to apply for these memberships in 2023. The president also sees the army's development as an opportunity for science and industry to advance in Ukraine. As journalists have recently uncovered, the Ukrainian military industry is still dependent on some products of the Russian military complex.[36] This dependence, as well as the embezzlement associated with it, was lately slammed by the US ambassador to Ukraine.

---

35 SGR, March 11, 2019, Op. cit.
36 Investigative Journalist Reports About Supplies to Ukroboronprom Based on Evidence from Official Investigation. *Interfax*, February 8, 2019, https://en.interfax.com.ua/news/general/571229.html.

The army's modernization should go hand in hand with the improved social safety net for citizens and improved pay scales for officers and soldiers. Also, all the victims of Russia's aggression should receive reimbursement and reparations for the lands, businesses, and loved ones they have lost.

These steps, in combination with the diplomatic efforts of Ukraine's transatlantic allies and international sanctions against Russia, should lead to the entire "de-occupation" of the Donbas and Crimea and peace for Ukraine, Poroshenko expects.

Thus the platforms of the current leading electoral candidates are closely aligned in how they plan to achieve peace through pursuing diplomatic measures, developing the Ukrainian army, and maintaining close ties with NATO. Diplomacy must help end the war, all agree, and Russia should pay for the damage it has caused. A reformed Ukrainian army should be able to defend citizens and the state from any immediate danger, while an alliance with NATO should put Ukraine in a stronger position with respect to fending off menacing actors in the future.

What divides the candidates is the issue of membership in NATO. Zelensky and Tymoshenko are less committed to it, while Poroshenko proposes to apply for it in the near future. Also, the diplomatic formats are seen differently: Zelensky prefers the Budapest format but also wants direct talks with Putin. Tymoshenko is more inclined to see the Budapest format as the main instrument, while Poroshenko prefers to have NATO as an ally in talks with Russia.

Despite the many issues dividing the current leaders in the presidential race, then, Zelensky's, Poroshenko's, and Tymoshenko's platforms all seem reasonably close in their proposals to end the war and secure peace for Ukraine. It appears that the Ukrainian political elites have a common position on the key steps needed to reintegrate the country and achieve a stable security for the citizenry.

Results of the first round of Ukraine's presidential elections

April 2019[37]

After a complex campaign marked by occasional violence and voter anxiety over the economy and the war in the East, and replete with "kompromat" leaks and mounting suspicions, the actual voting and tabulation of the first round of votes for Ukraine's next president passed in almost exemplary fashion.[38] The OSCE/ODIHR mission, the EU, and NATO's Parliamentary Assembly praised the quality of the first round of voting, mentioned some legal issues, and expressed hope that the second round would be up to the same standards as the first.[39]

As announced by Ukraine's CEC, with more than 99 percent of votes counted, it appears that more than 62 percent of Ukrainians voters, or more than 18.6 million people, officially expressed their support for one of thirty-nine presidential candidates. This relatively high turnout is not unusual: after the Euromaidan in 2014, 59 percent of voters participated in the presidential elections. More than 67 percent had done so in 2010, and more than 70 percent on the eve of the Orange Revolution in 2004. Although pollsters had

---

37 A shorter version of this column has previously been published as: Minakov, M. (2019). Ukraine's Presidential Elections: New Cycle, Same Names. *Focus Ukraine*, April 3, https://www.wilsoncenter.org/blog-post/ukraines-presidential-elections-new-cycle-same-names.

38 See the reports by the journalists of *Kyiv Post* in March – April 2019 at https://archive.kyivpost.com/hot/2019-presidential-election. See also: Istrate, D. (2019). Violent Clashes in Ukraine Ahead of Presidential Election. *Emerging Europe*, March 12, https://emerging-europe.com/analysis/violent-clashes-in-ukraine-ahead-of-presidential-election/; Roth, A. (2019). Ukraine Election: Will Voter Anger Propel TV Comic to Presidency? *The Guardian*, March 29, https://t.ly/Y_8hH; Miller, C. (2019). Sleaze Scandals Stalk Ukraine Campaign. *Politico*, March 5, https://t.ly/pDkEK.

39 Ukraine, Presidential Election, 31 March 2019: Statement of Preliminary Findings and Conclusions. *OSCE*, April 1, 2019, https://www.osce.org/odihr/elections/ukraine/415733; Statement by the Spokesperson Following the First Round of the Presidential Elections in Ukraine. *The EU Diplomatic Service*, April 1, 2019, https://www.eeas.europa.eu/node/60462_en; Ukraine Election Competitive, But Legal Issues Remain, International Observers Say. *NATO Parliamentary Assembly*, April 1, 2019, https://t.ly/9WSNP.

expected more than 80 percent of the electorate to actively participate in the first round of this year's presidential elections, the gap between intended and actual participation is also par for the course.[40]

On March 31, Ukrainians chose two politicians to compete for the post of president; a runoff will be necessary because neither achieved a majority. In one of the most surprising developments of the past few months, the businessman and actor Zelensky surged in the polls, ultimately receiving more than 30 percent of votes cast (almost 5.6 million ballots). President Petro Poroshenko, at 15.95 percent (3 million ballots), got just over half the votes of his principal competitor. The outcome of their struggle over the next three weeks will determine who will lead Ukraine for the next five years.

Yulia Tymoshenko, who was on roughly equal standing with Poroshenko in the most recent pre-election poll, fell back 2.5 percentage points from the incumbent in actual voting.[41] Her failure to make a stronger showing in the polls owes in part to the unexpected popularity of Ihor Smeshko, ex-chief of Ukraine's security services. Smeshko received 6 percent of votes cast, taking approximately half from Tymoshenko and the other half from Anatolii Hrytsenko's traditional electorate.

The Opposition Bloc, the remnant of the Party of Regions, which is supported mainly by traditional voters in the East, was divided between two candidates, Yuri Boyko and Oleksandr Vilkul. Together, Boyko (11.7 percent, or 2.2 million votes) and Vilkul (4.1 percent, or 782,000 votes) received approximately the same support as Petro Poroshenko did. Had their sponsors, Viktor Medvedchuk and Rinat Akhmetov, been able to avoid conflict, the former "regionnaires" might well have ended up in the second round. However, their divisiveness and competition led many eastern Ukraine voters to turn their sights toward Zelensky.

The final vote to determine Ukraine's next president is scheduled for April 21. Judging from Petro Poroshenko's initial reaction

---

40 Monitoring of Electoral Moods of Ukrainians (March 22–27, 2019). *SGR*, March 28, 2019, https://t.ly/mJaUM.
41 Ibid.

to national exit poll results after the March 31 vote, the next round of campaigning will be even more rancorous and personalized. For example, Poroshenko has called Zelensky "Kolomoysky's puppet," stressing the showman-candidate's alleged connection to the famous oligarch.[42] Zelensky lost no time in calling the president "Svynarchuk's puppet," referring to Poroshenko's business partner, who has recently been accused of corrupt activities connected to military procurements.[43] If the debate continues at this level, the campaign promises to be quite meaningless.

Zelensky has shown himself to be a unique candidate who managed to erase the curse of Ukraine's electoral East-West divide. According to CEC data, Zelensky won in nineteen (out of twenty-five) oblasts and in Kyiv. Petro Poroshenko won in two western Ukraine oblasts, Tymoshenko in one oblast of the same region, and Yuri Boyko got majority support in the controlled parts of Donetsk and Luhansk oblasts. But Zelensky achieved respectable to good results in all those communities and regions.

Being ideologically neutral and vague on policy matters, Zelensky seems to attract equally Ukrainian- and Russian-speaking voters, urban dwellers and small-town residents. Representative of a younger generation of Ukrainians, he won solid support from older audiences. It seems that different groups that had been marginalized in the reforms process invested in him their hopes and fears. All these factors coming together may give him the support needed to win the election.

On the other hand, Zelensky faces Petro Poroshenko, a savvy and mature politician who has publicly demonstrated his firm will to victory. His team has already started a new campaign, setting aside the patriotic and conservative slogans the candidate had leaned on heavily during the first round in favor of calls to "consolidate the pro-democracy candidates" around him. Poroshenko has

---

42 Zelensky Agrees to Hold Debate with Poroshenko. *UNIAN*, April 1, 2019, http://surl.li/mfhoha; Stern, D. L. (2019). Comedian Volodymyr Zelensky is Ahead in First Round of Ukraine's Election. *The Washington Post*, March 31, http://surl.li/mgofox.
43 Corruption in Ukroboronprom: Journalists Claim Anti-Corruption Watchdog, Prosecutors Involved. *UNIAN*, March 11, 2019, http://surl.li/rqxeyq.

also sought to reach out to Zelensky's supporters, saying he has heard their grievances and complaints.

Yulia Tymoshenko initially disagreed with her defeat in the polls, calling it the result of manipulations by the incumbent, but refused to organize a Maidan protest, as some of her supporters had urged.[44] She eventually conceded.[45] Tymoshenko and the other former presidential candidates now have some tough decisions to make — specifically, who should get their support? Who is the more appropriate candidate, and how would allying with him influence their own chances to gain more seats in the Rada for their party?

But while the former candidates ponder their next moves, Zelensky and Poroshenko have lost no time in squaring off against each other. A victory for one or the other will define the future of Ukraine — territorially the largest and economically the poorest European country — and its political, economic, societal, and international trajectory for the next five years.

Expectations from the newly elected President Zelensky

April 2019[46]

On April 21, Ukrainians elected a new president. He is Volodymyr Zelensky, an actor, comedian and political satirist, who won by a compelling margin of nearly three to one. When his five-year term begins next month, Zelensky will lead Europe's largest state by territory, a country divided by war with neighboring Russia and weary of corruption, but also wary of both external and internal "change" that could make an already difficult situation even worse.

---

44 Ukraine: Rival Accuses Incumbent President of Rigging Vote. *US News*, April 2, 2019, http://surl.li/bcxpdk.
45 Бобрицкий, Д. (2019). Третье поражение. Почему Юлия Тимошенко проиграла (from Russian: Third Defeat. Why Yulia Tymoshenko Lost). *Liga.Net*, April 3, http://surl.li/ocwonc.
46 A shorter version of this column has previously been published as: Minakov, M. & Rojansky, M. (2019). What to Expect from Ukraine's Next President. *Focus Ukraine*, April 25, https://www.wilsoncenter.org/blog-post/what-to-expect-ukraines-next-president.

Who is Zelensky and why did Ukrainians choose him?

Zelensky is an entertainer, a political satirist rather than a politician in any traditional sense. At 41, he is certainly young. He came of age well after the dissolution of Soviet Union and Ukraine's independence in 1991, and has therefore experienced firsthand the high hopes of the early independence years, but also the political chaos, economic collapse, and the rise of the oligarchs — people like incumbent president Petro Poroshenko and Zelensky's own business partner, Ihor Kolomoisky.

In his television appearances, Zelensky has been merciless in shredding the country's corrupt, oligarch-controlled political class. The younger generation of Ukrainians is especially familiar with his comic show "Block 95," which blended slapstick comedy and variety show acts with cutting political satire. Underscoring Ukraine's traditions of free speech and pluralism, Zelensky's show lampooned the absurdity of Ukrainian political events and figures from the pro-Western, reformist Orange Revolution (2004–2005) to the grossly corrupt Yanukovych years (2010–2014). Indeed it was on television, live on New Year's Eve last year, that he announced his presidential bid.

Zelensky's other signature television project "Servant of the People," in which he plays an upright and honest schoolteacher turned president, is now also the name and the manifesto of his political party. His landslide victory, defeating the incumbent by a 3-1 margin and winning majorities in all but one region of the country, was more than anything a resounding rejection of the status quo by voters who are justifiably outraged. These voters may well see Zelensky's television character as far preferable to the present political reality. As Zelensky himself said to Poroshenko in the pre-election debate, "I am not your opponent, I am your sentence."

Zelensky's own honesty was tested in the recent campaign: he has acknowledged his business partnership with Kolomoisky (who owns the TV channel on which Zelensky appears), as well his own commercial interests in Russia. When asked pointedly about Kolomoisky, Zelensky said that if the oligarch breaks the law in Ukraine under his presidency, he will go to jail. He also claims to have wound down his business in Russia and rightly pointed out that President Poroshenko has had extensive business dealings in Russia during his tenure. Despite intense attacks by opponents, Zelensky has not suffered any loss of popularity nor shed the image of a candidate of hope shaped to a large degree by his TV personality, "President" Holoborodko.

How will Zelensky's election impact the conflict in eastern Ukraine?

According to a recent study, Ukrainians expect the new president to deal with the seemingly endless war with Russia in addition to economic hardship and corruption.[47] Many are frustrated and angry that after five years of war and sacrifice, they are no better off. Zelensky addressed this frustration with a twofold message of hope.

First, he has offered an inclusive political alternative to the nationalist policies and rhetoric of the current president. A native Russian speaker himself, Zelensky was seen by his electorate as preferable to President Poroshenko and his nationalist campaign slogan, "army, language, faith." In his last years in office especially, Poroshenko has pushed hard to promote the dominance of the Ukrainian language over Ukrainian-Russian bilingualism (which is widespread in the center, east and south of the country), and touted his successful bid for the Orthodox Church's independence from the Moscow Patriarchate. Meanwhile he has prosecuted a grinding and bloody war of attrition against Russian-backed forces in Donbas, which has cost thousands of civilian and military lives but delivered no measurable progress on the ground.

Second, Zelensky has promised to negotiate with Russian President Vladimir Putin to end the conflict. While Poroshenko and other critics warn that the comedian would be no match for his wily Russian adversary, Ukrainians appear weary of endless conflict

---

47 Снизить тарифы и снять неприкосновенность: что украинцы хотят от президента в первые 100 дней—КМИС (from Russian: Reduce Tariffs and Remove Immunity: What Ukrainians Want from the President in the First 100 Days—KMIS). *Hromadske*, April 16, 2019, http://surl.li/klvywb.

and hopeful that a new president can at least bring peace and a chance to rebuild, if not restoration of territories seized by Russian forces in 2014. With his overwhelming victory over Poroshenko, Zelensky at least comes to any negotiation — whether with Russia or with local Donbas separatists — with a powerful mandate that can strengthen his hand.

Can Zelensky fulfill his promises to the Ukrainian people?

Any president can deliver on promises only to the extent he is able to cooperate with the parliament, which enjoys considerable power under Ukraine's constitution. Zelensky's compelling victory sets the stage for the next phase of political competition in Ukraine's parliamentary elections (to be held in October 2019). According to a recent poll, his party has the highest level of support among all Ukrainians (26 percent).[48] However, the party lacks any real infrastructure: it has neither members nor regional organizations, which are critical for mobilizing voters. Even if Zelensky's party wins a quarter of seats in the Rada. In October, he will still need allies from other factions to build a stable coalition and confirm his appointment of allies to the Cabinet of Ministers — especially to the powerful post of Prime Minister.

Without the political party infrastructure enjoyed by his vanquished presidential rivals, Zelensky faces the risk of not being able to deliver what is expected from him. Voters' disappointment with the slow pace of fulfilling the promises could already count against the new president by the fall, lowering his parliamentary result from the current 26% to far less and making the formation of a favorable coalition even more important. What Zelensky may then be ready to sacrifice to the political and oligarchic old guard to secure such a coalition and actually implement the remainder of his agenda has yet to be seen.

---

48 Social and Political Attitudes of The Population of Ukraine on The Eve of The Second Round of The Elections of The President of Ukraine: April 2019. *KIIS*, April 16, 2019, https://www.kiis.com.ua/?lang=eng&cat=reports&id=851&page=2.

How does Russia see Zelensky?

For the Kremlin, which has not yet formally congratulated Zelensky on his victory, the "anyone but Poroshenko" enthusiasm appears to be shared with Ukrainian voters. On the one hand, this might reflect a cynical calculation that Ukraine under a new, inexperienced president who is determined to trash the political status quo will be a weaker adversary and thus more easily pressured and manipulated. On the other hand, Russia has shown little appetite for "owning" the costly conflict it unleashed in eastern Ukraine and may be ready to settle the dispute on terms that permit outsiders, especially wealthy western countries, to step in and help reconstruct the Ukrainian economy.

Zelensky's focus on pursuing peace and fighting corruption would potentially facilitate these goals in the short term. In the longer term, though, Zelensky says he is fully committed to Ukraine's western orientation, including pursuing EU and NATO membership. These can hardly be to the Kremlin's liking, but Moscow may be willing to keep its powder dry and offer Zelensky some concessions just to help consolidate his defeat of Poroshenko and the national conservative constituency he represents. After all, Russia can always attack Zelensky with real or fake "kompromat" in the future, and can at any time escalate violence by its proxy forces in Donbas to discredit the new president as a peacemaker and demoralize his core constituents.

What does Zelensky's victory mean for the West?

In terms of implications for the United States and the European Union, Ukraine's election may become a critical turning point. With the Mueller investigation concluded, Ukraine remains the biggest sticking point for President Trump's long-standing goal of repairing US-Russia ties. Trump was among the first to congratulate Zelensky on his victory and may seek to highlight in the comedian's victory a version of his own message that only a political outsider can contain the "deep state" and deliver real change for the benefit of the majority of ordinary people.

In any case, if Zelensky is successful in tamping down the Donbas conflict and restoring some degree of normalcy to Ukraine's economic and political ties with Russia, then the impetus for further escalation of US sanctions on Russia will be reduced, and there will be less tension between Washington and European capitals like Berlin and Rome, which now strongly oppose piling on new sanctions. Such steps could likewise clear the air for a Trump-Putin summit in the near future and permit progress on a long-frozen list of US-Russia priorities, from getting nuclear arms control back on track to deescalating risks around regional conflicts in Latin America, the Middle East, the Black Sea and the Baltic, which would be broadly welcomed by Europeans as well.

In sum, President-elect Volodymyr Zelensky is for the moment more a symbol and a beneficiary of Ukrainians' rejection of the past than a figurehead for any concrete political movement or policy program. He won the election first and foremost because he is not a politician, and not a creature of the old system. But to be an effective president, he will have to master national politics and wrestle the old system into submission. Whether he can do that will depend on which domestic forces rally to his banner in the months leading up to the fall parliamentary elections, as well as on the attitudes of Washington, Moscow and European capitals. Amid Ukraine's ongoing severe economic difficulties and the costly war in the east, Zelensky can certainly use all the help he can get.

I. 2. Winner

Delayed start of Zelensky's presidency

June 2019[49]

Ukrainians knew at the start of 2019 that they were entering a super-election year, with both spring presidential and autumn parliamentary elections scheduled. What they did not anticipate was the new president, Volodymyr Zelensky, announcing in his inaugural speech to the Verkhovna Rada that he was dissolving parliament—and that parliamentary elections would therefore have to take place much sooner than expected, on July 21 rather than October 26.[50]

No one was prepared for this change in schedule.[51] The Central Electoral Commission has announced that it might not be able to produce the ballots in time for the earlier parliamentary elections. The main parties are rushing to create their lists of candidates. The major candidates are urgently meeting with their constituencies on building new roads and schools.

However, Ukrainians' plans for a summer vacation may still pan out, since the Constitutional Court has begun urgent deliberations to decide whether Zelensky's dismissal of parliament is constitutional. On the one hand, de facto, the country's governing coalition, comprising Arseny Yatsenyuk's People's Front party as the parliamentary faction and the Petr Poroshenko Bloc as the presidential party, as well as several other smaller factions, did not exist for more than three years, after Tymoshenko and Lyashko left it in 2016, and there were some unappointed ministers in the cabinet.

---

[49] A shorter version of this column has previously been published as: Minakov, M. (2019). Hot Summer in Kyiv: President Zelensky and The Rada. *Focus Ukraine*, June 6, https://www.wilsoncenter.org/blog-post/hot-summer-kyiv-president-Zelensky-and-the-rada.

[50] Full Text of Volodymyr Zelenskyy's First Speech as President of Ukraine. *Hromadske*, May 20, 2019, https://hromadske.ua/en/posts/full-text-of-volodymyr-zelenskyys-first-speech-as-president-of-ukraine.

[51] Ukraine's New President Dissolves Parliament and Calls a Snap Election. *The New York Times*, May 20, 2019, https://www.nytimes.com/2019/05/20/world/europe/ukraine-zelensky-parliament-election.html.

On the other hand, de jure, the parliamentary speaker announced the death of the coalition only in May 2019.[52]

Even though there is a chance the elections will be postponed beyond July 21 (the Court is expected to issue its verdict by the end of June), all the major Ukrainian parties have started preparations. The Petr Poroshenko Bloc was renamed European Solidarity, while the former president has declared he wants to be "the nation's father," like Jarosław Kaczyńsky, who has no position but defines today's Polish politics from behind the scenes.[53] Yatsenyuk's People's Front, facing vast unpopularity, has decided it will try to get seats in the new parliament through majoritarian districts.[54] Leaders of the different factions of the Opposition Bloc are holding talks on combining forces to regain the votes in Ukraine's South-East that went to Zelensky.[55] Yulia Tymoshenko's party has spread out to the regions to gain as much support for party and majoritarian elections as possible. An emerging political group, Voice, led by pop singer Svyatoslav Vakarchuk, has started an active campaign in the same regions and among the same demographics that gave their votes to Poroshenko.[56]

Unlike most of the older parties, which have managed to attract only modest support, Zelensky's party is garnering more and more support, even though it has neither a coherent platform nor a list in place. The party will be led by a young political expert and campaigner, Dmytro Razumkov. To fill in the echoing space left by

---

52 Ukraine Parliament Coalition Breaks Up – Speaker. *Euronews*, May 17, 2019, https://www.euronews.com/2019/05/17/ukraine-parliament-coalition-breaks-up-speaker.
53 Порошенко планирует стать не депутатом, а "отцом нации" (from Russian: Poroshenko Plans to Become Not a Deputy, But a "Father of the Nation"). *Ukrainiska Pravda*, June 3, 2019, https://www.pravda.com.ua/rus/news/2019/06/3/7216934/.
54 Members of People's Front to Run for Parliament in Majoritarian Districts. *Kyiv Post*, May 28, 2019, http://bassman.lnkiy.in/GabhV.
55 "Опозиційний блок" готується до возз'єднання партії і призначив з'їзд (from Ukrainian: "The Opposition Bloc Is Preparing to Reunite the Party And Has Scheduled a Congress". *Livy Bereh*, May 30, 2019, https://lb.ua/news/2019/05/30/428336_oppozitsionniy_blok_gotovitsya.html.
56 Vakarchuk Creates Holos Party for Running In Parliamentary Elections. *Interfax*, May 16, 2019, https://en.interfax.com.ua/news/general/587540.html.

an absent team, the Servant of the People party (named after the popular TV series starring Zelensky as an ethical schoolteacher who rises to become president) has requested e-applications from its supporters to nominate the best candidates.

So far the chances of the old and new parties have been assessed by Ukrainian voters this way.[57] The Servant of the People party has the support of 48.2 percent of those who plan to vote in the parliamentary elections and have settled on a party (in two weeks this metric moved up by nine percent). Its closest rival, the Opposition Bloc, is almost forty percentage points lower, with only 10.7 percent of likely voters supporting it. Poroshenko's European Solidarity is supported by 7.8 percent of likely voters, Tymoshenko's Batkivshchyna by 6.9 percent. Vakarchuk's Voice party stands a chance of winning seats in parliament with 5.6 percent. Other parties do not meet the 5 percent threshold in opinion polls.

With elections looming, relations between President Zelensky and the Verkhovna Rada remain hostile. After delaying the inauguration of the president-elect, a majority in parliament has consistently derailed all the president's initiatives. Zelensky failed to get a passing vote on changing the election law.[58] The Rada continues to ignore other presidential draft laws, such as legislation on impeachment and rescinding MPs' immunity. Also, the Rada did not approve Prime Minister Volodymyr Groysman's resignation, tendered at the request of the president.[59] The war between the president's office and parliament has already led to a stalemate in government and does not serve the nation.

In this hostile environment, President Zelensky has focused on areas where he can make a difference, his administration and international relations. The president appointed the key staff of his

---

57 Monitoring of Electoral Moods of Ukrainians (29 May – 3 June 2019). *SGR*, June 5, 2019, https://t.ly/7Acdq.
58 Verkhovna Rada Did Not Support The Amendments to The Electoral Law Despite the Agreements With The President—Ruslan Stefanchuk. *President of Ukraine official website*, May 22, 2019, https://www.president.gov.ua/en/news/verhovna-rada-ne-pidtrimala-zminu-viborchogo-zakonu-popri-do-55565.
59 Rada Refuses to Accept Resignation of Prime Minister Groysman. *Ukrainian News*, May 30, 2019, https://ukranews.com/en/news/634552-rada-refuses-to-accept-resignation-of-prime-minister-groysman.

administration during his first ten days in office.[60] My research shows that out of a dozen appointments to key administration, general staff, and security service positions, three have past links to the wealthy businessman Ihor Kolomoisky, who some allege aided Zelensky's bid for the presidency. A larger group of appointees come from Zelensky's media company, each of them counterbalancing the appointees in the previous group in case there should be divided loyalties. Others, such as Ruslan Ryaboshapka, Ruslan Stefanchuk, and Vadym Prystaiko, built solid careers in their sectors of responsibility—anticorruption efforts, the law, and diplomacy, respectively—and constitute a group of technocrats.

President Zelensky has also made a symbolic choice for his first visit abroad. He went to Brussels, where he met with EU and NATO leaders on June 4. There Zelensky issued an important statement that Euro-Atlantic integration remains a priority for his presidency.[61]

Even before setting out on his Brussels trip, Zelensky had started a dialogue with the International Monetary Fund. On May 28 he met with the IMF mission in Kyiv, where the parties opened a discussion of cooperation priorities. The next steps in the partnership will be discussed after parliamentary elections and the appointment of a new cabinet.

Which brings us back to the parliamentary elections. They are crucial for Ukraine, as they will effectively decide how the country will be led under a new president and new prime minister. The answer to that will become apparent only in August, when the results of the parliamentary elections are announced and a new governing coalition emerges, unless the Constitutional Court postpones the election until October.

---

60 Ukraine President Zelenskyy Appoints Core Team Members. Who Are They? *Hromadske*, May 22, 2019, https://hromadske.ua/en/posts/ukraine-president-zelenskyy-appoints-core-team-members.
61 The Course Towards Full Membership in the EU And NATO Remains the Unwavering Foreign Policy Priority of Ukraine – Volodymyr Zelenskyy. *President of Ukraine official website*, June 4, 2019, https://www.president.gov.ua/en/news/kurs-na-povnopravne-chlenstvo-u-yes-i-nato-zalishayetsya-nez-55745.

Parliamentary elections and political cleavages in Ukraine of the 2019 summer

July 2019[62]

Ukraine has reached the midpoint of a super-election year. With the somewhat surprising outcome of the presidential elections now in the rear-view mirror, the electorate is preparing for snap parliamentary elections on July 21. And with the elections have come a rearrangement of the political elite landscape in Ukraine and new political cleavages, which are expected to be on display in the upcoming Rada elections.

Even a year ago, no one could have imagined that Ukraine's leaders would become outsiders.[63] It looked as if the post-Euromaidan ruling elites would control the centers of power forever. However, the result of the presidential elections was a shock for both politicians and experts: Ukrainian voters preferred Volodymyr Zelensky, an actor with no experience in public matters, to run the country for the next five years. Unlike his main competitors, all seasoned if old-style political figures, Zelensky was seen by the voters as the proper person to take on the challenges of ending the war in the East, ending corruption, and mitigating economic hardship. Zelensky won 73 percent of the vote in twenty-four of twenty-five regions—an unprecedented result in a country that has long experienced a sharp division in the electorate between the eastern and western regions. Zelensky's landslide victory was even described by some as an "electoral Maidan," a radical attempt at regime change by constitutional means.[64]

---

62 A shorter version of this column has previously been published as: Minakov, M. (2019). Rearranging the Elite Landscape: Parliamentary Elections and New Political Cleavages in Ukraine. *Focus Ukraine*, July 17, https://www.wilsoncenter.org/blog-post/rearranging-the-elite-landscape-parliamentary-elections-and-new-political-cleavages.
63 Half A Year to the Elections: Candidate and Party Rankings, Voter Motivation, Public Expectations. *Democratic Initiatives*, September 6, 2018, https://t.ly/lz9wt.
64 Schreck, C. (2019). An Electoral Maidan: Hope and Change, Ukrainian-Style, Vaults Zelenskiy into Presidency. RFERL, April 21, https://t.ly/KShBb.

The shock of Zelensky's win soon deepened. The post-Euromaidan political elites, whose candidate, the incumbent Petro Poroshenko, received only 24 percent of the votes in the second round of elections, started undermining the efforts of the president-elect by refusing to accept the resignations of the existing chiefs of defense, security and foreign affairs (and in one case, by the minister of foreign affairs reusing parts of Poroshenko's speeches in a statement representing the new president to Brussels). In response, on his long-postponed inauguration day, President Zelensky called for early parliamentary elections.

This was a declaration of war by the new elite configuration against the ones that came into power in 2014, as well as against those who had held the reins of power before the Euromaidan. Thus a distinct new political cleavage emerged in April–May 2019.

The new elite group is still coalescing. Its creator is Volodymyr Zelensky, who believes that Ukraine needs "new faces" in politics.[65] Thus he and his administration have created a party whose major selection criterion apparently was nonparticipation in politics before 2019. Zelensky's party, Servant of the People (named after the TV serial in which Zelensky starred as a schoolteacher-turned-honest politician), has created a candidate list that seemingly supports this principle. And it looks like a large part of the electorate wants fresh faces, not well-known politicians. According to recent polls, Servant of the People is supported by 47 to 52 percent of likely voters in the upcoming parliamentary elections.[66]

As the Ukrainian parliament is elected through a mix of party lists (225 seats) and single-mandate-district candidates (225 seats), it is also important for President Zelensky to bring into parliament the same number of MPs from the single-mandate districts as arrive through party list voting. According to my observations, single-

---

[65] Grytsenko, O., Hnatyuk, V. (2019). What we know about people Zelensky will take to next parliament. *Kyiv Post*, July 8, https://www.kyivpost.com/post/7331.

[66] Monitoring of Electoral Moods of Ukrainians (6-10 July 2019). *SGR*, July 11, 2019, https://t.ly/zSLsr; Рейтинг підтримки політичних партій на виборах до Верховної Ради України: Липень 2019 року (from Ukrainian: Rating of Support for Political Parties in the Elections to the Verkhovna Rada of Ukraine: July 2019). *KIIS*, July 7, 2019, https://www.kiis.com.ua/?lang=eng&cat=reports&id=873&page=1.

mandate candidates receive a 15–20 percent bump in votes if they are nominated by the presidential party. This is how a new elite group tries to construct a power structure: by controlling the presidency and having a majority in parliament and the cabinet.[67]

Another means of rotating elites is to use lustration. Lustration, by purging older, embedded political groups, can be a tool to deprive certain groups of power when there is a transition from authoritarian to democratic rule. It was wielded for this purpose in 2014 by the post-Maidan elites. On July 12, President Zelensky submitted a draft law to parliament that envisages extending lustration to senior officials who have been in their positions since February 23, 2014, when the leaders of the Euromaidan started removing former president and Russia sympathizer Viktor Yanukovych and other major and middle-level officials from office.[68]

So much for the older elite group. A second political elite group consists of politicians who largely came to power after the Euromaidan, in the presidential and parliamentary elections of 2014. Their leaders include ex-president Poroshenko, ex-prime minister Yatsenyuk, Minister of Interior Arsen Avakov, Yulia Tymoshenko, Oleg Lyashko, Mikhail Saakashvili, Anatolii Hrytsenko, and a handful of other politicians who played crucial roles in developments between 2014 and 2019. According to a recent poll, their electoral value is minimal today. Poroshenko's party, European Solidarity (with 8.2 percent of expected electoral support), and Tymoshenko's Batkivshchyna (6.4 percent) may still make it into parliament.[69] The others will most likely not meet the

---

[67] Servant of The People Seeking One-Party Majority in Future Rada – Election HQ Head. *Interfax*, May 27, 2019, https://en.interfax.com.ua/news/general/589663.html.

[68] Проєкт Закону про внесення змін до деяких законодавчих актів України щодо очищення влади (from Ukrainian: Draft Law on Amendments to Certain Legislative Acts of Ukraine on the Purification of Government). *Official website of the Verkhovna Rada of Ukraine*, July 11, 2019, https://w1.c1.rada.gov.ua/pls/zweb2/webproc4_1?pf3511=66202; see also: Zelensky Proposes Extending Lustration Law to Senior Officials Holding Posts since February 23, 2014. *Interfax*, July 11, 2019, https://en.interfax.com.ua/news/general/599462.html.

[69] Monitoring of Electoral Moods of Ukrainians (6-10 July 2019). *SGR*, July 11, 2019, https://t.ly/nyZuF.

5 percent hurdle and so will not have representation in the Verkhovna Rada.

Still, these groups control upper-middle management positions in state bodies, law enforcement agencies, and most state-owned corporations. The struggle between this elite group and the new one coalescing around President Zelensky is visible in each ministry and each oblast of Ukraine today.

There is also a political party that tries to be in both camps. Svyatoslav Vakarchuk, a rock star, ex-MP (he served after the Orange Revolution, in 2005–2006), and a reemerging politician, has created a new party, Holos (Voice), that combines Zelensky's logic of new faces and Petro Poroshenko's national-conservative ideology. This party currently is supported by between 4 and 6.6 percent of likely voters.[70] It has a chance to send delegates to the Verkhovna Rada and to be a minor partner in the pro-Zelensky coalition.

The third political division that has become pronounced with this year's elections is associated with the power elites that ruled before the Euromaidan and survived after 2014 in the form of the Opposition Bloc. Today this bloc has split into several factions, which are fighting each other for votes in southeastern Ukraine. Only the Opposition Platform–For Life alliance has a chance to create solid representation in the Rada: it has 11.6 percent of likely voters' support.

For Life is led by the duumvirate of Yuri Boyko and Victor Medvedchuk. These politicians are openly pro-Russia, and often visit Moscow as part of their campaign. They were an integral part of the political regime since 2014 and are looking for new opportunities in Ukraine's power games.[71]

These three main elite groups — Zelensky's coalescing group, the just-defeated older power circles associated with Poroshenko, Tymoshensko, et al., and the Opposition Platform–For Life alliance — will define the future of Ukraine over the next political cycle.

---

70 SGR, July 11, 2019, Op. cit.; KIIS, July 7, 2019, Op. cit.
71 Viktor Medvedchuk and Yuriy Boyko Visited Moscow on July 10 to Meet with Russian Prime Minister Dmitry Medvedev. *UKRINFORM*, July 11, 2019, https://2cm.es/LQlO; Sukhov, O. (2019). Viktor Medvedchuk Comes Back with a Vengeance. *Kyiv Post*, April 5, https://www.kyivpost.com/post/10220.

Their battle for the Verkhovna Rada will take place very soon, on July 21, and will most likely continue in the local elections scheduled for later this year, which would make 2019 a unique super-election year in the history of contemporary Ukraine.

President Zelensky establishes one-party majority

July 2019[72]

Ukraine's snap parliamentary elections on July 21 yielded another sensational result in the country's super-election year. In an unprecedented victory, President Zelensky's Servant of the People party took 254 of 450 seats, a ballot-box result that amounts to a stable one-party majority in the Verkhovna Rada.[73] Just as in the presidential elections this spring, Zelensky and his party won a majority of votes in all but one oblast, Lviv.

Other parties met with much more humble results. The pro-Russia party Opposition Platform, led by Yuriy Boyko and Viktor Medvedchuk, won forty-three seats. Russian President Vladimir Putin's and Prime Minister Dmitry Medvedev's public support for this party did not translate into success.[74]

Yulia Tymoshenko's Batkivshchyna party and Petro Poroshenko's European Solidarity party won twenty-six and twenty-five seats respectively. The old "Orange" parties lost quite a bit of ground in Ukraine.

The Voice (Golos) party, led by rock singer Svyatoslav Vakarchuk, barely crossed the 5 percent threshold. Seen as a youth wing of Poroshenko's group, Voice brings twenty MPs into parliament

---

[72] A shorter version of this column has previously been published as: Minakov, M. (2019). One-Party Majority: Just Another Victory for Zelensky. *Focus Ukraine*, July 24, https://www.wilsoncenter.org/blog-post/one-party-majority-just-an other-victory-for-Zelensky.

[73] Результаты внеочередных выборов народных депутатов Украины 2019 (from Russian: Results of the Snap Election of People's Deputies of Ukraine 2019). *Ukrainska Pravda*, July 21, 2019, https://www.pravda.com.ua/rus/articl es/2019/07/21/7221526/.

[74] Sorokin, O. (2019). Kremlin-friendly Opposition Platform Becomes Second Largest Party in Parliament. *Kyiv Post*, July 22, https://2cm.es/ObkZ.

and is expected by many to try to form a coalition with the dominant party.

Another fifty-seven MPs will enter the Rada as winners of single-mandate districts. Most of them will want to join a coalition with the president's party, but party leaders have already warned that they will be very selective in whom they form alliances with.[75]

The remaining twenty-six seats in the Verkhovna Rada will remain empty because their voting constituencies live in the non-controlled territories of Donbas and Crimea.

I offer the following three takeaways from Ukraine's parliamentary elections.

Generational change in Ukrainian politics

Both the presidential and the parliamentary election results signal a radical generational change in Ukraine's political class. The results show that established and experienced politicians no longer enjoy the support of the vast majority of voters. Not only do the new political leaders have much greater support than the previous administration, but that support is spread equally across the country.

Zelensky won the presidential race with over 73 percent of the votes. His party received 43 percent of the votes for parliament. Together with the winners of the single-mandate districts, the party will form a stable majority in the Rada. In addition, Svyatoslav Vakarchuk and his team will bring in twenty new, young parliamentarians. In total, "young" (defined not only by age but also by their very recent entrance into politics) parliamentarians will hold more than 300 seats in the new Rada.

The older political generation, defined by the ideological cleavage of the 2004 Orange Revolution, is today represented by the Opposition Platform, Poroshenko's European Solidarity, and

---

75   Разумков: Самовыдвиженцы могут войти во фракцию "Слуги народа", но есть условие (from Russian: Razumkov: Self-Nominated Candidates Can Enter the Faction "Servants of the People", But There Is a Condition). *Ukrainska Pravda*, July 23, 2019, https://www.pravda.com.ua/rus/news/2019/07/23/7221712/.

Tymoshenko's Batkivshchyna. Together, these parties managed to send only around 100 MPs to parliament.

New power elites are rising in Ukraine. These individuals and their political leanings will likely define the country's future for the next ten to fifteen years, just as their predecessors did. The old cleavage, based on geopolitical orientation and ethnolinguistic policies, is fading. Today's political fault line seems to lie in the choice between waging peace or war.

Zelensky's test for Ukrainian political system

With a new cabinet in place and majority support in the Rada, the temporary obstruction of President Zelensky's agenda by the bureaucracy and parliament will likely come to a swift end. Ukraine should once again enjoy normal executive discipline in forming and enacting policy.

Majority support in the Rada also means that most of the reforms announced by the new president are likely to advance. Since many of the reforms promised by candidate Zelensky can only be implemented after some changes are made to Ukraine's constitution, however, the role of the opposition parties will remain significant. To change the constitution, Zelensky will need partners in parliament. If only for this reason, the potential for arbitrary one-party rule will be limited.

A one-party majority in the Rada will test the Ukrainian political system. Ukraine could actually benefit from the current situation: a cabinet and a president supported by a stable majority in the Rada can be efficient in enacting reforms, but the opposition's participation remains essential if lasting constitutional reform is to succeed.

Whether the new parliamentary majority will respect the opposition will become clearer once the parliamentary committees get their new leaders. In 2014, the ruling coalition put all committees under its control, and thus failed to respect the opposition's concerns. Hopefully, this parliament will draw some lessons from the post-Maidan developments and will be more balanced, inclusive, and committed to the national dialogue.

Green light for Zelensky's agenda

With his electoral wins, Zelensky is well positioned to address the major concerns of Ukrainian voters: achieving peace in the East, tackling corruption vigorously, and increasing household incomes.[76]

With respect to the pursuit of peace, Zelensky is currently testing his ability to craft a cease-fire agreement on the line of contact that will hold. On July 21 a "permanent" cease-fire went into effect. Unlike many previous cease-fire agreements, this one appears stable for the moment. Though the stipulated "silence" on the line of contact has been broken several times, with tragic results, every day it gets stronger and stronger.[77]

The new ruling group has also signaled its commitment to fighting corruption. Right after the parliamentary elections, President Zelensky announced that his candidate for general prosecutor was Ruslan Ryaboshapka, a dedicated and experienced lawyer who has proven his ability to fight corruption and make the necessary hard choices.

It is too early to know whether inclusive economic growth is a priority for Zelensky's team. Here the choice of prime minister will be decisive. However, it will be several days to weeks before Zelensky announces his choices for the cabinet.

In these several ways, the parliamentary elections of July 21 continue the trend of big change in Ukrainian politics, and buoy hopes for the country's future.

---

76 Monitoring of Electoral Moods of Ukrainians (13-17 July 2019). *SGR*, July 18, 2019, https://2cm.es/OcZm.

77 На Донбассе оккупанты нарушили "режим тишины" (from Russian: Occupiers Violated the "Silence Regime" in Donbas). *Ukrainska Pravda*, July 23, 2019, https://www.pravda.com.ua/rus/news/2019/07/23/7221691/.

I. 3. Reformer

The first Zelensky's reforms and challenge for checks and balances

September 2019[78]

Ukrainian president Volodymyr Zelensky, who took office more than a hundred days ago, has finally assembled the government that he will use to fulfill his political program. On September 2, 2019, at a joint meeting of the president, his office chiefs, the Cabinet members, the leadership of the Rada, and the general prosecutor, Zelensky conducted himself as a captain giving orders to his crew — perhaps forgetting that all of these assembled officials are representatives of different branches of power in a parliamentary-presidential republic. The abovementioned officials, however, seemed to be equally forgetful of their positions. Instead, the prime minister and the parliament's speaker accepted the situation as natural, and duly made notes of the tasks assigned to them.

The ruling team that now controls parliament, the Cabinet, the Office of the General Prosecutor, the army, and the security services seems to follow presidential orders in spite of the demands of the constitution.

Furthermore, on September 4, 2019, Ukrainian parliament has amended the Constitution abolishing parliamentary immunity.[79] The immunity of president and judges, however, remained intact. Zelensky's draft law on impeachment effectively makes dismissing

---

[78] A shorter version of this column has previously been published as: Minakov, M. (2019). Zelensky's Government and the Challenge for Checks and Balances. *Focus Ukraine*, September 9, https://www.wilsoncenter.org/blog-post/Zelens kys-government-and-the-challenge-for-checks-and-balances.

[79] Ukraine's MPs Cancelled Parliamentary Immunity. Why Is This Dangerous? *Hromadske*, September 4, 2019, https://hromadske.ua/en/posts/ukraines-mps -cancelled-parliamentary-immunity-why-is-this-dangerous.

a president impossible, while MPs can still easily be arrested or dismissed.[80]

This situation is not new. For example, in the post-Euromaidan government, President Petro Poroshenko also become a highly influential political figure, especially after Prime Minister Arseniy Yatseniuk resigned in April 2016. Poroshenko even sought to extend his authority into the Ukrainian church, an obvious contradiction of the constitution (Article 35).[81] However, Poroshenko's authority was limited by Interior Minister Arsen Avakov. Avakov, an ally of Yatsenyuk, provided some balance to the informal distribution of power in Ukraine. Since Ukraine's formal institutions are weak, and became even weaker after each maidan, the balance of power has long been mediated among informal groups within the country. This unspoken balance became particularly visible during the 2019 presidential elections, when Avakov demanded that the incumbent's political team abide by the law, a stricture that worked in favor of Poroshenko's rivals.[82]

Zelensky's group contains numerous people who are new to politics. It was Zelensky's idée fixe to avoid "old time" politicians and officials in his administration.[83] This idea was linked to his aim to bring an end to corruption in the public sector anymore. He brought into power his new Servant of the People (SP) party, which was built during his parliamentary campaign of June and July 2019 and which has a minimum of cadres with previous exposure to national politics or public service.[84]

---

80 Проект Закону про особливу процедуру усунення Президента України з поста (імпічмент) (from Ukrainian: Draft Law on a Special Procedure for Removing the President of Ukraine from Office (Impeachment)). *Official website of the VRU*, August 29, 2019, https://w1.c1.rada.gov.ua/pls/zweb2/webproc4_1?pf3511=66240.
81 Bershidsky, L. (2018). Religion Will Be on Ukraine's Ballot. *Bloomberg*, December 18, 2018, https://2cm.es/LRYd.
82 Stack, G. (2019). Law Enforcement Agencies Take Sides as Election Tensions Rise in Ukraine. *Intellinews*, March 20, https://2cm.es/OcZP.
83 Zelensky's Plan to Purge Ukraine Officials Draws Criticism. *Financial Times*, July 12, 2023, https://www.ft.com/content/f1f40060-a4ab-11e9-974c-ad1c6ab5efd1.
84 Luhn, A. (2019). Reformist President's New Party Set to Win Majority in Ukraine's Parliament. *The Telegraph*, July 22, 2019, https://2cm.es/OcZS.

However, in spite of Zelensky's declared mission to change Ukraine and end political corruption, his new team seems to be avoiding any effort to construct a more formal system of checks and balances. At least, this is the conclusion I have drawn from the political decisions made between August 29, 2019, when the newly elected Rada met for the first time, and the September 5, 2019. Within this short period, Ukraine's parliament appointed the new leadership of the Verkhovna Rada and the Cabinet, and President Zelensky issued his orders to the new senior officials.[85]

Let's look at the construction of Ukraine's current government.

Through the Ukrainian people's democratic choices, the SP is a one-party majority in the Rada. In this situation, the ruling faction is responsible for delivering their promises (which are identical to Zelensky's own promises) to the people, adhering to the Ukrainian constitution, protecting citizens' liberties, and distributing authority among the branches of power.

The composition of the new weakened Rada leadership and membership of the parliamentary committees demonstrate an attempt to balance efficacy and constitutional democratic principles. The SP majority diminished the number of parliamentary committees from 27 to 23. Of these 23 committees, SP members (254 of the Rada's 450 members [MPs]) will preside over 19 of them, and will have 49 deputy chairs and secretaries in the committees. The SP members also have a majority in each parliamentary committee.

Unlike in the previous, post-Euromaidan Rada, the SP majority has provided the diverse opposition groups of the noncoalition parties with an opportunity to chair four committees. Yuri Boyko's Opposition Platform – For Life faction (43 MPs) will chair the Freedom of Speech Committee; it will also have 14 deputy chairs and committee secretaries. Yulia Tymoshenko's Batkyvshchyna faction (26 MPs) will chair the Youth and Sports Committee and will have 10 deputy chairs and secretaries. Petro Poroshenko's European Solidarity (25 MPs) will chair the European Union Integration

---

85 Here's Every Member of Ukraine's New Cabinet of Ministers. *Kyiv Post*, August 29, 2019, https://www.kyivpost.com/post/7598.

Committee and will have a total of three deputy chairs and secretaries. Finally, Svyatoslav Vakarchuk's Voice (20 MPs) will have a total of 13 deputy chairs and secretaries. Although this composition strengthens the president's control of the legislative process, it also provides opposition groups with a more powerful voice than they had in the previous parliament.

The same Zelensky dominance is visible in the new Cabinet as well. The Cabinet, which also was reduced in size from 19 minsters and six vice prime ministers to 15 ministers and two vice ministers, now contains 11 men and six women with an average age of 39. The vast majority (80 percent) are political novices. With the exceptions of Arsen Avakov (who remained Interior Minister) and Oksana Markarova (retained as Minister of Finance), the new Cabinet consists solely of SP members or President Zelensky's appointees.

Prime Minister Oleksiy Honcharuk presides over this youthful Cabinet. At only 35 years of age, he is Ukraine's youngest ever prime minister. In spite of his previous sympathies for President Poroshenko, Honcharuk joined the Zelensky team in spring 2019 and soon became vice head of the presidential office. With no history of allegiance to any oligarch, he is a Zelensky loyalist who seemingly has agreed to run the Cabinet to fulfill the presidential program of reforms. For the time being at least, there does not appear to be any real competition between the president and the prime minister. Accordingly, the SP has shown goodwill to provide opposition with some influence, but its majority is too large for it to be outweighed. The president's control over the legislature and the executive is now significantly larger than under previous administrations, and it is much greater than envisaged by the constitution.

Three years ago, Tymofiy Mylovanov (now the Minister of Economy and an influential intellectual in the governing team) and I published a joint article on the threats that unchecked presidential power brings to post-Soviet political systems.[86] I hope that he and his comrades in Zelensky's crew will keep these risks in mind,

---

86 Minakov, M., Mylovanov, T. (2016). Why the Post-Soviet Presidential Institution Is Flawed. *Vox Ukraine*, June 14, https://voxukraine.org/en/why-is-the-post-soviet-presidential-institution-flawed-en/.

manage to avoid the negative results of imbalanced, personalized power, and are able to implement a more constitutional set of checks and balances in Ukraine.

Zelensky's Achievements after the first six months in power

November 2019[87]

In April, Volodymyr Zelensky was elected president of Ukraine by a relative landslide. As I wrote before, he won with a campaign based on three main promises—promises that reflected the hopes and expectations of Ukraine's deeply frustrated voters: (1) maximum efforts for peace in Donbas, (2) fighting corruption to deliver good and responsive governance, and (3) improving the well-being of ordinary Ukrainian people. In July, Ukrainian voters endorsed this platform again, handing Zelensky's Servant of the People party an absolute majority of seats in the Verkhovna Rada, paving the way for the new president to begin delivering on his lofty promises. So, how have the new president and his team met and managed these expectations during the first months in government?

War and Peace

Despite the many obstacles to Donbas conflict resolution, both domestic and external to Ukraine, and notwithstanding some missteps by the new government, President Zelensky deserves praise for his commitment to delivering on his biggest campaign promise.[88] Kyiv has restarted negotiations with Moscow, Paris, and Berlin to deescalate and resolve the conflict. The Minsk talks are now much more active and productive than they were in 2017 through early 2019.

---

87 A shorter version of this column has previously been published as: Minakov, M., Rojansky, M. (2019). The First Six Months: An Assessment of Zelensky's Achievements. *Focus Ukraine*, November 13, https://www.wilsoncenter.org/blog-post/the-first-six-months-assessment-Zelenskys-achievements.
88 Yaffa, J. (2019). Ukraine's Unlikely President, Promising a New Style of Politics, Gets a Taste of Trump's Swamp. *Newyorker*, October 25, 2019, https://2cm.es/Od08.

A highly visible achievement likely to bear fruit in tamping down heated relations with Russia was the prisoner swap, concluded after several years of waiting. Seventy prisoners—thirty-five held by Ukraine and thirty-five held by the Russia-backed separatists, though fifty-five of the total were in fact Ukrainian citizens—were exchanged in September 2019.[89] Another exchange involving a larger number of detainees is expected soon.[90] This step toward easing the conflict is definitely a tick mark on the success side of the president's ledger.

A second real accomplishment was the start of the front-line withdrawal of troops. Three areas considered appropriate for troop withdrawal had been identified in 2016, but the pullback was initiated only on November 1, 2019, in Stanytsia Luhanska, one of the three sites identified earlier.[91] Signaling the return of normalcy, reconstruction of the destroyed bridge over the Siverskyi Donets river will be finished shortly, reconnecting communities in the area of disengagement. Troops are expected to be withdrawn from two more areas, Petrivske and Zolote, by the end of November 2019. The areas of troop withdrawal were considered to be among the least dangerous on the front line. If effectively implemented, the troop withdrawal could mark the first in a series of steps bringing down the casualty toll among Ukrainian civilians and combatants alike.

However, the situation in the Donbas remains explosive. Despite the ongoing talks in Minsk and force disengagement on the line of contact, more cease-fire violations were committed in both Donetsk and Luhansk oblasts in September than in the previous

---

89 Nechypurenko, I., Higgins, J. (2019). Russia and Ukraine Swap Dozens of Prisoners, in a 'First Step to Stop the War'. *The New York Times*, September 7, https://www.nytimes.com/2019/09/07/world/europe/russia-ukraine-prisoner-swap.html.
90 New Prisoner Swap Not Synchronized with Normandy Summit—FM Prystaiko. *UNIAN*, November 1, 2019, https://2cm.es/Od0a.
91 President: The Liberation of Ukrainian Citizens and the Separation of Troops in Petrivske and Zolote was discussed at the TCG meeting in Minsk. *The President of Ukraine official website*, October 1, 2019, https://www.president.gov.ua/en/news/prezident-ukrayini-na-zasidanni-tkg-u-minsku-obgovoryuvalosy-57573.

month.[92] At this point, ending the conflict seems more an aspirational goal than one to be achieved on a timetable.

Russia's illegal annexation of Crimea seems to be excluded from the talks with Russia. Kyiv wants the issue back on the agenda; however, resolution of the conflict in the Donbas takes precedence.

Finally, Zelensky's peace plans are meeting growing resistance from pro-Poroshenko groups and nationalist forces.[93] Some radical groups tried to subvert the troop pullback in Stanytsia Luhanska. President Zelensky moved on the spot to talk to protesters in the war zone and to resolve the issue.[94] But the entire situation points to the lack of communication between the government, on the one hand, and the military, National Guard, and volunteer paramilitary organizations on the other — and the latter, those with the guns, are proving increasingly persuasive in their resistance to the government's plans to achieve peace.

Corruption and Good Governance

The Ukrainian government has taken some important steps on fighting corruption. Zelensky has met frequently with the heads of the anti-corruption institutes, including the Specialized Anti-Corruption Prosecutor's Office (SAPO), the National Anti-Corruption Bureau (NABU), the National Agency for Prevention of Corruption (NAPC), the State Bureau of Investigations (SBI), the Security Service of Ukraine (SSU), and the Anti-Corruption Court of Ukraine. Each time he has publicly demanded that these agencies prove their efficacy — to the Ukrainian people and to himself.

---

92 Special Monitoring Mission to Ukraine Daily Report 260/2019. *OSCE*, November 2, 2019, https://www.osce.org/special-monitoring-mission-to-ukraine/437753.
93 Roth, A. (2019). Thousands march in Kyiv to oppose east Ukraine peace plan. *The Guardian*, October 14, https://www.theguardian.com/world/2019/oct/14/thousands-march-kyiv-oppose-east-ukraine-peace-plan.
94 Volunteer veterans reportedly withdraw their firearms from Zolote-4 after meeting with Zelenskiy. *The Ukrainian Week*, October 28, 2019, https://ukrainiaweek.com/volunteer-veterans-reportedly-withdraw-their-firearms-from-zolote-4-after-meeting-with-zelenskiy/.

Most of these bodies have scored only modest achievements. They have arrested some of President Poroshenko's associates and launched investigations into their potential crimes. Among the most visible detainees are Oleg Hladkovsky, a top Defense official and business partner of Poroshenko; a People's Front party MP and the former head of the Rada's defense committee Serhii Pashinsky; and ex-deputy minister for the occupied territories Yuri Hrymchak.[95] Other current investigations are focusing on pro-Russia opposition leaders.

However, these arrests and investigations have not yet led to court rulings. And this will not be an easy or a fast process. Moreover, that the investigations were launched almost exclusively against members or associates of the previous President's administration following a power turnover is concerning. Will the anticorruption bodies be responsive to corrupt behavior in the current governing team, and will it thus confront corruption in real time, not merely waiting to read the political winds following every power shift?

An answer might soon be forthcoming in what happens to Privatbank, whose former owner, oligarch Ihor Kolomoisky, is seen by many as President Zelensky's supporter.[96] Kolomoisky is suing to have the nationalized bank returned to him even as the EBRD and IMF are pushing Zelensky to recover the billions in depositors' money that disappeared from Privatbank before the state took over. The IMF, for example, does not believe in the current ruler's independence, having told Zelensky he must clean up the financial system and reduce the influence of the oligarchs before a new loan deal can be concluded.[97]

---

95 Court Arrests Hladkovsky For Two Months With Hr 10 Million Bail. *Kyiv Post*, October 19, 2019, https://2cm.es/LR-z; Kyiv Court Arrests Ex-MP Pashynsky. *UNIAN*, October 7, 2019, https://www.unian.info/politics/10711902-kyiv-court-arrests-ex-mp-pashynsky.html; Court Arrests Deputy Minister Hrymchak For Two Months. *UKRINFORM*, August 17, 2019, https://2cm.es/LR-B.
96 "NABU and SSU Should Do Their Job on Privatbank" – EBRD Vice President. *Hromadske*, October 29, 2019, https://hromadske.ua/en/posts/nabu-and-sbu-should-do-their-job-on-privatbank-ebrds-vice-president.
97 See: Talley, I., Cullison, A. (2019). Ukraine Corruption Concerns Stall IMF Bailout. *The Wall Street Journal*, October 31, https://2cm.es/Od0l; Ukraine

Other achievements in this sector are more positive. The High Anti-Corruption Court, whose launch was delayed by President Poroshenko, has started work; its first ruling came at the end of October 2019.[98] New legislation has lifted Poroshenko-era constraints on the anti-corruption system: the NAPC was reformed to sever ties with the oligarchic clans, while the SSU leadership and other high law-enforcement officials became subject to open reporting requirements in the NAPC e-assets declaration.[99] Also, Zelensky's team has managed to pass a bill that reinstates criminal liability for the illegal enrichment of officials, thus restoring the personal responsibility that was canceled under the previous administration just before Poroshenko left office.[100]

August and September saw a number of cases brought against pro-presidential MPs either for violating the constitution (by voting instead of another MP), or for breaking the moral rules of membership in the legislature, or for receiving cash payments from the Servant of the People faction, Zelensky's party.[101] No legal or political action was taken to punish these breaches of trust and the law, however.

---

should tackle corruption to win new loan: IMF. *France 24*, November 7, 2019, https://www.france24.com/en/20191107-ukraine-should-tackle-corruption-to-win-new-loan-imf.

98 High Anti-Corruption Court Starts Work in Ukraine: How Will It Operate? *Ukraine Crisis*, September 6, 2019, https://uacrisis.org/en/73207-high-anti-corruption-court.

99 The President signed the law that restarts NACP and opens declarations of the SSU leadership. *Antac*, October 16, 2019, https://2cm.es/Od0p.

100 See: Joint Statement of the G7 and the World Bank on Constitutional Court Decision on Illicit Enrichment. *The EU Diplomatic Service*, March 7, 2019, https://www.eeas.europa.eu/node/59235_en; Ukrainian lawmakers reinstate criminal liability for illicit enrichment. UNIAN, November 1, 2019, https://2cm.es/LRYS.

101 See: Думанская, В. (2019). Кнопкодавы Зеленского: Нарушить обещание в первую неделю работы (from Russian: Zelensky's Buttonheads: Breaking a Promise in His First Week on the Job). *Ukrainska Pravda*, September 13, 2019, https://www.pravda.com.ua/rus/columns/2019/09/13/7226190/; Rannard, G., Zotsenko, D. (2019). Ukraine MP 'Sorry' for Prostitute Chat in Parliament. *BBC News*, October 31, 2019, https://www.bbc.com/news/blogs-trending-50249919; Пранкер "Джокер" обсуждал с депутатом Радуцким зарплату в конвертах для "слуг народа" (from Russian: Joker Pranker Discussed with MP Radutsky Envelope Salaries for "Servants of the People"). *Ukrainiski Novyny*, November 1, 2019, https://2cm.es/LRZ0.

Zelensky's fight against corruption has so far taken the form of punishing those adjudged to have engaged in corrupt behaviors. Although his team brings a bit less corruption related baggage than is usual into power in Ukraine, a further test will be how he handles the appearance or reality of corruption among his own allies. Broader good governance and concrete steps to change the longstanding culture of corruption remain as future challenges.

Economic Growth

Ukraine's economy is now in relatively good shape — a credit first of all to the country's hardworking and innovative population, but also to the work of the previous government with international stewardship and support. During Zelensky's first six months, the country's GDP has continued growing, notching up 3.5 percent growth in the first half of 2019, compared to 3.3 percent for same period in 2018 (World Bank's data). Also, household consumption has continued to grow.

According to recent data, since September, the hryvnia to dollar exchange rate appreciated by 3.2 percent, to around 24.36 hryvnia per $1 by the end of October, thanks to foreign exchange inflows by nonresidents who are purchasing government securities.[102] Also, though Ukraine's current account deficit had grown by 42 percent from $359 million in August 2018 to $512 million by the beginning of July 2019, this deficit was offset by $639 million in financial inflows. At the same time, manufacturing and FDI growth remained weak: as World Bank reports, fixed investment amounts to 20 percent of GDP, which is insufficient for sustainable growth.

There are other holes in the economic picture that may have far-reaching results for Zelensky. Small and medium-sized enterprises (SMEs), among Zelensky's biggest supporters in the presidential election, are now starting to resist some of the president's

---

102 Ustenko, O. et al. (2019). Ukraine – Macroeconomic Situation Report – October 2019. *The Bleyzer Foundation*, October, https://www.usubc.org/files/SB_Ukr_Monthly_Ec_Report_October_2019.pdf.

economic initiatives, which are seen as a crackdown on SMEs.[103] In October, for example, a set of new legal acts came into force that increase the tax burden on businesses and increase the power of tax inspectors. The goal of the reform is to eliminate the shadow economy. However, the crackdown should start with the oligarchs, not by putting pressure on small businesses. In response to complaints from SMEs, President Zelensky promised a breakthrough for the Ukrainian economy and a two-year period during which SMEs would not be liable to tax inspection.[104]

Meanwhile, Ukraine rose seven points in the World Bank's Doing Business 2020 ranking, reaching the 64th position.[105]

Even though most of the economic developments of 2019, both positive and negative, are not solely the result of Zelensky's team's decisions but are continuations of trends that started under his predecessor, voters do associate them with the young president.[106] It is a reflection of an almost euphoric change of the public mood that Ukrainians have started positively assessing the economic situation in polling data, and they even praise the state of roads, which have long been infamous for their derelict condition, and are in reality hardly different from what they were a year ago.

---

103 Петрук, Н. (2019). Нові правила для ФОПів: що підписав Зеленський (from Ukrainian: New Rules for Individual Entrepreneurs: What Zelensky Signed)? *Radio Svoboda*, October 18, 2019, https://www.radiosvoboda.org/a/novi-prav yla-dli-fopiv/30193436.html.
104 Ukraine on Verge of Economic Breakthrough – Zelensky. *Interfax*, October 29, 2019, https://en.interfax.com.ua/news/economic/621518.html; Зеленський ініціює запровадження дворічного мораторію на перевірки ФОП усіх категорій, окрім "ризикових" (from Ukrainian: Zelenskyy Introduces a Two-Year Moratorium on Inspecting Private Entrepreneurs of All Categories Except "Risky".). *Interfax*, October 15, 2019, https://ua.interfax.com.ua/news/econo mic/619027.html.
105 Doing business 2020 – Ukraine profile. *World Bank*, January 2021, https://www.doi ngbusiness.org/content/dam/doingBusiness/country/u/ukraine/UKR.pdf.
106 Assessment of the Situation in Ukraine (19-22 October 2019). *SGR*, October 24, 2019, http://ratinggroup.ua/en/research/ukraine/ocenka_situacii_v_strane_19-22_okt yabrya_2019_goda.html.

Trust in the Government

A recent poll conducted by the Sociological SGR shows that, despite the various scandals and disappointing decisions, Ukrainians' optimism prevails, and trust in President Zelensky and his government remains high.[107] Moreover, trust in public institutions in general has increased in comparison with the beginning of the year. The most trusted institutions are civilian volunteer organizations (69 percent), veterans of the Donbas war (67 percent), the president (66 percent), and the Ukrainian army (65 percent). The Cabinet of Ministers (45 percent) and the Verkhovna Rada (44 percent) also received very high trust ratings, especially when compared with the 9 percent trust in government measured in December 2018.[108]

The result for Zelensky, 66 percent, is high, but seven percentage points lower than in September 2019. This decline should be a wake-up call for the new administration, but it also reflects a more realistic recalibration of Ukrainians' earlier very high expectations. That said, Ukrainians still trust their new president and his team. And it is up to the president to ensure that this trust remains solidly grounded on his achievements.

Zelensky meets Putin in Paris

December 2019[109]

After a three-year break, the Normandy Format was once more activated earlier this week. The presidents of Ukraine, France, and Russia and the chancellor of Germany met in Paris on December 9, 2019, to resume talks on the fate of eastern Ukraine.[110] Though the

---

107 Ibid.
108 See the year old data at: Bikus, Z. (2019). World-Low 9% of Ukrainians Confident in Government. *Gallup*, March 21, 2019, https://news.gallup.com/poll/247976/world-low-ukrainians-confident-government.aspx.
109 A shorter version of this column has previously been published as: Minakov, M. (2019). Results of the Normandy Format Talks for Ukraine: Hope, with Reservations. *Focus Ukraine*, December 11, https://www.wilsoncenter.org/blog-post/results-the-normandy-format-talks-for-ukraine-hope-reservations.
110 More on the meeting, see: Parandii, Kh. (2019). Will the Normandy Four Summit Bring "Peace for Our Time" to Ukraine? *Center for European Reform*,

meeting did not lead to a breakthrough in finding a solution to the Russian-Ukrainian conflict, it did have some promising results.

President Volodymyr Zelensky arrived in Paris burdened by declining popularity and by political rivalry with Ukraine's former president, Petro Poroshenko. Poroshenko, during whose presidency the Minsk Memorandum and the Minsk Protocols were signed, now demands that these agreements not be implemented, saying that doing so would be capitulating to Russia.[111] By challenging Zelensky's authority in this fashion, Poroshenko appears to be using against the new president certain tactics that Saakashvili used against him in 2017, in the hope of consolidating various oppositional parliamentary parties and radical groups and becoming their new leader.[112] With a large hostile crowd gathered in Kyiv's center, near his office, expressing support for Ukraine's sovereignty and independence and decrying any possible deal with Russia, President Zelensky left to face Putin in Paris.[113]

A meeting of the four leaders, with documented conclusions, along with separate talks between the Ukrainian and Russian presidents and delegations, produced the following key results.[114]

First, political communication between Kyiv and Moscow has been revived, after being dormant since November 2016. It was the first face-to-face meeting of President Zelensky and President

---

December 5, https://www.cer.eu/insights/will-normandy-four-summit-bring-peace-our-time-ukraine; Putin and Zelensky Are Meeting for the First Time in Paris. What Could They Possibly Agree on? *Meduza*, December 9, 2019, https://2cm.es/LRZg; Hodge, N. (2019). In Paris, Putin and Zelensky Take Hesitant Steps Toward Peace. *CNN*, December 9, https://2cm.es/Od0T.
111 Kraner, A. (2019). Zelensky's Opponents Fear He Is Ready to Capitulate to Russia. *The New York Times*, December 5, https://www.nytimes.com/2019/12/05/world/europe/zelensky-ukraine-russia.html.
112 Thousands of Saakashvili Supporters Stage Protest against Ukraine President. *Reuters*, December 10, 2017, https://2cm.es/Od0Y.
113 Don't Cede Too Much to Putin, Ukrainians Tell Zelenskiy Ahead of Paris Summit. *EURACTIV*, December 9, 2019, https://2cm.es/LRZo.
114 Overall Agreed Conclusions of the Paris Summit in the Normandy Format of December 9, 2019. *President of Ukraine official website*, December 10, 2019, https://president.gov.ua/en/news/zagalni-uzgodzheni-visnovki-parizkogo-samitu-v-normandskomu-58797. See also: Gotev, G. (2019). Normandy Summit Upholds 'Steinmeier formula' for Eastern Ukraine. *Euractiv*, December 10, 2019, https://2cm.es/Od15.

Putin. The leaders of the two nations at war with each other had a chance to start resolving the conflict. Angela Merkel and Vladimir Putin, the Normandy talks' "old-timers," are now restarting the negotiations with new participants in the French and Ukrainian leaders. This meeting thus seemed to mark the start of the new period of enhanced communication in a format that has proven to be effective in preventing conflict from escalating.

Second, the status of the Minsk agreements seems to start changing. Both Minsk documents are the result of Russia's and the Russian-backed separatist military's successes in the campaign of August 2014 – February 2015. Since then the political and security situation has changed. And even though President Putin said at the meeting that there are "no alternatives" to the Minsk agreements, Zelensky's and, to some extent, Angela Merkel's statements at the press conference suggest that these agreements may be reviewed for the sake of conflict resolution.[115]

Third, the participants in the Paris talks reached some important decisions with regard to demilitarization and addressing humanitarian needs in the Donbas. Both Moscow and Kyiv agreed to implement a lasting cease-fire. At the press conference, Zelensky demanded that the Russian Federation use its influence in the region to make the cease-fire a reality, taking the same responsibility on himself on behalf of Ukrainian forces.[116] Other promising proposals that seemed to have mutual consent included troop withdrawal in three new places on the front line, an "all-for-all" prisoner swap by New Year's Eve, stepped-up mine clearance, extension of the Law on the Special Status of Certain Districts of the Donetsk and Luhansk Regions, and incorporation of the Steinmeier formula into Ukrainian legislation.[117]

---

115 First Normandy Four Summit in 3 Years: How It Happened. *Hromadske*, December 9, 2019, https://hromadske.ua/en/posts/first-normandy-four-summit-in-3-years-live-updates.
116 Ibid.
117 See: Volodymyr Zelenskyy: The Most Important Victory for Me Is That We Have Agreed to Release Captives on the Principle "All for All" by December 31. *President of Ukraine official website*, December 10, 2019, https://2cm.es/Od1h; The Law on Special Order of Local Self-Government in Certain Areas of Donbas

In several key areas, however, Kyiv and Moscow did not reach agreement: holding elections in the non-controlled territories, as called for under the Steinmeier formula; the handling of Russian-Ukrainian border control; and the status of the Donbas after reintegration.[118] These disagreements may help keep the street protests in Kyiv in check and assure protestors that the president is not capitulating. Also, the seemingly permanent interior minister, Arsen Avakov, has got a message to cool it out to some of the more radical groups that are allegedly under his influence.[119] Avakov has supported Zelensky and his position during talks on regaining control of the Donbas.[120]

In addition to the Donbas issue, the Ukrainian and Russian delegations discussed the gas issue in a bilateral format. The two presidents, together with several ministers and representatives of Naftogaz and Gazprom, have tried to find their way to agreeing on a new contract for transiting gas from Russia to the EU through Ukraine's pipelines. Both Paris and Berlin are very interested in seeing this issue resolved before the current contract between Ukraine and Russia expires on January 1, 2020.[121]

All parties made some progress in the fall of 2019 toward a new contract that would ensure Ukraine's and the EU's energy security. According to sources in Naftogaz and the European

---

May Be Extended for Another Year—President. *President of Ukraine official website*, December 10, 2019, https://2cm.es/LRZK.

118 See: The Parties Will Return to the Issue of Restoring Ukraine's Full Control Over the State Border During the Next Meeting in the Normandy Format—President. *President of Ukraine official website*, December 10, 2019, https://2cm.es/Od1u; Ukraine Will Never Give Up Its Territory and Will Not Allow to Influence the Vector of Its Movement and Development—President. *President of Ukraine official website*, December 10, 2019, https://www.president.gov.ua/en/news/ukrayina-nikoli-ne-postupitsya-svoyeyu-teritoriyeyu-j-ne-doz-58805.

119 Bennetts, M. (2018). Ukraine's National Militia: "We're not neo-Nazis, we just want to make our country better". *The Guardian*, March 13, https://2cm.es/LR-0.

120 Бега, В. (2019). Аваков: украинская полиция зайдет на оккупированные территории и будет патрулировать вместе с местными представителями (from Russian: Avakov: Ukrainian Police Will Enter Occupied Territories and Patrol Together with Local Representatives). *Hromadske*, December 10, 2019, https://2cm.es/LR-6.

121 On these interests, see: Rettman, A. (2019). EU Fears New Russia Gas Crisis, Amid Court Disputes. *The EU Observer*, November 28, https://euobserver.com/foreign/146753.

Commission, a draft agreement had been prepared in advance of the Paris talks and was ready to be signed and presented by the presidents as one of the meeting's successes. However, some new and as yet unclear disagreements among the parties appeared just hours before the meeting. Thus this part of the talks failed, though the involved parties plan to follow up soon and try to prevent Kyiv and Moscow from engaging in a new energy war.

The results of the Paris talks proved that the antecedent hopes and fears were both, to some extent, based in a realistic appraisal of the outcome. The Normandy Format has had new life breathed into it, and the two nations have restarted peace and trade negotiations. Some steps toward demilitarization of the line of contact and improving the quality of life in the war-affected communities were made. However, after almost six years of conflict, negotiations are still in an early stage. The old conflict can lead to many new ones: in the energy sector, in the radicalization of protests, in failure of the cease-fire and the resumption of hostilities. A stable peace in Ukraine and Eastern Europe thus remains a distant goal for all parties in Europe.

Political struggle and media wars in the winter of 2019–2020

February 2020[122]

In the recent three months, Ukrainian politics have been overtaken by information wars. These wars undermine two things vital to liberal democracy: citizens' control of government and the transparency of authorities' actions.

Both traditional and social media in Ukraine contribute to propagating leaks — insider information, secret records, political pranks — which in turn inform Ukrainian citizens of the habits of mind, moral values, and just plain oddities of the country's political

---

[122] A shorter version of this column has previously been published as: Minakov, M., Prokip, A. (2019). Ukraine's Democratic Leakocracy. *Focus Ukraine*, February 27, 2020, https://www.wilsoncenter.org/blog-post/ukraines-democratic-leakocracy.

leaders and officials.[123] However, in Ukraine as in many other countries, the "leakocracy" does not serve democracy well: instead of encouraging government accountability, it feeds resentment politics, destroys trust, and wreaks havoc on the public sphere as a space for meaningful discourse among citizens. And the information fed to the public through leaks may be intentionally falsified.

The most recent case is connected to an attack on Ukraine's prime minister, Oleksiy Honcharuk. Since January 15, secret recordings of a meeting convened by Honcharuk have been leaked to the media by an unknown source.[124] On these recordings, the prime minister, several cabinet ministers, representatives of the National Bank of Ukraine, and other top officials are heard discussing how to explain the country's economic situation to President Volodymyr Zelensky. Among the many uncomfortable matters surfaced in the recordings is that the head of the cabinet, who is responsible for economic policies, is in fact not an expert on economic development and has avoided informing President Zelensky about some troubling financial issues.

It is quite probable that the aim of releasing these recordings was to discredit the prime minister, undermine the unity of Zelensky's team, and try to use the ensuing scandal to topple the cabinet. Such a scandal did appear briefly to be taking shape, its further development nipped in the bud by President Zelensky's public show of support for Honcharuk and the cabinet. Simultaneously, President Zelensky demanded that law enforcement agencies find whoever made and leaked the illegal recordings.

In early February the Security Service of Ukraine searched some media outlets but did not uncover the source.[125] instead, the searches added to journalists' concerns over shrinking media

---

[123] For example, see: Ukraine Prime Minister Offers Resignation after Leaked Recording. *The Guardian*, January 17, 2020, https://2cm.es/LR-H; SSU Chief: We Do Not Render Services to Political Elites, But Ensure the National Security of the Country. *Interfax*, December 19, 2019, https://en.interfax.com.ua/news/interview/631440.html.

[124] Sorokin, O. (2020). Prime Minister Honcharuk Targeted in Latest Audio Leak. *Kyiv Post*, January 16, 2020, https://2cm.es/LR-N.

[125] Sukhov, O. (2020). Authorities Search Kolomoisky's TV Studio as Part of Honcharuk Leak Case. *Kyiv Post*, February 6, 2020, https://www.kyivpost.com/post/10659.

freedom in Ukraine.[126] Zelensky's approval rating dropped slightly in connection with the scandal. The greatest impact, however, showed up in loss of trust in elections as a means for citizens to express their interests and emphasize policy priorities important to them. In January 2020, politicians and citizens across the political spectrum were voicing the same concern in on-air talk shows: the elected leaders were not delivering what they had promised as candidates and what the voters thought they were getting. The major factor giving rise to this concern is the leaks, which feed suspicions and disbelief.

Thus 2019 appears in retrospect to have been a turning point in Ukrainian politics. Both the style and content of public political communication have changed drastically from what they were in the post-Maidan years. The very nature of what is being discussed, and how, has changed.

Wire-tape recordings and leaks are not new in Ukrainian politics. Since Kuchmagate of 2000, the secrets leaked from the offices of Ukrainian leaders have played into the political process in important ways. Petr Poroshenko's presidency, for example, was not immune to such influences.[127] Beginning in 2019, however, what was previously a marginal factor in shaping political processes has moved to center-stage.

The leakocracy's distinctive feature is the promotion to positions of authority of fledgling politicians who are unknown to citizen-voters and inexperienced in negotiating established democratic institutions. The people currently in power seem to be hewing narrowly to the principle of withholding information: the less one knows about an emerging decision-maker, the less ground one has to doubt that person's actions. And so not trust but resentment and mistrust are leading to certain choices made by citizens.

The effect of the leakocracy is strongest when the mass media proliferate into the political and private spheres to such an extent that they force a spectacle culture on media consumers. Just as

---

126 Dutsyk, D., Dyczok, M. (2020). Ukraine's New Media Laws: Fighting Disinformation or Targeting Freedom of Speech? *Focus Ukraine*, February 10, 2020, https://2cm.es/LR-O.

127 Sukhov, O. (2018). Onyshchenko Releases Alleged Recording Implicating Poroshenko, Zlochevsky In Graft. *Kyiv Post*, April 20, 2018, https://www.kyivpost.com/post/10319.

political philosophers and certain visionary sociologists feared, mediated images now control human attention, which changes the very logic of political and economic competition, as well as government behavior. Together, spectacle and resentment are creating a new political reality in Ukraine.

This reality works in the following way. The winner of the 2019 presidential elections was a candidate who communicated to voters through a satirical TV show.[128] The new ruling party, Servant of the People, is named after Zelensky's popular sitcom and is expected to act in accordance with the TV show's plot and the president's wishes.[129] People with no political experience whatsoever before 2019 now make decisions for a population of approximately 40 million and the largest European country by territory.

To compete with authorities of the Zelenskyan type, various opposition groups use leaks as the only tool that works against headliner politicians. In particular, they use new media to compete with new power—such as by leaking audio files of Honcharuk's meeting, which revealed some astonishing deficits in the administration. President Zelensky's support remains high among voters. But trust in public policy and political solidarity have both been dealt blows as the new media deliver a mixture of truth and falsity, with very troubling results.

Ukraine has reached a dangerous crossroad in its political development. In 2019, voters used a classic democratic instrument, elections, to deliver a definitive verdict on the post-Maidan elites and their policies.[130] Their use of leaks to control the new authorities now brings the country to an unknown land of spectacle politics, not democracy. Information tornados—a spiraling, toxic mix of truth and misdirection—are turning a modern democracy into a resentful leakocracy with an unpredictable future.

---

128 Nussbaum, E. (2019). In Ukraine, a TV President to Rival Trump. *The Newyorker*, September 30, 2019, https://www.newyorker.com/magazine/2019/10/07/in-ukraine-a-tv-president-to-rival-trump.
129 Wilson, J. (2019). Ukraine Elected a Sitcom Star President. His Show Tells Us What to Expect. *Slate*, April 26, 2019, https://2cm.es/LR-T.
130 Jacobsen, K. (2016). How a Fictional President Is Helping Ukrainians Rethink Their Absurd Politics. *Foreign Policy*, December 13, 2016, https://2cm.es/LR-U.

II. Master

New Zelensky's administration: arrival of Yermak and Shmyhal

March 2020[131]

"No story is ever over."[132]

On March 4, 2020, Ukraine's parliament approved a change of cabinet. Appointed on August 29, 2019, President Volodymyr Zelensky's first cabinet barely survived six months, a short tenure marked by chaos.[133] Thus the new political generation's first attempts to create a better Ukraine have failed, putting in doubt the newcomers' ability to effectively govern a large and culturally diverse European country.

In recent months, Ukrainian internal politics was marked by a series of mini-crises, mainly connected to the cabinet members and the Rada's ruling faction, Zelensky's Servant of the People party. A radical parliamentary opposition amplified the miscalculations of Zelensky's team, making sure each failure became a media scandal and each scandal became a sort of mini-referendum on trust in President Zelensky.

So far, the opposition's spoiler strategy has not proved effective. Volodymyr Zelensky remains the only politician whose trust rating is higher than distrust rating: in different polls, this ratio varies from 59 percent trust in the president to 32 percent distrust,[134] to

---

131 A shorter version of this column has previously been published as: Minakov, M. (2020). Zelensky Relaunches His Administration with a Fresh Cohort. *Focus Ukraine*, March 5, https://www.wilsoncenter.org/blog-post/Zelensky-relaunches-his-administration-fresh-cohort.

132 Quotation from: "But if anything is certain it is that no story is ever over, for the story which we think is over is only a chapter in a story which will not be over, and it isn't the game that is over, it is just an inning, and that game has a lot more than nine innings." Robert Penn Warren, *All the King's Men*.

133 Here's every member of Ukraine's new Cabinet of Ministers. *Kyiv Post*, August 29, 2019, https://www.kyivpost.com/post/7598.

134 Socio-political Moods of Population (22-26 January 2020). *SGR*, February 4, 2020, https://2cm.es/LR-Y.

51.5 percent versus 41 percent.[135] However, the same polls show that distrust in the cabinet and the Rada has soared to over 64 percent for both institutions, and it can be safely assumed that the president is losing support as well.

"Farewell, Youth!"[136]

On March 4, before Prime Minister Oleksiy Honcharuk, who was among those dismissed, spoke some parting words to the Rada, President Zelensky delivered a speech in which he blamed his own cabinet for unsatisfactory reforms. Specifically, reforms in the health care and social welfare spheres and the inexpensive provision of basic utilities were assessed as not responding to the core needs of Ukrainians. He also confessed that he did not control the *sylovyky*[137] sufficiently to be able to effectively punish corrupt officials. In a way, the president confessed to a mistake in putting together this particular cabinet.

In response, Prime Minister Honcharuk made a short, impassioned statement to the Rada in which he declared that his reforms had been quite successful but were clearly underappreciated.[138] He also thanked the president for the opportunity to try to change Ukraine for the better.

At the conclusion of these exercises in blaming and thanking, the Rada issued its verdict: the prime minister was sacked by 353 votes (226 were needed). The youngest Ukrainian prime minister in

---

135 Оцінка громадянами діяльності влади, рівень довіри до соціальних інститутів та політиків, електоральні орієнтації громадян (лютий 2020 р.) (from Ukrainian: Citizens' Assessment of the Government's Performance, the Level of Trust in Social Institutions and Politicians, the Electoral Orientations of Citizens (Late 2020)). *Razumkov Center*, February 24, 2020, https://2cm.es/LR--.
136 Quotation from: "Farewell, Youth, I'm afraid I hardly got to know you." Grunge punk band The Menzingers, *Farewell Youth*.
137 *Sylovyky* or "securocrats" are officials and politicians associated with the security or military services who are now presiding as heads of the law enforcement agencies.
138 Остання промова Гончарука як прем'єра (from Ukrainian: Remaining Promotion of Goncharuk as Prime Minister). *Channel 24*, March 4, 2020, https://www.youtube.com/watch?v=OI85jTyjyp0.

the history of independent Ukraine and the cabinet have been abruptly dismissed.

"Greetings, youthful and unfamiliar clan!"[139]

In line with information leaked before the vote in the Rada, President Zelensky proposed to the Rada appointing Denys Shmyhal as the new prime minister.[140]

Shmyhal was named deputy prime minister in February 2020. Educated in Belgian, Canadian, and Finnish universities, he had previously worked as head of the administration of Ivano-Frankivsk oblast (in 2019-2020), as an executive at Rinat Akhmetov's DTEK energy company (2017-2019), and as an official and businessman in various organizations (before 2017). Though coming with a strong economic and administrative background, Shmyhal is a novice in politics, just as his predecessor was on the day of his appointment.

Shmyhal offered the Rada his plan, which includes (1) economic reforms that promote the social welfare of citizens and deliver revenues to the state budget; (2) reform of the public health system; and (3) continued decentralization and ensuring the reintegration of non-controlled communities in the Donbas and Crimea. After a short deliberation, parliament approved Shmyhal as Ukraine's prime minister with 291 votes. President Zelensky showed that he still controls parliament and can get the MPs' approval of relatively unknown candidates at will for any post in the government.

Several positions in the new cabinet were also approved. The share of the cabinet that constitutionally belongs to the Verkhovna Rada, with appointments proposed by the prime minister,

---

139 Quotation from: "But apart / Their sullen comrade stood in lonely splendour / Like aged bachelor, and, just as before, / Around it all was barren. / Greetings, youthful / And unfamiliar clan! I shall not see / The mighty growth of your maturing summers, / When you'll outstrip these trees I've known for ages...." Alexander Pushkin, *Life Again Has Brought Me* (Вновь я посетил), tr. by Rupert Moreton.

140 Talant, B. (2020). Leaked Memo from Presidential Office Outlines Targets for Cabinet Shuffle. *Kyiv Post*, March 3, 2020, https://2cm.es/Od31.

delivered 277 yea votes (out of 381) to affirm the choices of Shmygal. Shmyhal proposed thirteen ministers and vice prime ministers, five of whom were members of the retiring Honcharuk cabinet.[141] The ever-constant Arsen Avakov remains as minister of interior affairs, a position he has held since 2014 under multiple presidents. So far the new cabinet is overall more experienced, but four important ministerial positions remained unfilled: those of culture, education, energy, and economy (some of these ministries may actually be divided into two, so the open posts might amount to six, not four).

The president also received the Rada's approval for his share of cabinet appointments. Dmytro Kuleba became minister of foreign affairs, and retired general Andrii Taran was approved as the new minister of defense.

According to sources in parliament, President Zelensky has described the new cabinet as "new faces with brains."[142] Indeed, Zelensky's signature policy of appointing novices to strategically important positions has continued. This time, however, several appointees do have some experience in public office, including the prime minister, the minister of finance, and the minister of social policy. But the major characteristics of the new cabinet members are better alignment with the goals and objectives of the president and his recently appointed chief of staff, Andriy Yermak, and less entanglement with politicians in the West.

The desire for better alignment of cabinet members' views with the administration's goals likely stems from the rapid appointment of Andriy Bohdan as chief of staff within 24 hours after Zelensky's May 2019 inauguration, and Bohdan's subsequent assemblage of the cabinet under Prime Minister Honcharuk. With time, too many differences surfaced, and Bohdan left office in in early

---

141 Рада избрала новый состав правительства (from Russian: The Rada Elected a New Government). *Ukrainska Pravda*, March 4, 2020, https://www.pravda.com.ua/rus/news/2020/03/4/7242543/.

142 A New Government for Ukraine: One Female Minister and "Indispensable" Arsen Avakov. *Hromadske*, March 4, 2020, https://hromadske.ua/en/posts/ukrainian-parliament-votes-in-new-pm-denys-shmyhal.

February. Yermak has now reassembled the cabinet in a way that better fits his operating style.

But the rising wave of anti-Western resentment should also be taken into account in understanding the cabinet reshaping. In my talks with pro-presidential politicians and officials over the past two weeks, I constantly encountered hidden antipathy toward the West. Many young and educated politicians and administrators believe that Western governments and financial-political clans have representatives in Ukraine; the common name for these traitors of the national interest is *sorosiata* (roughly, "Uncle Soros's kids"). Despite diverse attitudes toward Ukraine in the West, for Ukraine's many politicians the *sorosiata* represent a threat equal to Russia's, and their dominance in Honcharuk's cabinet was not acceptable.

Another important step taken yesterday was intended to dilute the influence of the *sylovyky*. The Rada has split the positions of head of the army and head of army staff; candidates to fill these positions are currently under discussion. Also, the president and the Rada agreed to review how law enforcement agencies fight crime and corruption in the public sphere in Ukraine on September 5. Although G-7 ambassadors have publicly expressed support for Ukraine's general prosecutor Ruslan Ryaboshapka,[143] the parliamentary committee recommended a vote of no confidence in him.[144] Ryaboshapka seems to have evolved into another scapegoat for the entire *sylovyky* team's failure to punish officials suspected of corruption.

"The seeds of time."[145]

Prime Minister Shmyhal now faces the daunting task of fulfilling the many expectations of Ukraine's president and, to a somewhat

---

[143] G7 Ambassadors to Meet with Prosecutor General Riaboshapka Today. *Interfax*, March 3, 2020, https://en.interfax.com.ua/news/general/644605.html.

[144] Rada's Committee Recommends MPs to Consider Draft Resolution on Vote of No Confidence in Riaboshapka. *Interfax*, March 4, 2020, https://en.interfax.com.ua/news/general/644898.html.

[145] Quotation from: "If you can look into the seeds of time, / And say which grain will grow and which will not, / Speak then to me, who neither beg nor fear / Your favors, nor your hate." Shakespeare, *Macbeth*, Act 1, Scene 3.

lesser extent, of meeting the hopes of the Ukrainian citizenry. However, he will also have his work cut out to restore citizens' trust in government. Without that social capital, another wave of Ukrainian reforms will be doomed to the same fate as all previous waves.

President Zelensky proved that he remains in full control of the central government and parliament. However, his room for maneuver has considerably narrowed. With the dismissal of his first cabinet, the president will now have to own any mistakes made by his ministers—and he can't afford mistakes. This is part of the reason why key ministerial posts remain unfilled: the president is looking for success and surety in the spheres of civic unity (contra ethnonationalism; here, under the aegis of the Ministry of Culture and Ministry of Education) and the economy (Ministry of Economic Development and Ministry of Energy).

Ukraine's government underwent a generational change last year. But yesterday's political shake-up and the failure of President Zelensky's first cabinet have shown that the new generation of politicians was poorly prepared to face the challenges that have confronted Ukraine for the past six years. It is unknown just yet whether the newly appointed, more experienced hands in the cabinet and ministries will be able to right the ship of state quickly enough to stanch civilian demands and induce economic development adequately to answer the IMF's concerns.

Zelensky's version of *perestroika* and the oligarchs

March 2020[146]

As a student of the post-Soviet human, I am amazed to see how often political processes in contemporary Ukraine resemble those of its Soviet past. One such resemblance I see is between Volodymyr Zelensky's policies and Mikhail Gorbachev's *perestroika*.

---

[146] A shorter version of this column has previously been published as: Minakov, M. (2020). Zelensky's Version of Perestroika and the Role of the Oligarchs. *Focus Ukraine*, March 19, 2020, https://www.wilsoncenter.org/blog-post/Zelenskys-version-perestroika-and-role-oligarchs.

Here I use the word "perestroika" (literally "reshaping" or "rebuilding") as a term for a political action that offers an alternative to the usual choice of revolution or reform, between overthrowing everything and starting anew or molding what one has into a different shape. In this context, then, revolution denotes an event of radical innovation and a new beginning in politics (or some other sphere of human activity). Reform, by contrast, is a change within a given political regime aimed at making it more effective and viable. Perestroika is in between.

When Gorbachev started to change the Soviet Union thirty-five years ago, he had in mind reforms, especially industrial, economic, and political. But he soon learned that the Soviet system could not be reformed and he needed *perestroika*, something more than reform. In essence, he tried to open up the political and socio-economic sectors to innovation while keeping intact the ruling regime. Thus he enforced some controlled political liberalization, some media freedom, called glasnost, some limited religious and economic freedoms, and the "new thinking," or a new approach to foreign relations. However, these steps were naïve and contradictory. And these contradictions ultimately led the USSR to self-destruct.

Zelensky electorally won on all political fronts in 2019. The mere fact of his victory introduced a Khrushchev-style *thaw* to Poroshenko-era ideocratic politics. Diversity of opinion has increased in the mass media, along with a more openly critical stance on the national government. Zelensky's first cabinet, that put together by former prime minister Oleksiy Honcharuk, was an outsider to systemic corruption, and the business community seemed to be happy with it. Inter-church conflicts also appeared to quiet down. And a hopeful belief that young people without political, policy, or administrative experience could bring lasting change to the system has been driving Zelensky's perestroika of 2019–early 2020.

Beneath all this, however, the essence of Zelensky's perestroika lies in the attempt to tease apart two parts of Ukraine's political system: the democratic façade and the shadow oligarchic state.

In my book *Development and Dystopia*, I analyzed how post-Soviet political systems evolved into a specific chiasm of formal and informal power institutions.[147] There I showed that the formal façade of Ukraine was constructed as a set of weak democratic institutions that were under the invisible—yet undeniable—control of informal institutions. The main informal institutions were organized as oligarchic clans. These clans constantly competed, both among themselves and with sporadically independent government agencies, for control over official structures. The official structures included parliamentary factions, judges in courts, senior officials in the cabinet, governors, mayors, and so forth. Thus, by the time Zelensky entered the picture, Ukraine was a pluralist semi-free polity in which democracy was mixed with competitive authoritarianism and patronal politics.[148]

The more I study it, the more I am convinced: the *perestroika* of Volodymyr Zelensky in 2019 was actually directed at separating the formal institutions from the impact of the informal underworld. Unlike his predecessor, Zelensky did not belong to a clan, his own or any other. With the presidential administration under former chief of staff Andriy Bohdan, he tried to create a balanced system of clans, all held at arm's length, that would not be able to intervene in the actions of the formal institutions. The policy of "new faces" was conceived to bring into parliament and the cabinet people with no connections to the clans. The new president-led, single-party majority in government would function as a formal organization ensuring that the president's agenda was supported by the Rada. Inexperienced but honest ministers would guarantee the ministries worked for the public good. A prosecutor general whose thinking was aligned with the president's and who respected the rule of law would direct new and old law enforcement agencies to achieve a

---

147 Minakov, M. (2018). *Development and Dystopia*. Stuttgart: ibidem Verlag.
148 See: Hale, H. E., & Orttung, R. W. (eds.). (2016). *Beyond the Euromaidan: Comparative Perspectives on Advancing Reform in Ukraine*. Stanford University Press; Minakov, M. (2016). A Decisive Turn? Risks for Ukrainian Democracy After the Euromaidan. *Carnegie Regional Insight,* February 3, https://2cm.es/Odbb; Sorokin, O. (2019). Freedom House: Ukraine Remains Partly Free, According to 2019 report. *Kyiv Post,* February 5, https://2cm.es/Odbe.

more just society in Ukraine. All these desiderata were expected to become part of officially sanctioned constitutional amendments and laws (and often these amendments are not of a liberal democratic nature). In this way the government would actually start working according to formal rules and for the public good.

Unlike Gorbachev, Volodymyr Zelensky turned out to be a fast learner. Simple solutions proved not to work in the dire conditions of Ukraine's reality. One cannot make peace just by stopping the shooting. And one cannot rebuild the Ukrainian state just by ignoring the informal groups that own vast portions of the nation's economic wealth, still financially support many MPs, judges, and mayors, and control the mass media.[149]

The recent personnel changes in the offices of the chief of staff, cabinet, and prosecutor general might actually reflect Zelensky's learning from the experiences of 2019. Now the new head of the presidential administration, Andriy Yermak, will have to find a new way to cope with Ukraine's crises by negotiating deals with big business. President Zelensky's March 16 meeting with Ukrainian tycoons was dedicated to exploring ways his government could cooperate with the private sector on the most pressing national challenges, including the COVID-19 pandemic and economic issues.[150] The new cabinet is in the hands of people who, like Prime Minister Denys Shmyhal and Minister of Economy Ihor Petrashko, are the "new faces with brains and hearts" sought by Zelensky and have broad experience working for oligarchic corporations, Ukrainian public establishments, and Western companies. Simultaneously, Prosecutor General Iryna Venediktova, approved on March 17 by the Rada and the first woman in the post, is expected to exercise a "strong hand" in keeping the oligarchs (both supportive of

---

149 Shavalyuk, L. (2018). Twilight of the Oligarchs. *The Ukrainian Week*, November 11, https://ukrainianweek.com/twilight-of-the-oligarchs/; Grytsenko, O., Sorokin, O. (2019). Media Grab: Oligarchs, Pro-Russian Forces Use TV to Push Political Agenda. *Kyiv Post*, June 21, https://www.kyivpost.com/post/10260.
150 Zelenskiy Calls on Oligarchs to Help Finance Virus Fight as China's Ma Donates Testing Kits. *RFE/RL*, March 17, 2020, https://www.rferl.org/a/ukraine-coronavirus-oligarchs-medicine/30492082.html.

and rival to Zelensky) and other informal groups under strict control.

Many experts have already negatively assessed Zelensky's overhaul of the administration: they lean toward viewing the change of cabinet and prosecutor general as a sign of the oligarchs regaining their usual role.[151] I do not necessarily find the personnel changes to be a sign of the administration's defeat by the oligarchs. From the perspective of the oligarchic clans, the new cabinet remains the president-controlled executive. However, the new cadres on the presidential staff, in the cabinet, and heading up the law enforcement agencies may reflect a change of tactics in dealing with big business on Zelensky's part — and he might be more open to striking compromises with them — but with the prior aim of his *perestroika* firmly in place: to prevent the oligarchs from misusing public institutions. It remains for the future to reveal whether the concessions lead to a return of (oligarchic-controlled) business as usual or whether they contribute to advancing Zelensky's brand of *perestroika*, but with new means and at a different pace. And lurking on the periphery is the biggest question of all: whether Zelensky's *perestroika* might end in failure, just as Gorbachev's did.

Ukraine's politics in the fall of 2020

August 2020[152]

Typically, Ukrainian politics works in five-month periods: from February to June and from late August to mid-December. The autumn period starts on August 24, Ukraine's Independence Day. However, that tradition was broken this year since President Volodymyr Zelensky's team and the major opposition groups were actively competing over the political agenda for the autumn period during all the summer.

---

151 Ben, B. (2020). Ukraine's New Government: More Oligarchic, More Pro-Russian. *Euromaidan Press*, March 6, https://euromaidanpress.com/2020/03/06/ukraines-new-government-more-oligarchic-more-pro-russian/.

152 A shorter version of this column has previously been published as: Minakov, M. (2020). Ukraine's Current Political Agenda. *Focus Ukraine*, August 31, https://www.wilsoncenter.org/blog-post/ukraines-current-political-agenda.

President Zelensky spent most of the summer actively visiting Ukraine's regions, meeting with local officials, politicians, and journalists. Judging by the time spent and the media coverage, his major attention was dedicated to the communities in the southeastern oblasts. Ex-president Petro Poroshenko, former vice prime minister Yuriy Boiko, and the two irreconcilable opposition groups they head were also very active in the regions and received ample media coverage.

This competition—both open and covert—ended up with the formation of a political agenda for the second half of the Ukrainian political year. Three key issues seem to be in play: (1) how to proceed with conflict management and resolution in the Donbas; (2) which parties will be victorious in the upcoming local elections and will Zelensky's Servant of the People repeat the electoral miracle of 2019; (3) the well-being of Ukrainians as the country struggles with COVID-19, an economic crisis, and huge payments due on international debt.

The Donbas War

The start of the new political cycle was marked by a thus far durable ceasefire on the front line in the Donbas.[153] The ceasefire took effect on July 27 and, despite some violations,[154] for the first time in six years the number of those killed from shooting has fallen to zero.

President Zelensky has tried to leverage this success to nail down a new summit with Emmanuel Macron, Angela Merkel, and Vladimir Putin in the Normandy Four format.[155] Kyiv insists on the summit taking place this fall, while Moscow waffles or outright refuses to consider it.[156] As President Zelensky explained in a recent

---

153 President personally inspects compliance with ceasefire in Donbas. *President of Ukraine official website*, August 6, 2020, https://2cm.es/Odc4.
154 Special Monitoring Mission to Ukraine (SMM) Daily Report 202/2020. *OSCE*, August 25, 2020, https://www.osce.org/special-monitoring-mission-to-ukraine/461716.
155 President's Office: Normandy Four Berlin Summit Closer After Political Advisers' Meeting. *UNIAN*, July 4, 2020, https://2cm.es/Odcb.
156 Socor, V. (2020). Kozak Celebrates Diplomatic Victory over Ukraine in Rude Letter to Normandy Forum. *Euromaidan Press*, August 8, https://2cm.es/Odcd.

interview with Euronews, he sees the possibility of ending the Donbas war this year with the support of Western allies, and despite Russia's resistance.[157]

To advance on the conflict resolution agenda, Zelensky has changed the head of the Trilateral Contact Group on Donbas (ex-president Leonid Kuchma ceded the chair to ex-president Leonid Kravchuk) and appointed a new chief of Ukraine's special forces in the Donbas.[158] These changes have in turn changed the dynamics of the talks with Russia and the separatists: a new POW swap is to take place, and both demining operations and troop pullbacks are expected to occur soon in the Donbas.[159]

Both opposition wings have criticized the president for the ceasefire and its implications. For one wing, that headed by Petro Poroshenko, Zelensky's peacebuilding efforts point to a betrayal of the national interest and "capitulation" to Russia.[160] The other wing, headed by Yuriy Boiko, demands additional and more radical steps toward resolving the conflict while offering itself as a competitor to Zelensky for the moniker of "real peace-maker."

Resolving the conflict in the Donbas remains, perhaps, the key issue underpinning Ukraine's political agenda and defining the differences between political parties. An end to the fighting is also a key demand of Ukrainian people, as recent polls show.[161]

---

[157] Vakulina, S. (2020). Volodymyr Zelenskyy: "High Chance" of Ending War in Ukraine "This Year". *Euronews*, Augst 25, https://2cm.es/LS9s.
[158] President Changed the Leadership of the Special Operations Forces. *President of Ukraine official website*, August 25, 2020, https://2cm.es/Odcs.
[159] Ceasefire Regime Continues: 20 Demining Sites and 4 New Disengagement Sites Have Been Agreed at the TCG Meeting. *President of Ukraine official website*, August 20, 2020, https://2cm.es/LS9B.
[160] Zelensky's Opponents Fear He Is Ready to Capitulate to Russia. *The New York Times*, December 25, 2019, https://www.nytimes.com/2019/12/05/world/eu rope/zelensky-ukraine-russia.html.
[161] Соціально-політична ситуація в Україні – Липень 2020 (from Ukrainian: Socio-Political Situation in Ukraine — July 2020). *SOCIS*, August 13, 2020, https://socis.kiev.ua/ua/2020-08-13/.

Local elections

This summer, twenty-nine years after the dissolution of the USSR, Ukraine took an important step toward redefining its administrative-territorial structure: it introduced 136 new rayons, replacing the previous 490 rayons. (A rayon is the second level of administrative division, below oblast.) More than 300 townships lost their administrative significance of rayon centers, along with relevant budgets and government positions. Also, the Rada amended some rules pertaining to local elections; among many other novelties, the changes increased the role of parties in local election. The reorganization of the rayons has somewhat disoriented local elites, who, during the quarantine, became very hostile toward the presidential team. The amendments to the electoral rules provide the presidential party with the opportunity for a larger presence on local councils and force local clans to seek cooperation with it.

However, the opposition parties look at the local elections—which usually have been of limited significance in Ukraine—as a battlefield on which Volodymyr Zelensky could face his first electoral defeat. Nationally, the Servant of the People party currently enjoys the support of almost 30 percent of active and decided voters, while Boiko's Opposition Platform–For Life is supported by 22 percent and Poroshenko's European Solidarity is supported by 16 percent of voters.[162]

But at the regional level these sympathies change dramatically: local communities prefer local leaders, and their party affiliation plays a much lesser role. Currently, the Zelensky team seems to have problems finding strong candidates for the mayors of Ukraine's biggest cities. In Kyiv, Kharkiv, Odessa, Dnipro, and Lviv, the most popular candidate are either rivals of or neutral toward the ruling group. Zelensky's party may have its factions in most local councils, but their role could be insignificant in the western rayons, where Poroshenko's party is strong, and the

---

162 Ukraine Turns 29. Where Are We Now, and What Is Our Way? Results of the Nationwide Opinion Poll. *Democratic Initiatives*, August 24, 2020, https://2cm.es/Odcm.

southeastern rayons, where the Opposition Platform and some associated smaller parties may win majorities.

Local elections will definitely be at the center of public attention and political competition this fall.

Socioeconomic issues

Finally, the pandemic and its socioeconomic impact are also helping shape the political struggle in Ukraine. Now, at the end of August, Ukraine's COVID-19 contagion appears to be peaking, with more than 2,000 new cases a day. For purposes of control measures, Ukrainian regions have been divided into three categories, with the most infected regions put under strict quarantine.

However, these measures are highly unpopular. Even though Ukrainians acknowledge the seriousness of the pandemic and the government's efforts to protect the population, when it comes to quarantine, this acknowledgement disappears.[163] For example, in the last week of August the cabinet of ministers, responding to the worsening situation, introduced the most severe quarantine measures yet. This decision has sparked elite and popular protests in several regions, leading to conflict between the central and local governments over the "easing" of the regime.

The community overreaction is connected with the dire economic situation nationally and with growing economic problems for households. According to OECD data, Ukraine's GDP fell 5.9 percent year-over-year in January–May 2020; by the end of this year, the projected GDP decline is expected to be 8 percent, inflation is expected to be 8.7 percent, and unemployment is expected to be 9.5 percent. This last figure relates to the official economy. According to three small-town mayors with whom I spoke, in the "shadow economy" — which feeds the populations of small towns and rural areas — unemployment seems to be three to four times higher.[164]

---

163 One Step from the Second Wave of COVID-19 Epidemic: What Bothers Ukrainians about the Healthcare System. *Democratic Initiatives Foundation*, August 17, 2020, https://2cm.es/LS9K.

164 Istrate, D. (2019). Ukraine's Shadow Economy Nearly Half of GDP. *Emerging Europe*, October 16, https://emerging-europe.com/analysis/study-ukraines-shadow-economy-nearly-half-of-gdp/.

The country's economic stability is also at risk because of the more than $5 billion in payments due on external debt this fall and a growing state budget deficit (about $10 billion). However, Prime Minister Denis Shmyhal and his cabinet have assured they will deal with the economic storm and bring the national economy back to calmer waters early next year.[165]

All three issues—the Donbas war, local elections, and the socioeconomic crisis—are at the center of attention for the Ukrainian government and politicians this fall. They will also define the major cleavages and disputes for the new political period.

President Zelensky's personnel problem

September 2020[166]

President Volodymyr Zelensky achieved a victory in the presidential elections of 2019 in part by hammering on the weaknesses of his major rival, then-president Petro Poroshenko. One of Poroshenko's biggest faults, which Zelensky returned to frequently during the presidential debates, was his inclination to appoint his alleged cronies to key government positions. Voters agreed and delivered the win to Zelensky. Zelensky dissolved parliament within hours after being sworn in and—finding a legal pretext to do so—in anticipation of getting a majority in the Rada—something he achieved. But the president then faced a difficult moment of truth: who would become the key players on his team—professionals or friends, statesmen or former business partners?

The abrupt dismissal of the Rada, and the subsequent revolving door in key administrative posts, introduced an unexpected difficulty for Zelensky. A political novice himself, he was elected on the wave of voters' distrust of "old professionals" in politics and

---

[165] Шмыгаль убеждает, что "дырки" в бюджете нет (from Russian: Shmyhal Assures That There Is No 'Hole' in the Budget). *Ekonomicheskaya Pravda*, August 21, 2020, https://www.epravda.com.ua/rus/news/2020/08/21/664261/.

[166] A shorter version of this column has previously been published as: Minakov, M., Prokip, A. (2020). President Zelensky's Personnel Problem. *Focus Ukraine*, September 18, https://www.wilsoncenter.org/blog-post/president-zelenskys-personnel-problem.

public administration. Ukrainians wanted big changes and new faces. Thus Zelensky's close associates came from media circles and show business. His choices for top positions in the new government thus began to bend in a traditional direction.

A significant number of the top officials appointed to the new government did not have political experience but met the important qualification: they enjoyed the trust of the president, mainly based on personal ties and friendship. For example, Ivan Bakanov, Zelensky's childhood friend and executive of his media business (Kvartal/Block 95), was appointed chief of the Security Service of Ukraine. Serhiy Shefir, a former scriptwriter and producer of Kvartal 95, became chief assistant to the president. Serhiy Trofimov, former executive producer at Kvartal 95, and Yuriy Kostyuk, a former screenwriter, became deputy chiefs of the presidential office. Kvartal 95 managers were also appointed to the national TV and radio broadcasting regulator and the Anti-Monopoly Committee.

Appointing trusted people to the executive suite is nothing new. It is common in some older democracies, especially presidential republics. But in those republics, it typically is done with strong oversight from the legislature, coupled with an approval requirement. In Ukraine, the Rada and the cabinet, as well as other oligarchic clans, were able to somewhat counterbalance Poroshenko's clan's authority. But this balance of powers disappeared with the 2019 parliamentary elections, which put Zelensky's party in charge of everything.

As of September 2020, the Servant of the People party has 247 votes (out of 450) in parliament, which gives it a governing majority. Moreover, the core of the party is also under the control of a dozen trusted partners of President Zelensky. The largest part of the ruling faction and of the two cabinets (so far) have lacked appropriate political or public sector experience when they took up their positions, a deficit that contributed to numerous mistakes on their part, some public scandals, and at least one change of cabinet.

Andrii Bohdan, Zelensky's ex-chief of staff, in a recent interview said that the president appoints top officials based on personal sympathy.[167] And it looks as though the bitter mistakes of the past sixteen months have not persuaded President Zelensky to alter how he chooses candidates for government positions. According to Bohdan, candidates for the upcoming local elections were selected based on the same "sympathy" factor. This is why, for example, the Servant of the People party nominated Oleh Filimonov, once a popular comedian, to run for mayor of Odesa and Viktor Hevko, an actor and stand-up performer, to run for mayor of Ternopil.

To be fair, it is not only Zelensky's team that promotes media- and show-people into positions of power. The Holos (Voice) opposition political party, established by the well-known singer Svyatoslav Vakarchuk, nominated Serhii Prytula, comedian and showman, to run for mayor of Kyiv. Thus show business seems to be supplying the cadres for political and administrative posts. It is a strange turn of events.

In fairness, Zelensky's choices are somewhat reduced by the fact that professionals—established politicians, public administrators, lawyers and economists—are not rushing to join the ruling parties and enter high public office, even when invited to do so. That complicates the picture. Experienced hands, aware of the selection criterion and wary of the seemingly endless reshuffling of key personnel around the president, are not confident they would last long in a government position or be able to make a difference. Worse, many professionals who could bring greater effectiveness to Ukraine's government in these difficult times often say that working for the government would undermine their reputation.

Thus the deficit among the ranks of likely contenders for positions in government has become a serious obstacle to the current administration. To fill the void, the ruling party has started hiring government professionals with tarnished reputations, including people who were associated with the Yanukovych clan or had a record of plagiarizing their Ph.D. theses.

The current government has an enormous problem with the cadres. Why does this matter? Continuing to hew to inappropriate

---

167 Talant, B. (2020). In Rare Interview, Ex-Chief of Staff Bogdan Talks about Zelensky, Yermak. *Kyiv Post*, September 10, https://www.kyivpost.com/post/7031.

selection criteria for key government positions in Ukraine reduces the quality of decision-making and policymaking, the efficacy of governance, nonpartisan law-making and judicial independence, national security, and political stability. Those are major drags on Ukraine's effort to define its national identity and its aspiration to join its western European neighbors. If the problem is not tackled properly and fast, it also stands to shatter President Zelensky's once enormous popular support.

Ukraine's politics in the first half of 2021

January 2021[168]

Ukrainian politicians are about to return to Kyiv after the holiday break and immerse themselves in the new political season of February–June 2021. A quick review of the political achievements of 2020 is in order before we take up the major issues likely to dominate the new season of political competition.

Achievements of 2020

As I wrote last August, Ukraine's political agenda of the preceding six months was structured around (1) conflict in the Donbas, (2) local elections, and (3) social issues born of the COVID-19 pandemic and related government policies to mitigate the pandemic's effects. With the passage of another six months, Ukraine's political year 2020 appears resolutely framed by those same issues.

There was no major breakthrough in resolving the conflict in the Donbas. The Minsk Trilateral Contact Group (TCG) and its Political Working Group discussed issues related to the implementation of the mandate given by the TCG to develop a draft action plan in full compliance with the Minsk Agreements. The positions of the Ukrainian and Russian delegations were rapidly moving away

---

[168] A shorter version of this column has previously been published as: Minakov, M. (2021). Ukraine's Political Agenda for the First Half of 2021. *Focus Ukraine*, January 22, https://www.wilsoncenter.org/blog-post/ukraines-political-agenda-first-half-2021.

from each other, which considerably hamstrung the work of the TCG. The only two visible achievements here were (1) fulfillment of measures to keep the ceasefire that went into force on July 27, 2020, and (2) the Verkhovna Rada's reapproval of the law "On the Special Order of Local Self-Government in Certain Areas of Donetsk and Luhansk Regions," which upheld the status quo and authorized continuation of the talks. However, as the TCG's chair, OSCE ambassador Heidi Grau, reported, people continued dying from arms fire in the war zone.[169]

According to my calculations, based on material openly available from the OSCE's Special Monitoring Mission to Ukraine, the Ukrainian Ministry of Defense, and reports in conventional mass media, the number of victims of the conflict, including both civilians and combatants, fell significantly, to one-fourth or one-fifth of their number prior to the ceasefire. Also, according to OSCE SMM reports, the intensity of fire declined by more than four times in the conflict zone since August 2020. So the ceasefire has had a significant impact on the death toll in the Donbas, but the conflict is still in its military phase.

Local elections were not a disaster for the ruling party but showed that Zelensky's political magic in 2019, which churned out election winners, faded in 2020.[170] Some 15 percent of all members of local councils were elected from Servant of the People party and 10.5 percent from Yulia Tymoshenko's Fatherland party, with the Opposition Platform — For Life having the third-best result (9.9 percent) in the elections. Only one mayor of twenty big cities (Poltava) is from President Zelensky's party; even the mayor of his native city of Kryvyi Rih was elected from the Opposition Platform — For Life. However, the ruling party has managed to create ruling majorities

---

[169] Press Statement of Special Representative Grau after the Regular Meeting of Trilateral Contact Group on 16 December 2020. *OSCE SMM*, December 17, 2020, https://www.osce.org/chairmanship/473889.

[170] Temnycky, M. (2020). Zelensky, Servant of the People Experience Major Setback in Ukraine Local Elections. *Focus Ukraine*, November 9, https://2cm.es/Oddn; Dumanska, V., Fedoriv, I. (2021). Ukraine's Local Elections: A Reality Check for Decentralization and Electoral Reforms. *Focus Ukraine*, January 12, https://2cm.es/LSaB.

on fifteen oblast councils, and in four more oblasts the party participates in the ruling majority as a minor partner.

According to not entirely trustworthy statistical data, the epidemic situation in Ukraine started to improve in November, even in the absence of strong lockdown regulations. From approximately 15,000 cases daily in early December 2020 the number dropped to 7,000 new cases daily in mid-January 2021. Despite such inspiring figures, however, the government imposed a lockdown on January 8 (effective through January 24), 2021. Quarantine measures and the increased spending on public health have made their impact felt on Ukraine's economy: the country's GDP has declined approximately 5 percent.

Altogether, the problems of 2020 changed the political sympathies of Ukrainians. According to recent polls, Ukrainian citizens still trust President Zelensky: 33 percent trust him and 60 do not trust him (in November 2019 this ratio was 52 percent to 19 percent).[171] His major rivals are still lagging behind him: Yuri Boyko is trusted by 26 percent, but 51 percent do not trust him; Petro Poroshenko is trusted by 20 percent, while 76 percent of citizens do not support the former president. At the same time, the presidential party has lost its electoral dominance: only 21 percent of those voters who have definite preferences support Servant of the People party, while Opposition Platform—For Life has become the most popular party, with 23 percent of voters' support. Poroshenko's European Solidarity party is in third place, with 14 percent.[172]

With an ongoing war, a faltering economy, and the pandemic weighing on them, Ukrainians seem to have lost the uplift they felt in 2019 with the political change from Poroshenko politics to the younger Zelensky's vision of the future: the collective feeling of happiness has dropped from 33 percent in 2019 to 14 percent in

---

171 Assessment of the Work of Authorities and Reaction to Current Events. *KIIS*, November 27, 2019, https://www.kiis.com.ua/?lang=eng&cat=reports&id=905&page=11; Level of Trust in Politicians and Electoral Rating: December 2020. *KIIS*, December 12, 2020, https://www.kiis.com.ua/?lang=eng&cat=reports&id=992&page=1.

172 *KIIS*, December 12, 2020, Op. cit.

2020, which made Ukraine among the ten least happy nations in the past year.¹⁷³

Major political issues facing Ukraine in 2021

To overcome the ills of 2020, Ukrainian politicians will need to put in place effective measures against COVID-19 and ensure the stable growth of the economy in general and of household income in particular. The president's team will face the special challenge of resolving the constitutional crisis without further harm to the rule of law, the constitution, or the political order.

Vaccination is becoming a central issue of Ukrainian politics. The president's team has denied any talks with Russia about getting the Russian vaccine and has turned instead to China for the Sinovac Biotech vaccine.¹⁷⁴ Also, Ukraine is waiting for eight million vaccine doses under the COVAX program, which may start first deliveries in March. In the political fight, the issue of vaccination is becoming a super-bioweapon capable of demolishing or restoring the president's favorability rating.

The Ukrainian Ministry of Finance expects 4.6 percent economic growth in 2021. This means that the country's economy will regain what it lost a year before. According to IMF forecasts, the trend in unemployment, which was heavily affected by the negative economic impact of the COVID-19 pandemic, reaching 10.1 percent in 2020, will fall off only slightly, to 9.3 percent in 2021. The situation in the shadow economy is stable: it is constantly over 30 percent of the official GDP.¹⁷⁵ The poorest part of Ukrainian society was deriving its income from the shadow economy. Now that unemployment in the shadow economy is much higher than the

---

173 Index of Happiness: In the World and in Ukraine. *KIIS*, January 14, 2021, https://www.kiis.com.ua/?lang=eng&cat=reports&id=993&page=1.
174 In Vaccine Geopolitics, a Great Game Played with Ukrainians' Health. *The New York Times*, January 1, 2021, https://www.nytimes.com/2021/01/09/world/europe/covid-vaccines-ukraine.html?auth=login-facebook.
175 Momot, T., Chekh, N., Prylypko, S., Filonych, O., & Cherednychenko, O. (2023). Corruption in Business: Motives and Influence on Shadow Economy. *Business: Theory and Practice*, 24(1), 206-215.

official unemployment figure, the least lucky Ukrainian families are on the verge of survival mode once again.

The government is now also hostage to a difficult economic situation resulting from the losses associated with the COVID-19 pandemic and the introduction of an energy market, a requirement of the IMF for Ukraine to continue receiving loan tranches—and it is households that will be most affected. The energy reform led to an increase in gas and electricity tariffs beginning January 1, 2021. With all the multiplier effects, the end price of energy for households, which previously had been subsidized by the state, has increased tremendously. This in turn has provoked mass protests around the country. Under pressure from protesters, Prime Minister Denys Shmyhal has promised to return to state regulation of the energy sector, which in its turn has prompted concern on the part of the IMF.[176]

The antitariff protests follow the antilockdown protests and merge with the efforts of the opposition to topple Zelensky's cabinet and get more participation in decision-making in the one-party-ruled Ukraine.[177] The merger of the political opposition's interests with growing social protests may pose a critical threat to the stability of order in Ukraine.

That order was also undermined by the ongoing constitutional crisis, which has pitted President Zelensky against the Constitutional Court of Ukraine and bores into the legality of several anticorruption reform measures dating from 2015. The current phase of the conflict began in October 2020, when the court ruled that some norms of the laws directing the work of anticorruption system were unconstitutional. Zelensky believes the anticorruption agencies must be upheld and their work strengthened or Ukraine will face losing foreign investment, IMF loans, and visa-free access to the EU.

In response to the CCU's rulings, on December 29, 2019, President Zelensky suspended Oleksandr Tupytsky, head of the CCU,

---

[176] Guz, S. (2021). In Ukraine, Anger over Fuel Poverty Is Bringing People out into the Streets. *OpenDemocracy*, March 15, 2021, https://www.opendemocracy.net/en/odr/tariff-protests-ukraine/.

[177] Ukraine says dozens of police hurt in clashes with lockdown protesters. *Reuters*, December 15, 2020, https://2cm.es/LSaK.

from serving as a judge of the CCU for a period of two months.[178] The constitutional law experts whom I contacted doubt that the president has the legal authority to act in that manner. However, as the Financial Times' Roman Olearczik rightly writes: "Mr. Zelensky appears to be trying to gradually squeeze out Mr. Tupytsky and other judges."[179] And the president is doing so using administrative levers that are in conflict with constitutional norms. Also, the presidential team has promoted a draft law that would strengthen the responsibility of persons in state or local government to submit accurate income declarations, a move that stands to infringe on judicial independence.[180]

The draft law in its current form (based on explanations on the presidential website; the draft remains unpublished at the time of this writing) seems to follow the recommendations of the Venice Commission as of December 9, 2020.[181] If the president's team does not find a way to compromise with the court, the political opposition, which is slowly gaining in popularity even as the president and his team are losing it, may use certain legal acts signed by the president to try to start impeachment proceedings.

Finally, the conflict in the Donbas and the situation of annexed Crimea remain issues for Ukrainian foreign and domestic politics. The Trilateral Contact Group's return to normal work and reaching agreement on a new summit to be held in the Normandy format,

---

178 President of Ukraine Signed a Decree on the Suspension of Oleksandr Tupytsky from the Post of a Judge of the Constitutional Court for a Period of Two Months. *President of Ukriane official website*, December 29, 2020, https://2cm.es/OddB.
179 Olearczik, R. (2020). Ukraine's Constitutional Court Crisis Escalates. *Financial Times*, December 20, 2020, https://www.ft.com/content/733a91e2-6ec8-4c5a-9f52-8bd38dfebc5b.
180 National Security and Defense Council Approved a Bill to Improve the Liability for False Declarations, Which the President Will Submit to the Parliament as an Urgent after Revision. *President of Ukraine official website*, December 29, 2020, https://2cm.es/OddE.
181 Urgent Joint Opinion of the Venice Commission and the Directorate General of Human Rights and Rule of Law (DGI) of the Council of Europe on the Legislative Situation Regarding Anti-Corruption Mechanisms Following Decision No. 13-R/2020 of the Constitutional Court Of Ukraine - CDL-PI(2020)018. *The Venice Commission*, pp. 18-20, https://www.venice.coe.int/webforms/documents/default.aspx?pdffile=CDL-PI(2020)018-e.

which may open up new perspectives for managing and settling the conflict, are the goals to achieve in 2021.

With all these issue on the front burner simultaneously, 2021 is shaping up to be as challenging a year for Ukraine as 2020 was. But the presidential team has gained some political and administrative experience, which may make its work more successful and Ukrainians happier.

Zelensky's presidency at the two-year mark

June 2021[182]

Approximately two years ago, in April 2019, Volodymyr Zelensky came to power. On May 20, 2021, the presidential team put together a big press event at which President Zelensky was to report on his achievements as president and discuss his administration's plans for the remaining three years of his tenure.[183]

The team decided to hold the event in a hangar of the Antonov aircraft company, in front of a huge AN-225 "Mriya" (Dream) plane. Such a background was chosen to send an optimistic message to the nation and underline the president's dream of a bright future for Ukraine. Instead, the disappointed journalists reported that the late Soviet era Mriya was without engines and the press event moderator took questions only from representatives of the media loyal to the president.

So the question about the results of President Zelensky's first two years in office remained largely unanswered at the presser. I will try to provide an assessment here, continuing the logic of my previous assessments: by comparing the interim results with the three promises Zelensky made as a candidate, peace in the Donbas, an end to corruption, and the improved well-being of ordinary Ukrainians. How well has President Zelensky and his team met

---

[182] A shorter version of this column has previously been published as: Minakov, M. (2021). Zelensky's Presidency at the Two-Year Mark. *Focus Ukraine*, June 3, https://www.wilsoncenter.org/blog-post/zelenskys-presidency-two-year-mark.

[183] President of Ukraine: My main goal is a country that is on top. *President of Ukraine official website*, May 20, 2021, https://www.president.gov.ua/en/news/prezident-ukrayini-moya-golovna-meta-krayina-yaka-na-visoti-68557.

these expectations as the president approaches the midpoint of his first term?

The situation in the Donbas and Russia-Ukraine relations

As of early June 2021, the situation in the Donbas has become rather threatening. After a period of active talks between Kyiv, Moscow, Paris, and Berlin, as well as talks with the Russia-backed separatists operating in eastern Ukraine, the immediate risk to Ukraine posed by activities on the Donbas front line fell. In 2019–2020 the conflicting sides conducted prisoner exchanges and pulled their armed forces out of three zones along the line of conflict. A July 2020 ceasefire was followed by a decrease in the number of victims, with attacks on either side being kept to a minimum. There were expectations that the ceasefire would evolve into a stable conflict resolution process.[184]

The situation did not hold, however. In the winter of 2020–2021 the situation on the front line worsened significantly. The Minsk process stalled, and meetings of the Trilateral Contact Group became less and less fruitful.[185] According to the daily OSCE SMM reports, the number of victims on both sides now has returned to pre-July 2020 levels (fifteen to twenty-five killed each month on both sides of the front line). The number of attacks has doubled, and the number of shots fired during each attack has quadrupled since early February 2021. The rhetoric of Moscow and Kyiv has grown hostile, and military forces were moved closer to the Donbas

---

184 Polishchuk, O., Holcomb, F. (2020). Breaking the pattern: the relative success of the latest ceasefire agreement in Ukraine. *ReliefWeb*, November 24, 2020, https://reliefweb.int/report/ukraine/breaking-pattern-relative-success-latest-ceasefire-agreement-ukraine.
185 Eastern Ukraine Situation Will Remain Fragile without Means to Calm Mounting Tensions, Under-Secretary-General Tells Security Council. *United Nations*, February 11, 2021, https://press.un.org/en/2021/sc14434.doc.htm.

and Crimea. Russian troops were also moved closer to the Ukrainian border in March–May 2021.[186]

Today the talks are mired in disputes over how to implement the Minsk agreements.[187] President Zelensky has been pushed into the same corner as his predecessor: no Ukrainian president can implement the Minsk agreements since the provisions of the agreements are not accepted by Ukrainian society. Yet this document is the only agreement that keeps Eastern Europe from returning to an active war situation.

There is a small silver lining to this difficult turn of events, and one that can be chalked up on the achievement side of the ledger. The looming risk of a more consequential Russia-Ukraine military conflict has returned the Ukraine issue to the front burner of international politics. President Biden made a long-delayed phone call to President Zelensky that launched engagement and cooperation between Kyiv and the new US administration.[188] Cooperation was deepened after a recent visit of US secretary of state Antony Blinken to Kyiv.[189] And Kyiv's European partners have become more active after the meeting of President Zelensky and France's President Macron.[190]

In addition, President Zelensky's administration has launched a Crimean Platform initiative, which has increased political

---

186 80,000 Russian Troops Remain at Ukraine Border as US and NATO Hold Exercises. *The New York Times*, May 5, 2021, https://www.nytimes.com/2021/05/05/us/politics/biden-putin-russia-ukraine.html.
187 Zolkina, M. (2021). Everything about Yermak's new plan: what the Normandy Format proposes to update the Minsk agreements. *Democratic Initiatives Foundation*, March 29, https://dif.org.ua/en/article/everything-about-yermaks-new-plan-what-the-normandy-format-proposes-to-update-the-minsk-agreements.
188 Cullison, A. (2021). President Biden Holds Call With Ukrainian President Zelensky, Part of Effort to Reassure Kyiv. *Wall Street Jounral*, April 2, https://www.wsj.com/articles/president-biden-holds-call-with-ukrainian-president-zelensky-ukrainian-officials-say-11617376424.
189 Blinken, on Ukraine Trip, Will Offer Support on Russia but Also Pressure on Corruption. *The New York Times*, May 5, 2021, https://www.nytimes.com/2021/05/05/world/europe/antony-blinken-ukraine-trip.html.
190 Ukraine's Zelensky says open to four-way talks with Putin to ease tensions with Russia. *France 24*, April 16, 2021, https://www.france24.com/en/europe/20210416-russia-tensions-on-menu-as-macron-holds-talks-with-ukraine-s-zelensky.

pressure on Russia regarding the annexed Crimea. Western participation in Kyiv's initiative is growing steadily: the first forum of the platform, scheduled for August 23, 2021, will be attended by the presidents of Latvia, Poland, and Slovakia, with representation from the United States and the EU.

The good governance and the fight against corruption

Zelensky's team has constructed an informal "vertical" that is far from any good governance or rule of law principles. In this new power vertical, the major role belongs to the Office of the President, while the Verkhovna Rada and the Cabinet of Ministers have lost their Realpolitik authority. The security services and general prosecutor's office proved unable to cooperate effectively to both fight corruption and promote the interests of the ruling group. As a result, since October 2020, the National Security Council, de jure an advisory organ, has become the center of the presidential team's decision-making. This decision-making is conducted in the style of "emergency politics," without the requisite respect for Ukraine's constitution and the division of powers stipulated therein.

So far, this vertical of power has functioned effectively, endowing the president with the image of a strong leader defending his people against "corrupt judges" (especially the judges of the Constitutional Court)[191] and pro-Russia politicians (mainly Viktor Medvedchuk and his allies).[192] Unlike many presidents before him, Volodymyr Zelensky enjoys an astonishingly high level of trust nationwide: two years into his presidency, 46 percent of Ukrainians trust the sitting president (while 51 percent do not trust him).[193] At the same period of his presidency, President Poroshenko enjoyed a

---

191 Zelensky: In 2021, Ukraine to Launch Major Judicial Reform. *UNIAN*, December 20, 2020, https://www.unian.info/politics/judiciary-zelensky-says-ukraine-to-launch-global-judicial-reform-in-2021-11261969.html.
192 Zelensky Risks Putin's Wrath With Swoop against Ukraine Oligarch. *Financial Times*, May 15, 2021, https://www.ft.com/content/8bb48865-ec57-44b9-9ed4-4782df798584.
193 Два года Президента Зеленского: оценки граждан (in Russian: Two Years of President Zelensky: Citizen Evaluations). *SG "Rating"*, May 20, 2021, http://ratinggroup.ua/ru/research/ukraine/dva_goda_prezidenta_zelenskogo_ocenki_grazhdan.html.

trust rating of 20 percent (with 71 percent of respondents distrusting) and President Yanukovych had a trust rating of 22 percent (with 70 percent distrusting).

This is not the first power vertical to have emerged in Ukraine over the past thirty years: power verticals existed during the administrations of Presidents Kuchma, Yanukovych, and Poroshenko.[194] But it is the first informal power structure that may be prepared to take on all the old guard Ukrainian oligarchs.[195] The draft of an anti-oligarch law offers a radically different approach to this fight: it aims not to correct the root causes leading to the perpetual reemergence of the clans but at the assets and actions of the clan leaders themselves.[196] It remains to be seen whether the draft law will survive scrutiny by the parliamentary committees without losing its teeth.

Outside the presidential vertical, the anti-corruption agencies and the Ministry of Interior have remained autonomous. The Western governments have managed to insist on the autonomy of the anti-corruption institutes created in the wave of reforms after the Euromaidan—at least until 2022, when the mandate of Artem Sytnyk, director of NABU, expires.[197]

The Ministry of Interior has remained in the hands of the unchanging minister Arsen Avakov, who has served in succession Presidents Turchynov, Poroshenko, and Zelensky, though signs are

---

[194] Minakov, M. (2017). Reconstructing the Power Vertical: the Authoritarian Threat in Ukraine. *OpenDemocracy*, June 29, https://www.opendemocracy.net/en/odr/reconstructing-power-vertical-authoritarian-threat-in-ukraine/.

[195] Ukraine Wants to Show Biden It's Serious about Ending 'Oligarch Era.' That's Not So Easy. *The Washington Post*, March 28, 2021, https://www.washingtonpost.com/world/europe/ukraine-biden-corruption-oligarchs/2021/03/28/e6e05bb0-8d7f-11eb-a33e-da28941cb9ac_story.html.

[196] Самаева, Ю. (2021). Законопроект «Об олигархах»: основные положения vs главные ожидания (From Russian: Draft Law 'On Oligarchs': Main Provisions vs Main Expectations). *Zerkalo Nedeli*, May 27, https://zn.ua/internal/zakonoproekt-ob-oliharkhakh-osnovnye-polozhenija-vs-hlavnye-ozhidanija.html.

[197] Experts Mull Anti-Corruption Next Steps in Ukraine. *Eurasianet*, April 27, 2021, https://eurasianet.org/event-experts-mull-anti-corruption-next-steps-in-ukraine; The AntAC Analyzed the Draft Law with the Help of which Activities of the NABU Will Be Blocked and Controlled Director Will Be Selected. *Antac*, March 16, 2021, https://antac.org.ua/en/news/analysys-draft-law-nabu-will-be-blocked/.

emerging that Minister Avakov is finally losing his autonomy and authority.

Unlike his predecessors, President Zelensky personally has remained beyond suspicion in matters relating to corruption.[198] Yet there is growing concern about the behavior of his entourage, especially in connection with the presidential flag project, Great Construction, which allocated a record amount from Ukraine's national budget for infrastructure projects but appears to have become bogged down, dogged by charges of politicization and unrealistic goals.[199]

The Well-being of Ukrainians

The issue of Ukrainians' well-being has drawn critical attention in light of the COVID-19 pandemic. The socioeconomic situation for many Ukrainians is difficult indeed. Ukraine's GDP dropped 4.2 percentage points in 2020, though it is expected to regain 4 percentage points in 2021. Unemployment is growing and prices are increasing, especially for communal services and housing, even as fewer households are eligible for subsidies.[200] Ukraine has one of the lowest vaccination rates in Europe, which forced Zelensky's team to install a new minister of health in May 2021.[201] Household

---

198 Ukraine's President Again Comes Under US Pressure—This Time, For Good Reason. *The Washington Post*, March 12, 2021, https://www.washingtonpost.co m/opinions/global-opinions/ukraines-president-again-comes-under-us-press ure--this-time-for-good-reason/2021/03/12/5da8f148-828c-11eb-ac37-4383f77 09abe_story.html.
199 Топалов, М. (2020). Питання на 120 мільярдів: куди пішли гроші з програми Зеленського "Велике будівництво" (from Ukrainian: The 120 billion Question: Where Did the Money Go from Zelensky's Big Construction Programme?). *Ekonomichna Pravda*, December 15, 2020, https://www.epravda.com .ua/publications/2020/12/15/669050/.
200 Oliynyk, S. (2020). How the Government "Optimizes" Subsidies. *Ukrainska Energrtyka*, December 18, https://ua-energy.org/en/posts/18-12-2020-5a644404- 1465-4fbc-8265-f233c8509ff9; Ukraine Unemployment Rate. *Trading Economics*, 2021, https://tradingeconomics.com/ukraine/unemployment-rate#:~:text=U nemployment%20Rate%20in%20Ukraine%20is,10.10%20in%2012%20months %20time.
201 New Ukraine Health Minister Vows to Speed Up COVID-19 Vaccinations. *Reuters*, May 20, 2021, https://www.reuters.com/world/europe/new-ukraine-he alth-minister-vows-speed-up-covid-19-vaccinations-2021-05-20/.

income and the health of family members remain among the key issues for Ukrainians.[202]

Yet the socioeconomic grievances do not translate into lack of trust in the president. Instead, a growing number of Ukrainians view the future with optimism. According to a recent poll, from January 2021 (when Zelensky's ratings reached their nadir) to May 2021, the share of optimists increased by nine percentage points, reaching 25 percent of those surveyed, while the share of skeptics dropped from 73 percent to 65 percent in the same period.[203]

Moreover, President Zelensky is regarded by Ukrainians as the second best president the country has had in its thirty years of independence. Leonid Kuchma (presided 1994–2005) was regarded by 23 percent of those polled as the best president ever, while Volodymyr Zelensky was designated the best president by 18 percent. The subsequent rankings proceeded as follows: Petro Poroshenko (2014–19, 14 percent), Viktor Yanukovych (2010–14, 13 percent), Leonid Kravchuk (1991–94, 12 percent), and Viktor Yushchenko (2005–10, 7 percent).

Two years after entering the stormy waters of Ukrainian politics, Volodymyr Zelensky is a politically engaged leader who has managed to mobilize support from the citizenry despite unmet expectations and a deteriorating quality of governance. President Zelensky is good at keeping himself at a remove from the corruption scandals and at delivering a political show that helps retain the sympathies of a relative majority of voters. There is no political figure in today's Ukraine who could challenge the president, and there is no political figure or force that could undermine the newly constructed power vertical. If the Zelensky team ever fails, it will be of its own doing.

---

202 Общественно-политические настроения населения (6-7 апреля 2021) (from Russian: Public and Political Attitudes of the Population (6-7 April 2021)). *SGR*, April 9, 2021, http://ratinggroup.ua/ru/research/ukraine/obschestvenno-politicheskie_nastroeniya_naseleniya_6-7_aprelya_2021.html.

203 Два года Президента Зеленского: оценки граждан (from Russian: Two Years of President Zelensky: Citizen Evaluations). *SGR*, May 20, 2021, http://ratinggroup.ua/ru/research/ukraine/dva_goda_prezidenta_zelenskogo_ocenki_grazhdan.html.

Zelensky starts the fight against oligarchs

June 2021[204]

With the dissolution of the USSR, the creation of national states, and the emergence of post-Soviet market economies, the new nations of Eastern Europe and northern Eurasia developed under the strong influence of oligarchic groups. The decommunization of the early 1990s, with its destruction of the Communist Party and KGB networks and the creation of relatively free economies and competitive politics, resulted in a vacuum of institutionalized power. This vacuum was filled with informal groups that took over emerging public institutions and subjugated them to their rent-seeking agendas.

In the early twenty-first century, post-Soviet governments and societies tried to end the oligarchy in two major ways: either by subduing it and integrating its elements into pyramid-like power system consisting of official public institutions and informal oligarchic groups, or by fighting corruption in the public sector through strengthening the rule of law and insisting on a clear division between the public and private sectors. The pyramid-like power system can be in the form of single-pyramid autocracies or multi-pyramid hybrid regimes with democratic and nondemocratic political elements. The success of the single-pyramid model in Azerbaijan, Belarus, and Russia has given birth to the current autocratic regimes in those countries. Multiple attempts to fight corruption have kept Georgia and Ukraine as hybrid regimes interpolated by many oligarchic groups and repeatedly oscillating between more and fewer political and economic freedoms.

Today we are witnessing another attempt to eradicate the oligarchy in Ukraine. This time, President Volodymyr Zelensky is going after the oligarchs individually. Is there any chance for success?

---

[204] A shorter version of this column has previously been published as: Minakov, M. (2021). Fighting Oligarchy or the Oligarchs? *Focus Ukraine*, June 10, https://www.wilsoncenter.org/blog-post/fighting-oligarchy-or-oligarchs.

Nature of the post-Soviet oligarchy

From the perspective of political economy, the post-Soviet oligarchy is a system in which private groups establish control over public institutions through rent-seeking activities.

After about thirty years of developing without hindrance in those states where they were not reined in by autocrats, the oligarchic groups have matured and evolved into stable and sophisticated informal structures. These structures typically consist of a core (comprising several oligarchic figures), public politicians (ministers, officials, MPs, mayors, etc.), and parties serving the interests of one or more of the following: their clan, individual judges or entire courts, parts of the law enforcement agencies, private companies, public companies informally controlled by the clan's management, media holdings, NGOs, philanthropic organizations, criminal and paramilitary groups, and foreign partners in the West and Russia. By controlling parts of the executive, legislative, and judicial branches of government, some governors, mayors, and local councils, the media, and civil society, each clan has a tendency to form a single pyramid in itself. And as the clans compete with each other for influence and control, they open a space for relatively free politics based on a zero-sum game.

The key foundational element of the oligarchy is a specific political culture based on neopatrimonialism and personal relations with the core figures of clans.[205] Informal groups exist as hierarchies of personal relations and as a permanent test of lower-level members' loyalty.

In Ukraine, the multi-pyramidal oligarchy developed based on the Soviet nomenklatura system and its efflorescence into regional clans.[206] These regional groups had their own ideologies, religious preferences, and geopolitical orientations. Whenever one group managed to take control of government, its informal

---

[205] Fisun, O. (2012). Rethinking Post-Soviet Politics from a Neopatrimonial Perspective. *Demokratizatsiya. The Journal of Post-Soviet Democratization*, 1: 87-96.

[206] Minakov, M. (2019). Republic of Clans: The Evolution of the Ukrainian Political System. In Magyar, B. (ed.). *Stubborn structures: reconceptualizing post-communist regimes*. Budapest: Central European University Press, 217-245.

subcultures would heavily influence the cultural politics. This description fits both President Viktor Yanukovych's administration (2010–14) and President Petr Poroshenko's (2014–19). Despite functioning in remarkably different political times, these administrations had in common a conservative worldview, hostility to the principles undergirding the rule of law, and an affinity for a personalist regime.

President Zelensky against the oligarchs

The electoral victory of Volodymyr Zelensky in 2019 provided Ukrainian society with another opportunity to overthrow the clans' control. Earlier opportunities were connected with the maidans of 2004 and 2013–14, but attempts then failed because the oligarchic clans managed to successfully adapt to the changed political situation.[207] In 2019, however, the opportunity for deoligarchization arose with the electorate's decision to change the president and parliamentary majority, and to some extent with the arrival of a new generation of politicians in Ukrainian power structures. Most of these newcomers were most probably not part of any oligarchic clan, although some doubt it.[208]

It took President Zelensky almost two years to launch the promised and long-awaited war on the oligarchs.[209] On June 2, 2021, the president submitted a draft law against the oligarchs to the Verkhovna Rada.[210] In keeping with the recent fashion in Kyiv

---

[207] Minakov, M. (2016). A Decisive Turn? Risks for Ukrainian Democracy After the Euromaidan. *Carnegie Regional Insight*, February 3, https://carnegieendowmen t.org/research/2016/02/a-decisive-turn-risks-for-ukrainian-democracy-after-t he-euromaidan?lang=en.

[208] Williams, M., Zinets, N. (2019). Comedian Faces Scrutiny over Oligarch Ties in Ukraine Presidential Race. *Rueters*, April 1, 2019, https://www.reuters.com/ar ticle/us-ukraine-election-zelenskiy-oligarch-idUSKCN1RD30L/.

[209] The future of the Ukrainian oligarchs (report). *Ukrainian Institute of Future*, June 13, 2019, https://uifuture.org/en/news-en/reportmaybutnieukrainskycholigarchiv/.

[210] Проєкт Закону про запобігання загрозам національній безпеці, пов'язаним із надмірним впливом осіб, які мають значну економічну або політичну вагу в суспільному житті (олігархів) (from Ukrainian: Draft Law on Prevention of Threats to National Security Associated with Excessive Influence of Persons with Significant Economic or Political Weight in Public Life

to place security concerns above the constitution, the draft law is named "Law on Prevention of Threats to National Security Related to Excessive Influence of Persons Who Have Significant Economic or Political Weight in Public Life (Oligarchs)."

The draft law implies that if a citizen meets three of the following four criteria, that person can be recognized as an oligarch:

> The citizen in question participates in the political life of the country; that is, the citizen holds a government office or is associated with someone in such a position, as, for example, someone who heads or finances a political party.
> The citizen owns a monopoly, either a natural monopoly or one in a particular economic sphere.
> The citizen has a significant impact on the media, either as an owner or as an influencer of editorial policies, or as someone who has sold the media to a related person or to a person lacking an impeccable business reputation.
> The citizen owns assets whose value exceeds 1 million subsistence minimums (currently almost 2.3 billion UAH or approximately $80 million).

If someone is adjudged to meet three of these four criteria, that person is to be acknowledged as an oligarch.

According to the draft law, the decision to recognize a person as an oligarch is made by the National Security and Defense Council (NSDC), a body that in the constitution is mentioned as a consultative organ only. This decision can be made if the council is asked to take up the matter by a member of the NSDC, by the National Bank, by the Security Service, or by the Antimonopoly Committee.

The act prohibits public officials from meeting or conversing with recognized oligarchs. If public officials violate this norm, they are required to submit an appropriate declaration on the meeting or face termination.

If a citizen is recognized as an oligarch, he or she will not be able to contribute financially to supporting a political party, will not be able to participate in privatization tenders of government-owned plants, and will not be able to hold a high position in government.

(Oligarchs). *The VRU Official Website*, June 2, 2021, https://w1.c1.rada.gov.ua/pls/zweb2/webproc4_1?pf3511=72105.

The Anti-Oligarchs Law is not the right way to go

This act, though brave on its surface, has several fundamental drawbacks. First, it is directed at persons, but not at the oligarchic groups or political structures that enable such persons to flourish.

Second, the act does not make use of any traditional institutions (the antimonopoly system, public finance reporting requirement of parties, etc.) or new ones (the post-Euromaidan anti-corruption bodies) with the legal authority to force oligarchic clans to transition into conventional big business groups.

Third, the entire spirit of the act is against the rule of law, the division of powers enshrined in Ukraine's constitution, and citizens' rights. A consultative authority cannot make decisions of the kind described in the draft law; only a court can do so. This act, if approved, will violate the constitution and grant the government extraordinary power, which in a post-Soviet context is more than risky.

Fourth, there are many ways for the oligarchs to continue doing business as usual since most of the illegal connections within clan structures would be hard to prove.

Finally, civil servants would find themselves in a situation in which any contact with a person not known to them could result in dismissal if that person turned out to be associated with an oligarch in the view of the NSDC.

President Zelensky's presenting the draft anti-oligarchs law was indeed a brave act, and one well received by Ukrainians and the international community. Even if it is approved by the Rada, however, it will not bring down the oligarchy. Some oligarchic figures would most likely be switched out for new ones, but clans and the oligarchic principle would prevail. The most likely effect of the law, if approved, will be to throw a monkey wrench into efforts to restore the rule of law in Ukraine.

Waiting for the storm? Ukraine's political situation before the autumn of 2021

September 2021[211]

Among Ukrainian politicians and analysts there is seemingly an unusual consensus: everyone expects a political tempest this autumn in Kyiv, once lawmakers and politicians return to work after the summer recess. Judging from the public debates over the last two months in Ukraine, there are two reasons to expect turmoil: the changing nature of President Volodymyr Zelensky's regime and the changing geopolitical context. Both kinds of changes are thought capable of bringing Ukraine to the brink of a political crisis that could see the consolidation of the opposition and more intense social protests.

Zelensky's political education has been steep and uneven over the past two years, and he has not avoided the strong centralizing tendencies that are characteristic of other post-Soviet states. The next few months will be a test of Zelensky's political acumen and whether he is flexible enough to turn various domestic and geopolitical problems into opportunities.

A changing regime

Notably, the content, form, and style of President Zelensky's policies have changed dramatically. From a perestroika-style reformist and a populist leader of the new political generation, President Zelensky has fallen back on the traditional agenda of post-Soviet presidents: he has started creating his own 'power vertical' that erodes the constitutional system of checks and balances.

Zelensky approaches the November midpoint of his five-year term with some sort of power vertical assembled. A power vertical is a structure that destroys the separation of powers into branches

---

[211] A shorter version of this column has previously been published as: Minakov, M. (2021). Waiting for the Storm? Ukraine's Political Situation before the Autumn of 2021. *Focus Ukraine*, September 2, https://www.wilsoncenter.org/blog-post/waiting-storm-ukraines-political-situation-autumn-2021.

and tiers and establishes a chain of subordination of the executive, the legislature, the judiciary, and local government to the presidential administration. Unlike Ukraine's previous presidents, Zelensky does not have his own clan, a stable political adopted family, which has resulted in a much lower level of corruption around him. But the unhappy logic of the post-Soviet presidential institution has inevitably led him to need the power vertical formation.

Today the Zelensky administration controls the Verkhovna Rada through a loyal majority of Servants of the People MPs and several allied MP groups. The current Cabinet of Ministers is fully loyal to the president, while the prime minister has shown no personal political program (though formally the prime minister can be a very influential power figure). The Constitutional Court is in continuous crisis owing to its conflict with the president. The judiciary at large is operating at a nadir of efficiency owing to unfinished reforms, endemic corruption, and constant clashes with the executive.[212] Since the recent local elections did not see the Servant of People party establishing effective control over the local councils,[213] the Zelensky administration has begun promoting a semiformal congress of local and regional authorities presided over by the head of the presidential staff.[214] So far the informal presidential control over the formal branches and tiers of power is neither absolute nor efficient. But it is definitely very different from the constitutionally mandated separation of powers and from Zelensky's policies during his first-year office.

The core of the vertical is now vested in the hard power institutions. Since October 2020, the Security Council has become the center of decision-making in Ukraine. In less than a year, the council has already sanctioned — bypassing court procedures to do so —

---

212 Evaluation of the judicial systems (2018 - 2020). *Council of Europe*, September 24, 2020, https://rm.coe.int/en-ukraine-2018/16809fe0cb.
213 Local Election Results in Ukraine: New Political Landscape on Ground? *Reanimation Package of Reforms*, January 13, 2021, https://rpr.org.ua/en/news/local-election-results-in-ukraine-new-political-landscape-on-ground/.
214 Yermak Elected Chairman of Presidium of Congress of Local and Regional Authorities. *UKRINFORM*, July 30, 2021, https://www.ukrinform.net/rubric-polytics/3289381-yermak-elected-chairman-of-presidium-of-congress-of-local-and-regional-authorities.html.

Constitutional Court judges, several oligarchs, many criminals, and some opposition (mainly Russia-leaning) leaders and their businesses and media outlets.[215] In July and August the presidential team increased control over the Ministry of Interior and key positions in the Ukrainian Army. With the resignation of former interior minister Arsen Avakov, a holdover from the Poroshenko and Turchynov administrations, in July,[216] and the confirmation of Denys Monastyrskiy to the post, the police service returned to the hands of a pro-presidential minister,[217] and radical—usually anti-Zelensky—groups were temporarily distracted from their street protests while looking for a new sponsor. The appointment of a new generation of officials to the army and police service helps the presidential team feel much safer in the face of the upcoming autumn turmoil. Thus the team's leaders appear to agree with analysts' predictions of a coming political tempest and are making anticipatory moves to withstand whatever crisis might emerge.

By-Blows from Recent Actions

Certain negative effects of recent regime actions, while not unexpected, have become unavoidably clear. The concentration of power in the hands of the presidential team has caused snowballing conflicts with the political groups and oligarchic clans in Kyiv and in the regions. Zelensky's approval rating, a key part of his political capital, is still in good shape, however: in September 2020 he was supported by 32 percent of decided voters, and after a January 2021 decline to 22 percent, in August 2021 his support rebounded almost to the previous level, a result mainly attributable to his playing

---

215 Matuszak, S., Żochowski, P. (2021). Growing Importance of the Security Council in Ukraine. *Center for Eastern Studies*, April 1, https://www.osw.waw.pl/en/publikacje/analyses/2021-04-01/growing-importance-security-council-ukraine.
216 Bezruk, T. (2021). Ukraine's All-Powerful Interior Minister Resigns – and Leaves a Legacy of Impunity Behind. *OpenDemocracy*, July 16, https://www.opendemocracy.net/en/odr/ukraine-avakov-resignation-impunity/.
217 Ukrainian Parliament Approves Denys Monastyrskiy as New Interior Minister. *RFE/RL*, July 16, 2021, https://www.rferl.org/a/ukraine-interior-minister-monastyrskiy/31362321.html.

hardline politics.[218] Also, the polls show that Zelensky is at least 15 percentage points ahead of his nearest rival, former president Petro Poroshenko.[219] Counterbalancing these positive findings, the same polls show that the level of Zelensky's disapproval rating has grown to well over 50 percent, and almost half of voters do not want him to participate in future presidential elections.

As a new political season opens in Kyiv, the presidential team is indeed well prepared to face possible internal turmoil. But changes on the international political scene could undermine its dominant position.

The Changing Geopolitical Context

Over the past nine months, the presidential team has defined the fight against Russia's Nord Stream 2 pipeline (NS-2) as one of its key foreign policy priorities. The prospect of the United States softening its position on the completion of NS-2 has provoked a harsh reaction from Zelensky's team against the country's Western partners. The July 21 US-German deal to allow the pipeline to be finished and giving Berlin the authority to control Russia's pipeline operations in Eastern Europe came as a shock to Ukraine's government and Western-oriented groups.[220] The talks between President

---

218 Рейтинг підтримки політичних лідерів і партій: Вересень 2020 року (from Ukrainian: Rating of Support for Political Leaders and Parties: September 2020). *KIIS*, September 21, 2020, https://www.kiis.com.ua/?lang=eng&cat=reports&id=969&page=10; Level of trust in politicians, electoral rating and attitude to certain initiatives / events: January 2021. *KIIS*, February 2, 2021, https://www.kiis.com.ua/?lang=eng&cat=reports&id=1003&page=7; Суспільно-політичні настрої населення України: результати опитування, проведеного 24 липня-1 серпня 2021 року (from Ukrainian: Socio- Political Attitudes of the Population of Ukraine: Results of the Survey Conducted on 24 July-1 August 2021). *KIIS*, August 4, 2021, https://www.kiis.com.ua/?lang=eng&cat=reports&id=1055&page=1.

219 Общественно-политические настроения населения (23-25 июля 2021) (from Russian: Public and Political Attitudes of the Population (23-25 July 2021)). *SGR*, July 27, 2021, http://ratinggroup.ua/ru/research/ukraine/obschestvenno-politicheskie_nastroeniya_naseleniya_23-25_iyulya_2021.html.

220 Lewis, S., Shala, A. (2021). US, Germany Strike Nord Stream 2 Pipeline Deal to Push Back on Russian 'Aggression'. *Reuters*, July 22, 2021, https://www.reuters.com/business/energy/us-germany-deal-nord-stream-2-pipeline-draws-ire-lawmakers-both-countries-2021-07-21/; Ukrainian Leaders to Biden: Standing

Zelensky and German chancellor Angela Merkel in Kyiv on August 21, 2021, were unsatisfactory for the Ukrainian side.[221] Thwarted expectations in regard to the constantly deferred summit between the US and Ukrainian presidents have also fed dissatisfaction with the West.[222]

The political sentiment toward Ukraine's Western partners has only hardened with the West's withdrawal from Afghanistan. For many pro-Western politicians and activists, the joy of the August 24 celebrations of Ukraine's thirtieth anniversary of independence was tempered by concern that Kyiv could be similarly abandoned by its Western partners sometime in the future. Anti-Western groups in Ukraine are using the Afghanistan case to undermine perspectives on Ukraine's cooperation with the United States, the EU, and NATO. And the debates over Ukraine's geopolitical future have had a negative impact on the country's political stability and the presidential team's hegemony.

Turning Threats into Opportunities

I do not subscribe to the apocalyptic expectations of some of my Ukrainian colleagues. The autumn political season will indeed kick off with the country facing new internal and external threats. But there is a way to reduce risks and turn threats into opportunities. The internal and external political changes of this year need to be taken seriously, but they are probably not a sign of approaching end times. With a return to rational, balanced, and constitutionally based politics, both kinds of challenges can be used by President

---

with the World's Democracies Means Changing Course on Nord Stream 2. *Atlantic Council*, August 27, 2021, https://www.atlanticcouncil.org/blogs/ukrainealert/ukrainian-leaders-to-biden-standing-with-the-worlds-democracies-means-changing-course-on-nord-stream-2/.

221 Key ally Merkel visits Ukraine before Leaving Office. *France24*, August 22, 2021, https://www.france24.com/en/live-news/20210822-key-ally-merkel-visits-ukraine-before-leaving-office; Goncharenko, R. (2021). Merkel leaves Ukraine with a difficult legacy. *Deutsche Well*, August 23, 2021, https://www.dw.com/en/opinion-merkel-leaves-ukraine-with-a-difficult-legacy/a-58961385.

222 Prince, T. (2021). As Washington Summit Nears, Disappointment Looms Over Ukraine-U.S. Relations. *RFE/RL*, August 29, https://www.rferl.org/a/biden-zelenskiy-ukraine-meeting/31433599.html.

Zelensky to seed an improved national dialogue on the aims of Ukraine's development and alliances. The president just needs to recall the aspirational policies that got him elected.

Three decades of Ukraine's independence: outcomes so far

September 2021[223]

Around thirty years ago the final phase of the Soviet Union's dissolution got under way. The coup attempt launched by Soviet conservatives against President Mikhail Gorbachev and his reforms on August 18, 1991, had failed to control the government three days later, when it was aborted, but it did succeed in railroading the process for approving the new Soviet Union treaty. Despite a majority of Soviet citizens expressing support for a "renovated Union" in March 1991 polls (with 71 percent of those living in the socialist republic of Ukraine supporting it), the Soviet republican governments started preparing for the USSR's dissolution by the end of August 1991.

The dissolution was guided by very different aspirations of the republican elites.[224] Some wanted to strengthen their position in advance of expected negotiations to renew the Union treaty; others pursued the national communist agenda, trying to preserve their rule by distancing themselves from the too liberal Yeltsin's Moscow; yet others saw an opportunity to establish independent nation-states. These aspirations can be seen in the texts of the declarations of independence that were approved by the republican Supreme Councils after Yeltsin emerged as the de facto leader after the coup attempt. The Ukrainian Declaration of independence, approved on August 24, 1991, is an example of the compromises that

---

223 A shorter version of this column has previously been published as: Minakov, M. (2021). Three Decades of Ukraine's Independence. *Focus Ukraine*, September 13, 2021, https://www.wilsoncenter.org/blog-post/three-decades-ukraines-independence.
224 On this, see: Plokhy, S. (2015). *The Last Empire: The Final Days of the Soviet Union*. London: Hachette UK.

had to be reached among contending interests and hopes of the founders of contemporary Ukraine.

The practical steps entailed in dissolving the old Union and forming a new, independent state—a creative-destructive process—became more clearly visible in the decommunization efforts of 1991–1992. In Ukraine, from the end of August through December 1991, the Communist Party of Ukraine was dissolved, its property was nationalized, and the KGB was banned, while party and ideological pluralism was established and all individuals living on the soil of the Ukrainian socialist republic were granted citizenship in the emerging independent state. Unlike in many of the other socialist republics, these steps prevented civil conflict from breaking out. Ukraine's national communists and national democrats had a consensus on establishing a new state, and no political force questioned it. The elites' decision was supported by 90 percent of Ukrainians on a referendum of December 1, 1991.

Now, thirty years later, it is not easy to find proper criteria by which to assess what has happened to us, the citizens of Ukraine, during this period. One place to start is by comparing what we have today with the expectations of those who established a new state in 1991.

These expectations are not an absolute point of reference, of course: 1991 marked a historical caesura, a profound change in the cultural, social, political, and economic life of many peoples living in Eastern Europe and northern Eurasia. The change was guided by hopes for the better, hopes that were shared equally among experts and citizenry, external observers and the people living through the transformative events. These boundless hopes almost inevitably spilled over into wishful thinking and political daydreaming.

Such wishful thinking appears to have guided the preparation of a famous report commissioned by Deutsche Bank to assess the prospects of the Soviet republics' economic development in 1990.[225] The report's authors—a group of experts, led by Jürgen Corbet— expressed a mixture of truly prophetic vision and blindness to what

---

[225] Corbet, J. et al. (1990). *The Soviet Union at the Crossroads: Facts and Figures on the Soviet Republics*. Frankfurt am Main: Deutsche Bank.

was coming in the post-communist future. They did anticipate the USSR's imminent dissolution but failed in their prediction that Ukraine would undergo the most successful economic transition of all the socialist republics and would "draw level with the economic and cultural standards of Western Europe." The conclusions of this report were widely used in the campaign for Ukrainian independence and resonated with late Soviet Ukrainians' aspirations regarding a possible future.

This mixture of hopes of 1991 can be assorted into three major tracks of the post-communist transformation: democratization, marketization, and Europeanization. Accordingly, I propose to assess the thirtieth anniversary of Ukraine's independence on these tracks.

Democratization Track

Post-Soviet democratization implied the establishment of a nation-state, ideological pluralism, freedom of association and of the press, a multiparty system, free and fair elections, and a strong civil society.[226] Thirty years of democratization have seen ups and downs on this track, but overall, Ukraine exists as a fully recognized independent and sovereign state. That sovereignty, however, has been threatened by the illegal annexation of Crimea, the continuous existence of non-government-controlled territories in the eastern Donbas, and ongoing military conflict in the Donbas.

Ukraine is one of the freest political regimes among the post-Soviet states, yet neither according to Freedom House reports nor according to Varieties of Democracy data can Ukraine be regarded as a full-fledged democracy. Rather, Ukrainian politics have oscillated between more and less free, hybrid political orders, with the best periods for liberal democracy in the first half of the 1990s and in 2005–2009. This uneven political development has provoked two deep political crises – the Orange Revolution of 2004 and the

---

[226] Minakov, M. (2019). Democratisation and Europeanisation in 21st Century Ukraine. *The Struggle for Good Governance in Eastern Europe. Second Edition*. Brussels: CEPS, 83-121, https://3dcftas.eu/publications/democratisation-and-europeanisation-in-21st-century-ukraine.

Euromaidan of 2013–2014 — that put Ukraine' existence as a country at risk. Despite a vibrant history of freedom of expression and debate in recent decades, in 2021 Ukrainians have also seen the authorities, including elected officials, take disturbing steps to limit such freedoms.[227] The democratization track thus exhibits mixed achievements, with freedom and its opposite co-occurring and clashing in the continuing political transformation of Ukraine. It would be difficult to say the founding fathers' and mothers' dream of a free Ukrainian state and an open Ukrainian society has been fully realized.

Economic Track

Ukraine's post-Soviet economic development has been guided by the goals of transformation toward a free market economy and a wealthy society.[228] In pursuit of these goals, Ukrainians have experienced (and survived) the huge economic decline of the early 1990s, an economic growth spurt in 2002–2007, and unstable stagnation the rest of the time.[229] The privatization process went quickly in the early post-Soviet years but was later put on hold by the newly created oligarchs. As in other post-Soviet nations, Ukrainians had to reinvent wealth and poverty, which created economic grounds for unstable politics and the rule of oligarchs. Marketization, the dream of 1991, is still incomplete, though the process continues, doggedly: only in 2020 did Ukraine finally launch its energy sector and agricultural land markets. And, like political liberty, economic freedom has oscillated between extremes. The slow pace of economic reforms, the dominance of the oligarchs in the economy, and ongoing war have kept Ukraine — despite some progress in human

---

227 Ukraine: Freedom House President Sends Letter to Biden Ahead of Zelenskyy Visit. *Freedom House*, August 26, 2021, https://freedomhouse.org/article/ukraine-freedom-house-president-sends-letter-biden-ahead-zelenskyy-visit.
228 Mylovanov, T., Sologoub, I. (2021). The Development of Ukraine's Private Sector. In: Minakov, M. et al. (eds.). *From "The Ukraine" to Ukraine: A Contemporary History, 1991–2021*. Stuttgart: ibidem Verlag, 53–94.
229 Sutela, P. (2012). The Underachiever: Ukraine's Economy Since 1991. Carnegie Endowment for International Peace, March 9, 2012, https://carnegieendowment.org/research/2012/03/the-underachiever-ukraines-economy-since-1991?lang=en.

development and quality of life—among the poorest countries of Europe. In this respect, the dreamers of 1991 would definitely be disappointed with the results of Ukraine's economic development.

Europeanization Track

Finally, the Europeanization track has also brought many surprises. The heady dream of Eastern and Western Europeans coming together to create a single culturally and socially united region of peace and collaboration, which shined so brightly in 1989-1991, has been a strong motivation for the post-communist transformation. Regretfully, this dream has never been fully realized: Europe today is a geopolitically divided region experiencing a growing number of conflicts and antagonisms.

Unlike its Central European and Baltic neighbors, Ukraine did not always have European integration as a goal. A multivector foreign policy was more influential in 1991-2004 and again in 2010-2014, while European- (and US-) oriented foreign policy was dominant (but also "declaratively dominant," with declarations not followed by sufficient actions) in 2005-2009 and after the Euromaidan in 2014,[230] which saw the ouster of the pro-Russia president Viktor Yanukovych and a decisive turn toward Europeanization among the citizenry, especially in the western portions of the country. Ukraine succeeded in gaining an Association Agreement with the EU in 2017, and that became the framework for some post-Euromaidan reforms. Today Ukrainian politicians and the government are in constant dialogue with their EU member-state peers. EU-Ukraine economic ties are strengthening. The security of Ukraine is now an important factor in the EU's security. Millions of Ukrainian labor migrants are now part of European societies, while their remittances hugely support the Ukrainian economy. However, further integration with the EU is limited by obstacles posed by both

---

[230] Wolczuk, K. (2003). Ukraine's Policy towards the European Union: a Case of 'Declarative Europeanization'. *Stefan Batory Foundation, The Enlarged EU and Ukraine: New Relations,* 1-28, https://www.batory.org.pl/ftp/program/forum/eu_ukraine/ukraine_eu_policy.pdf.

Ukraine's and the EU's political and socioeconomic factors.[231] While Europeanization—in the form of cooperation and integration with the EU—remains an important aspirational milestone for Ukraine, other developmental priorities may limit or even prevent it. Indeed, Ukraine has moved far ahead in becoming part of the European political, economic, and security agenda, yet I am not entirely sure that the forms of Ukraine's Europeanization correspond to the intentions of the dreamers of 1991.

Whither the Dream?

The year 2021 is not the end of independent Ukraine's history. I hope that in the future we will see more peace, freedom, and wealth in Ukraine and wider Europe. Yet my hope is constantly in conflict with the facts of what happened to the hopes of the founding fathers and mothers of Ukraine.

The Afghanistan Syndrome and US–Ukraine Relations

September 2021[232]

American politicians and experts are divided in their assessments of the US troop withdrawal from Afghanistan in August 2021. It has been called chaotic, "an unmitigated disaster of epic proportions," a sign of the "American empire's death"—and an "extraordinary success."[233]

---

231 European Council Conclusions on Ukraine. *European Council*, December 15, 2016, https://www.consilium.europa.eu/media/24151/15-euco-conclusions-ukraine.pdf; Kuleba Comments on Kaljulaid's View of Ukraine's EU Membership Prospects. *UKRINFORM*, August 28, 2021, https://www.ukrinform.net/rubric-polytics/3305586-kuleba-comments-on-kaljulaids-view-of-ukraines-eu-membership-prospects.html.

232 A shorter version of this column has previously been published as: Minakov, M. (2021). The Afghanistan Syndrome and US–Ukraine Relations. *Focus Ukraine*, September 27, 2021, https://www.wilsoncenter.org/blog-post/afghanistan-syndrome-and-us-ukraine-relations.

233 See: Kristian, B. (2021). The US Withdrawal from Afghanistan Is Chaotic, Tragic, and Necessary. *The Business Insider*, August 24, https://www.businessinsider.com/the-us-withdrawal-from-afghanistan-is-chaotic-tragic-and-necessary-2021

The Afghanistan government's inability to govern and control the country without the support of its Western allies and the Taliban's easy takeover were both planned and unexpected by the Western powers. Those two developments have left their mark on the self-perception — and self-esteem — of the United States, the UK, and other NATO member states participating in the Afghanistan campaign.[234]

The rapid political change in the center of Eurasia has also had a strong and direct impact on the security and political perspectives of China, India, Iran, Russia, Turkey, and the Central Asian nations, and has altered their understanding of the West's decreasing global presence.[235] "Westlessness" — a sense of unease arising from what the Munich Security Report 2020 describes as "increasing uncertainty about the enduring purpose of the West" — seems to be coloring many nations' global reorientations.

This new perception of the United States' and NATO's role and their relations with non-Western allies has many different manifestations in international and national, political, and mass media dimensions, all of which can be summed up in a common term, the Afghanistan syndrome. Combining opinion, emotion, and

---

-8?r=US&IR=T; Bredemeier, K. (2021). Blinken Defends US Withdrawal from Afghanistan. *VOA News*, September 13, https://www.voanews.com/a/622424 9.html; Anderson, J. L. (2021). Is the US Withdrawal from Afghanistan the End of the American Empire? *The New Yorker*, September 1, https://www.newyork er.com/news/daily-comment/is-the-us-withdrawal-from-afghanistan-the-en d-of-the-american-empire; Biden Defends Afghan Pullout and Declares an End to Nation-Building. *The New York Times*, August 31, 2021, https://www.nytim es.com/2021/08/31/us/politics/biden-defends-afghanistan-withdrawal.html. Anderson, J. L. (2021). Is the US Withdrawal from Afghanistan the End of the American Empire? The New Yorker, September 1, https://www.newyorker.co m/news/daily-comment/is-the-us-withdrawal-from-afghanistan-the-end-of-t he-american-empire.

234 See: Bowden, G., Turner, L. (2021). Afghanistan: Tony Blair Says Withdrawal Was Driven by Imbecilic Slogan. *BBC News*, August 22, https://www.bbc.com /news/uk-58295384.

235 On this see: Kurby, J. (2021). NATO Allies Are Preparing for a Future without America's "Forever Wars". *VOX*, August 31, https://www.vox.com/22639474 /afghanistan-nato-europe-refugees-germany-uk; Lynch, C., Gramer, R. (2021). China, Russia Look to Outflank US in Afghanistan. *Foregn Policy*, September 2, https://foreignpolicy.com/2021/09/02/afghanistan-withdrawal-china-russia -outflank-geopolitics-united-nations/.

imagery, the term conveys a loss of trust in the military and in political leaders, especially war hawks, and a feeling that the war had no just basis. When applied to the United States, the term implies a loss of confidence in the country as an ally and the suspicion of an inefficient US army. "Afghanistan syndrome" thus subsumes a number of attitudes and emotions arising from previous historical events, whether connected to the US past (such as the fall of Saigon) or part of the Afghan resistance to yet another foreign intervention (such as Britain's or the USSR's) on national soil, and is now a factor in the global political imagination, influencing the behavior of political elites in every nation and region of the world.

Effect of Afghanistan Syndrome on Ukraine

The syndrome's influence is readily seen in Ukraine, a country whose survival and development, in the face of Russia's aggression in Crimea and ongoing conflict with the secessionists in Donbas, depend on US, EU, and NATO support.

Since the winter of 2020–2021, the presidential team's political agenda has been strongly oriented toward cooperation with the United States and NATO. Fast integration into NATO and the EU, the return of the Crimea issue to the center of international attention, and the fight against the Nord Stream 2 (NS2) pipeline project have been at the heart of this agenda. Membership in NATO and the EU was regarded as a guarantee of, respectively, the security and economic development of Ukraine. Participation in the Crimean Platform Summit on August 23, 2021, was designed to garner the West's active support for Ukraine's territorial integrity and to start a new track of coordinated international pressure on Russia to deoccupy the Crimean Peninsula. And halting the NS2 pipeline was sought as a first step in underscoring the seriousness of US and EU support for Ukraine's interests.

By the beginning of September 2021, however, all three major agenda items appeared not to be moving forward. At the June 14, 2021, NATO summit, Ukraine did not advance from NATO aspiring member status, accorded in 2018, to participation in the "open-door policy." Later in September, at the YES Brainstorming event,

President of Estonia Kersti Kaljulaid expressed an informed opinion that Ukraine was still far from meeting the standards for EU membership and that without more work on reforms—a point also made earlier by US Department of State spokesperson Ned Price with regard to NATO membership—meaningful negotiations of EU accession would be impossible.[236] Even though the Crimean Platform Summit managed to bring together a respectable group of participants, the major Western countries—the United States, France, Germany, and the UK—were represented by high level officials but not by presidents or heads of government as official Kyiv had expected. Simultaneously, the United States and Germany agreed to continue the NS2 pipeline project, underscoring that Germany's economic interests are more important than Ukraine's.[237]

In this context, the Afghanistan syndrome was on full display in the responses of the Ukrainian elites—both the ruling group and opposition—to the news of the US withdrawal from Afghanistan.

President Zelensky's team is obviously frustrated, but tries to resist the potentially grim message. In his recent interview with CNN, Zelensky mentioned the Afghanistan issue several times.[238] His major message to Ukrainian citizens and Western elites was that Ukraine's case is completely different from Afghanistan's. In his opinion, Ukraine is less dependent on the West than Kabul was, yet Russia poses a much greater threat to Ukraine and the West than the Taliban ever did. Finally, President Zelensky stated:

> I really believe that in four or five or seven days, you can't take such a big country geographically as Ukraine with such a big population and simply occupy it like that. [239]

---

236 Decision on Ukraine's Admission to the EU Largely Depends on Its Members' Political Will—Dmytro Kuleba. *Yalta European Summit*, September 11, 2021, https://2cm.es/LSjq.
237 Formuszewicz, R., Łoskot-Strachota, A. (2021). Deal between Germany and the US on Nord Stream 2. *Center for Eastern Studies*, July 2, https://2cm.es/LSjx.
238 Ukraine Cannot Be Compared to Afghanistan, We Are Holding Up against World's Most Powerful Armies Over Seven Years – President. *President of Ukraine Official Website*, September 13, 2021, https://2cm.es/Odmv.
239 Ibid.

Indeed, Ukraine is more important for the security of Europe than Afghanistan, and Russia's military strength is undeniably greater than the Taliban's. But the strongest emotion that came through in this interview was frustration, accompanied by a poorly disguised distrust of Ukraine's Western partners that were avoiding becoming allies. This frustration was probably a result of the formally successful White House meeting of Presidents Biden and Zelensky on September 1, 2021, but it increased under the influence of the Afghanistan syndrome.[240]

President Zelensky again expressed frustration at the Yalta European Summit on September 10, 2021:

> Everyone unanimously sympathizes with Afghanistan or Ukraine, against which Russia is waging a war. But this is virtual reality. And for seven years in a row, the Yalta European Strategy Forum has been held in Kyiv. Therefore, Yalta is still far from Europe, it is occupied, and we do not know whether the world has a strategy to change this and restore respect for international law.[241]

The same frustration has recently been expressed by Minister of Foreign Affairs Dmytro Kuleba. In his interview with Western media, Mr. Kuleba said that the United States was in the midst of a "leadership crisis." However, he expressed the hope that Ukraine's security "was one issue where the United States could demonstrate how serious it was again." Fighting to repress his own feelings, the minister pointed to bipartisan support for Ukraine in the US Congress and to President Biden's personal connection to Ukraine, despite past scandals. In the end, the minister laid bare his frustration, saying that Ukraine "has learned a number of bitter lessons that Western promises are likely [to be] unfulfilled.... We do not believe in promises."[242]

---

240 Istrate, D. (2021). Reasons to Be Cheerful: The Biden-Zelensky Summit. *CEPA*, September 9, https://cepa.org/article/reasons-to-be-cheerful-the-biden-zelensky-summit/.
241 President at YES Brainstorming: We Must Put a Stop to Wars among Humans before Wars Do Away with Humanity. *President of Ukraine Official Website*, September 10, 2021, https://2cm.es/OdmC.
242 Caroll, O. (2021). 'We Don't Believe Western Promises': Kyiv's Foreign Minister Says Ukraine Needs to Militarise to Survive. *The Independent*, September 13,

While sharing the idea that the West's failure in Afghanistan is a threat to trusting relations among Ukraine, the United States, and NATO, diverse domestic opposition groups use it in their struggle with the authorities. Pro-Western groups around Petro Poroshenko demand more radical reforms (which they themselves had failed to inaugurate during the Poroshenko presidency in 2014–19). Russia-leaning groups demand reconsideration of Kyiv's strategy based on European and Euro-Atlantic integration. They also recall the "more successful" Soviet troop withdrawal in 1989, in which many of today's Ukrainians personally participated. And the isolationists declare that the Afghanistan case proves that Ukraine must rely only on its own army and resources; all hopes for foreign support are wrongheaded.

The Afghanistan syndrome is here in its fullest expression. Emotionally, it increases distrust among partners. Rationally, it leads to questions about how such military and state-building operations conducted under the aegis of the strongest world power and its allies could have failed. And the media keep alive images of bodies falling from US planes over Kabul.

Among many other steps toward repairing the United States' reputation, a speech by Victoria Nuland, undersecretary of the US State Department, directed to Ukraine's elites at the last Yalta European Summit on September 10, 2021, stands out. In her statement (now missing on YouTube), she used the concerns of Ukrainian politicians and the Afghan case as an argument in favor of closer US-Ukraine cooperation: in her (and the administration's) view, the US withdrawal from Afghanistan freed up bandwidth so that the United States could pay more attention to Ukraine and its security.

Judging from subsequent debates at the Yalta European Summit, this message was heard, but was not sufficient. The US government has a long road ahead to reassure its allies and partners of its commitment to a common security regime.

And in Ukraine, trust in the alliance with the United States and the West at large is significantly damaged. The Afghanistan

---

https://www.independent.co.uk/news/world/europe/ukraine-russia-war-west-b1919145.html.

syndrome has weakened the position of the current administration and is a direct challenge to a political agenda aimed at European and Euro-Atlantic integration. How the current agenda's deficit will be responded to by the Ukrainian elites remains to be seen.

Growing disenchantment with President Zelensky

November 2021[243]

Volodymyr Zelensky has reached the midpoint of his presidency: two and a half years ago he took office as head of the Ukrainian state, with an equal amount of time remaining to his mandate. In this chapter I want to take a look at what has happened to President Zelensky's image, and specifically at how from a radical alternative to political cynicism of Poroshenko's rule he has turned into a "just like all the others" politician whose popular support is waning.

Those were the days!

In the spring of 2019 a showman converted himself into a politician, then a statesman. The 73 percent of voters who supported him (or who voted against the incumbent, Petro Poroshenko) in the presidential elections had a clear set of change demands. Even though Zelensky's platform as candidate was at best hazy, one thing was crystal clear—here was a man who was different in every way from the hungry hordes of the old elites. A person without political experience or ties to established political groups, Volodymyr Zelensky was seen as a radical alternative to everything Ukrainian voters had come to expect from presidential aspirants and their politics. And the harsh, often pitiless light in which Zelensky depicted former presidents Yushchenko, Yanukovych, and Poroshenko seemed to promise that the newly minted politician would not follow in the footsteps of his predecessors.

---

[243] A shorter version of this column has previously been published as: Minakov, M. (2021). Just Like All the Others: The End of the Zelensky Alternative? *Focus Ukraine*, November 2, 2021, https://www.wilsoncenter.org/blog-post/just-all-others-end-zelensky-alternative.

The "total alternative" image worked perfectly for Zelensky. In the spring of 2019 he won the presidency, and in the summer of that year the voters gave him an unprecedented one-party majority in parliament. But the time was rapidly approaching to turn image into reality: there were no visible obstacles standing in the way of Ukraine's transformation from an oligarchic polity into an all-citizens' republic.

What's in a name?

Volodymyr Zelensky enjoyed unusual Ukrainian presidents' popularity for more than two years. But the general optimism about the direction Ukraine was heading — the uplift Zelensky had brought to Ukrainians in 2019 — had already evaporated by 2020: from polls showing 52 percent of Ukrainians optimistic and 18 percent pessimistic in September 2019, the mood shifted to 23 percent optimistic and 60 percent pessimistic in March 2020, and since then pessimism has prevailed.[244] In July 2020, the number of those who did not trust Zelensky exceeded the number of those who still believed in him (51 percent versus 43 percent).[245] Despite these sobering poll figures, however, Zelensky has personally remained the politician with more support by far than anyone else: in August 2021 his support from likely voters was well over 30 percent, while his closest contender for a future presidency, Petro Poroshenko, was supported by just 13 percent.[246]

Zelensky's rating was both a blessing and the Achilles' heel of the emerging power vertical in his administration. As a president without his own clan or a stable group of political, administrative, financial, and law enforcement supporters, Zelensky enjoyed a truly democratic legitimacy: it stemmed from citizens' sympathy

---

[244] Socio-political Moods of Population (5 August 2020). *SGR*, June 8, 2020, http://ratinggroup.ua/en/research/ukraine/6ee9e5cc92da48d67b1965102dc3c529.html.

[245] Украина на карантине: мониторинг общественных настроений (15-17 ноября) (from Russian: Ukraine under Quarantine: Monitoring of Public Sentiment (November 15–17)). *SGR*, November 19, 2020, https://2cm.es/LSjS.

[246] Общественно-политические настроения населения (2-4 сентября 2021) (from Russian: Socio-Political Moods of the Population (September 2-4 2021)). *SGR*, September 7, 2021, https://2cm.es/OdmS.

with his goals and apparent lack of dissimulation. This response may have been populist, but it did not derive from oligarchic consent, as in the previous presidency.[247]

Grapes of wrath

The October 2021 polls delivered a shock to the presidential team. According to the Kyiv International Institute of Sociology, Zelensky's approval rating as president dropped from 33.3 percent in September to 24.7 percent in October, separated from Poroshenko's approval rating by fewer than ten percentage points.[248] The Razumkov Center's poll demonstrates that Volodymyr Zelensky overtook Petro Poroshenko and now has the biggest "anti-rating" among Ukrainian politicians.[249] What has happened to the once beloved leader?

My answer: at the midpoint of his presidency, Zelensky himself has destroyed his image as an alternative politician. Here is what he did. First, Zelensky and his team started promoting the idea that he was "like any other businessperson in Ukraine." This statement was repeated by everyone on the presidential team in response to the revelations of Zelensky's offshore holdings, suddenly exposed in the Pandora Papers.

The disclosures contained in the Pandora Papers shook many societies around the globe this fall. The leaked documents were analyzed by a consortium of journalists, who found "financial secrets of 35 current and former world leaders, more than 330 politicians and public officials in 91 countries and territories, and a global

---

247 Konończuk, W. (2015). Oligarchs after the Maidan: The Old System in a "New" Ukraine. *Center for Eastern Studies*, February 16, https://2cm.es/OdmW.
248 Socio-Political Moods of the Population of Ukraine: The Election of the President of Ukraine and Current Political Events Based on the Results of a Telephone Survey Conducted on October 15–18, 2021. *KIIS*, October 19, 2021, https://www.kiis.com.ua/?lang=eng&cat=reports&id=1063&page=1.
249 Електоральні орієнтації громадян України та їх ставлення до резонансних подій останнього часу (жовтень 2021р.) (from Ukrainian: Electoral Orientations of Ukrainian Citizens and Their Attitudes toward Recent Resonant Events (October 2021)). *Razumkov Center*, November 1, 2024, https://2cm.es/Odn1.

lineup of fugitives, con artists and murderers."[250] To the surprise of the general public, Volodymyr Zelensky's name appeared on the list of offshore company holders.[251] The documents are testament that Zelensky and his partners (now the heads of security agencies and part of the executive branch of government) owned offshore companies in the British Virgin Islands, Cyprus, and Belize. These companies were used to "defend his business in Ukraine," the president explained.[252] Prior to the 2019 election campaign, Zelensky had turned over control of his shares to his current chief aide and head of the country's Security Service, but Zelensky's family continues "receiving money from the offshore [business operations]."[253]

In truth, the fact of Zelensky's offshore holdings was known and debated during the presidential campaign in 2019. Now, however, the media campaign in defense of the president is promoting the idea that offshore holdings are indeed a mirky business, yet everyone does it. And these words were heard by Ukrainian voters as "Volodymyr Zelensky is just like any other businessman, he is not an alternative."

The second hit to Zelensky's image was similarly engineered by the president and his entourage themselves. They did it by sacking Dmytro Razumkov from his position of speaker of the Verkhovna Rada.

In 2019 Razumkov was one of the key figures who brought Zelensky and the Servant of the People party to power. The young spin doctor soon became the official leader of the party, number one on the party's electoral list, and then the Rada's speaker.

---

250 Offshore Havens and Hidden Riches of World Leaders and Billionaires Exposed in Unprecedented Leak. *International Consortium of Investigative Journalism*, October 3, 2021, https://www.icij.org/investigations/pandora-papers/global-investigation-tax-havens-offshore/.
251 Loginova, E. (2021). Pandora Papers Reveal Offshore Holdings of Ukrainian President and his Inner Circle. *Organized Crime and Corruption Reporting Project*, October 3, https://2cm.es/Odn3.
252 Зеленский заявил, что не занимался отмыванием денег, хотя оффшоры использовал (from Russian: Zelensky Stated That He Did Not Engage in Money Laundering, Although He Used Offshore Vehicles). *Ukrainska Pravda*, October 17, 2021, https://www.pravda.com.ua/rus/news/2021/10/17/7310715/.
253 See the above sited OCCRP material.

The paths of Zelensky and Razumkov began to diverge last spring when the speaker found himself more frequently at odds with the president over the Security Council's rule in Ukraine. Razumkov stood up in defense of the constitution—even when the fight with the oligarchs was in question—and of the "presidential promises of 2019." On October 7, Razumkov was dismissed as speaker by an unusual coalition comprising a large part of the presidential faction in parliament, Yulia Tymoshenko's Batkivshchyna, and several oligarch-controlled MP groups.

Razumkov used his sacking as the basis for a future political campaign, emphasizing that he had remained true to the promises of 2019 that had enticed voters, while Zelensky had forgotten them. This immediately gave the rising politician the support of 7 percent of likely voters. And for a Ukrainian voter, the entire Razumkov drama was a reminder of Zelensky's now thoroughly buried 2019 campaign platform and its nonspecific change orientation.

Zelensky's political image long remained indestructible from the outside. But the two almost suicidal actions of the presidential team—the clumsy justification of the president's offshore business holdings revealed in the Pandora Papers and the ouster of Razumkov—came together at a time of energy-related hardships for Ukrainians and a new wave of COVID-19.[254] Together, these internal and external factors launched the processes of destruction of President Zelensky's image—and potentially of his popular legitimacy.

---

254 See: Polityuk, P., Zinets, N. (2021). Ukraine Shuts Schools as Coronavirus Death Toll Hits New Record. *Reuters*, October 22, https://2cm.es/Odnd; Prokip, A. (2021). Balancing between Debts and Regulations: Ukraine's Gas Market in Winter. *Focus Ukraine*, October 26, https://www.wilsoncenter.org/blog-post/balancing-between-debts-and-regulations-ukraines-gas-market-winter.

Expectations from Ukraine's political processes in the beginning of 2022

January 2022[255]

The new political season in Ukraine launched in a highly difficult situation. Expectations of major Russian aggression, the united stance of Western nations in support of Ukraine following President Joe Biden's infelicitous comments, and mounting economic challenges have made Ukrainian domestic politics even more complex since these three major issues stand in a contradictory relationship to one another.[256] This new political complexity tests the ability of the Zelensky administration to successfully lead Ukraine in what promises to be a stormy 2022.

Ukraine's security and new twists to European and Euro-Atlantic integration

Last year, the presidential team expended enormous effort to quickly achieve a membership perspective in the EU and NATO. Despite that effort, integration with the EU is so far limited to an Association Agreement and closer ad hoc cooperation. Membership in NATO has been declared possible, but seemingly not soon. Now that the risks of a direct military conflict between Russia and Ukraine have grown, this result is bitter indeed.

The dispiriting results of 2021 are unlikely to dissuade the Zelensky administration from continuing its attempts at European and Euro-Atlantic integration. However, official Kyiv has moved

---

255 A shorter version of this column has previously been published as: Minakov, M. (2021). Ukraine's Political Agenda for 2022. *Focus Ukraine*, January 25, 2022 https://www.wilsoncenter.org/blog-post/ukraines-political-agenda-2022-european-integration-deoligarchization-and-economic-growth.
256 Alper, A. et al. (2022). Biden Sees Russia Moving on Ukraine, Sows Doubt on Western Response. *Reuters*, January 20, https://2cm.es/LSLY; Siebold, S., Polityuk, P. (2022). West Stresses Unified Stance on Ukraine After Biden's "Minor Incursion" Remark. *Reuters*, January 20, https://www.reuters.com/world/blinken-arrives-berlin-ukraine-talks-with-european-allies-2022-01-20/; How a Russian-Ukraine Conflict Might Hit Global Markets. *US News*, January 21, 2022, https://2cm.es/LSLZ.

on to other possibilities of forming a strategic partnership with European nations. In January 2022 the Ukrainian political class seems to be inspired by the idea of an alliance with the UK and Poland. The Lublin triangle—an informal grouping comprising Ukraine, Lithuania, and Poland—offers some hope in the way of indirect Euro-Atlantic integration; the latter two countries are already NATO members. The UK and the Baltic countries have started delivering military supplies to increase Ukraine's capacity to resist a possible Russian attack.[257]

Kyiv's Western geopolitical choice seems to unite the ruling party and some opposition parties (European Solidarity, Holos/Voice, and Batkivshchyna). Also, over 50 percent of Ukrainians support membership in the EU (58 percent) and NATO (54 percent).[258]

Despite the Zelensky administration's endeavors and a growing need for support of Ukraine as it faces the threat of a Russian military incursion, the policy priority of European and Euro-Atlantic integration will need to be pursued and united around for a much longer time—longer than a single presidential term. The Western nations do support Ukraine financially, politically, and with weapons. Yet in the winter of 2021–2022, Ukraine is on its own on a possible battlefield.

Deoligarchization: further steps, with disheartening results

The second political priority for President Volodymyr Zelensky's team is deoligarchization. Indeed, Zelensky has entered a critical phase of his presidency with the approval of the acts "against oligarchs" and against their incomes. In order to destroy the oligarchs' influence on society (through their control of mass media) and their illegitimate sources of wealth (siphoning funds from the state

---

[257] Is the Ukrainian Military Really a David Against the Russian Goliath? *France24*, January 20, 2022, https://2cm.es/LSL-.

[258] IRI Ukraine Poll Shows Support for EU/NATO Membership, Concerns over Economy and Vaccines for COVID-19. *International Republican Institute*, December 17, 2021, https://2cm.es/OdPt.

budget, tax evasion, ongoing privatization), two legal acts have already been approved, Act 5599 and Act 5600.[259] The first act stipulates the creation of a special institution to identify individual oligarchs through an assets test and limit their influence on society, political groups, and government. The second act increases the costs of doing business for certain oligarchic groups. According to the calculations of Forbes.ua experts, the proper implementation of these laws could cost the billionaire Rinat Akhmetov, a prominent opponent of Zelensky, up to $1 billion, while the costs for other oligarchs allegedly would be inconsequential.[260]

These acts indeed hit some oligarchic groups, which led to an uptick in the media wars and political pressure on the president. But they failed to undermine the systemic nexus of business and government or help reform Ukraine's established anticorruption organizations, such as the Anti-Monopoly Committee, the state authority regulating competition, the SAPO and the NABU.

The president's team plans to address these drawbacks in its 20-step plan to combat the influence of the oligarchs.[261] The plan document has not yet been made public, but leaked drafts show Zelensky's seriousness in fighting oligarchy at a more systemic

---

[259] Проект Закону про запобігання загрозам національній безпеці, пов'язаним із надмірним впливом осіб, які мають значну економічну або політичну вагу в суспільному житті (олігархів) 5599 від 02.06.2021 (from Ukrainian: Draft Law on Prevention of Threats to National Security Associated with Excessive Influence of Persons with Significant Economic or Political Weight in Public Life (Oligarchs) No. 5599 as of June 2, 2021). *The VRU Official Website*, https://w1.c1.rada.gov.ua/pls/zweb2/webproc4_1?pf3511=72105; Проект Закону про внесення змін до Податкового кодексу України та деяких законодавчих актів України щодо забезпечення збалансованості бюджетних надходжень 5600 від 02.06.2021 (from Ukrainian: Draft Law on Amendments to the Tax Code of Ukraine and Certain Legislative Acts of Ukraine on Ensuring the Balance of Budget Revenues 5600 as of June 2, 2021). *The VRU Official Website*, https://w1.c1.rada.gov.ua/pls/zweb2/webproc4_1?pf3511=72106.

[260] Крицкая, И., Гненный, К. (2021). Проблемы на $880 млн. Какие бизнесы Ахметова пострадали из-за конфликта с Зеленским (from Russian: Problems for $880 mln. What Akhmetov's Businesses Suffered Because of the Conflict with Zelenskiy). *Forbes Ukraine*, December 8, https://2cm.es/OdR4.

[261] Кабмин разработал план по борьбе с "олигархами" на 20 шагов: что в нем (from Russian: The Cabinet of Ministers Has Developed a 20-Step Plan to Fight "Oligarchs": What's In It). *Ekonomichna Pravda*, November 24, 2021, https://www.epravda.com.ua/rus/news/2021/11/24/680082/.

level. The plan envisages strengthening the Anti-Monopoly Committee, reforming the Energy Commission, ensuring that penalties and limitations for oligarchs would touch their assets in foreign jurisdictions and offshore accounts, legalizing and normalizing some forms of lobbying, and taking several other steps that would sever the corrupt ties between the government and the oligarchic clans.

Deoligarchization efforts have already turned a number of parties and clans into the president's enemies. In 2021 the Medvedchuk group was sanctioned and its political influence was radically decreased; late in the year the media war between the presidential team and Rinat Akhmetov's group heated up;[262] and ex-president Petro Poroshenko was accused of high treason, along with Medvedchuk, for alleged involvement in sales of Donbas coal.[263] Poroshenko's assets were seized, and the court has obliged him to remain in Kyiv while free on bond.

Unlike European and Euro-Atlantic integration, deoligarchization does not unite the Ukrainian elites. Many of the steps taken against the oligarchs are seen as dubious in terms of their legality and constitutionality.[264] The sanctions levied against Medvedchuk or Poroshenko, who are not only oligarchic figures but also leaders of opposition groups, may be politically motivated.[265] The clashes with these rivals have contributed to the decline in Zelensky's popularity. A recent poll shows Poroshenko's popularity rating rising three percentage points, to 15.5 percent, while Volodymyr Zelensky's dropped more than two percentage points, to 17.4 percent. According to the same poll, support for Poroshenko's European Solidarity party rose from 13 percent to 16 percent, while support

---

262 Zelenskyy v. Akhmetov: War Has Not Yet Begun. *The Page*, December 1, 2021, https://en.thepage.ua/politics/war-of-zelensky-and-akhmetov-how-the-conflict-is-now-proceeding.
263 Zinets, N., Lewis, S. (2022). Ukraine's Ex-President Avoids Detention in Treason Case as Thousands Rally. *Rueters*, January 19, https://2cm.es/LSNG.
264 Wilson, A. (2021). Faltering Fightback: Zelensky's Piecemeal Campaign Against Ukraine's Oligarchs. *European Council on Foreign Relations*, July 6, https://ecfr.eu/publication/faltering-fightback-zelenskys-piecemeal-campaign-against-ukraines-oligarchs/.
265 Poroshenko, Ex-President, Returns to Ukraine, Roiling Politics. *The New Yourk Times*, January 17, 2022, https://www.nytimes.com/2022/01/17/world/europe/petro-poroshenko-russia-ukraine.html.

for Zelensky's Servant of People party dropped from 14.5 percent to 11.6 percent.[266]

In the face of a possible Russian incursion, any intensification of deoligarchization efforts at this time may weaken the political resilience of Ukraine. In that regard, ex-president Poroshenko issued a call for solidarity among Ukrainians and offered President Zelensky his help in uniting the people and defending the state — a broadly political jab at the incumbent.[267]

Issues with economic growth and infrastructural development

According to the National Bank of Ukraine, the pace of Ukraine's economic growth has been slower than expected: GDP growth in 2021 barely reached 3 percent.[268] Several economic sectors were hit by skyrocketing gas prices, the pandemics had a strong negative impact on household income for the second year in a row, and fiscal consolidation failed to support economic growth. And the threat of Russia's attack scares away investors — a factor that undermines the possibilities for economic growth even more.

One of President Zelensky's flagship projects, the Big Construction, was expected to boost Ukraine's economy and improve the country's aging infrastructure. In the framework of the project, Ukrainians are to get new roads and bridges, as well as rebuilt schools, hospitals, railway stations, and sport facilities. However, the project faces several challenges. First of all, many companies

---

[266] Socio-Political Moods of the Population of Ukraine: Elections of the President of Ukraine and the Verkhovna Rada of Ukraine Based on the Results of a Telephone Survey Conducted on January 20-21, 2022. *KIIS*, January 24, 2022, https://www.kiis.com.ua/?lang=eng&cat=reports&id=1090&page=1.

[267] Порошенко на Національному круглому столі «Єдність народу. Захист демократії. Оборона держави»: інтереси держави понад усе, закликаю всіх до єдності заради України (from Ukrainian: Poroshenko at the National Round Table "Unity of the People. Protection of Democracy. Defense of the State": The Interests of the State Are Above All, I Call on Everyone to Unite for the Sake of Ukraine). *Evropeiska Solidarnist Party Official Website*, January 22, 2022, https://2cm.es/OdRn.

[268] НБУ погіршив прогноз зростання економіки України (from Ukrainian: NBU Downgrades Ukraine's Economic Growth Forecast). *Ekonomichna Pravda*, Jabuary 20, 2022, https://www.epravda.com.ua/news/2022/01/20/681624/.

that implement the construction works derive the bulk of their materials from abroad, thus supporting more foreign than Ukrainian industries. Second, a project with a multibillion-hryvnia budget was an easy prey for corruption. According to the Ministry of Finance report for 2021, out of an audited 60 billion UAH (slightly more than 2 billion USD), more than 30 billion UAH in spending was recognized as "used ineffectively." Some was allegedly misused in corrupt schemes promulgated by a younger generation of politicians.[269]

Economic growth is sorely needed for the impoverished population and for Ukraine's defense sector. Even though the Big Construction is supported by over 90 percent of Ukrainians, it does not create many jobs or help shore up the defense infrastructure.[270] This issue is ever more contested between the pro-government and opposition groups and undermines the possibility of a productive dialogue for the common good in the coming months.

These three issues on the current Ukrainian political agenda can generate both stronger unity and deeper conflict, victory and disaster. Progress on these issues is likely to be severely affected by bellicose actions from Russia. So the coming weeks and months are a critical time for Ukraine's leaders and the international community to demonstrate wisdom and virtue in finding solutions to all three challenges.

---

[269] Показники виконання Зведеного бюджету України за 2021 рік (from Ukrainian: Performance Indicators of the Consolidated Budget of Ukraine for 2021). *Ministry of Finance Official Website*, December 2021, https://mof.gov.ua/uk/budget-process-projects-declaration. See also data of the investigative journalism Yuri Nikolov: «Чинна влада гарантує безпеку Коломойського» – Юрій Ніколов про корупцію й рукодуп'я влади, «обілечування» олігархів (from Ukrainian: "The Current Government Guarantees Kolomoisky's Safety" — Yuriy Nikolov on Corruption and Governmental Mismanagement, 'Curing' Oligarchs). *Nashi Groshi*, October 9, 2021, https://2cm.es/LSOb.

[270] Інфраструктура – це ставлення держави до своїх людей (from Ukrainian: Infrastructure Is the Attitude of the State towards Its People). *President of Ukraine Official Website*, February 22, 2021, https://www.president.gov.ua/news/prezident-infrastruktura-ce-stavlennya-derzhavi-do-svoyih-ly-66665.

Separatists threaten Ukrainian sovereignty

February 2022[271]

On February 15, 2022, deputies of the State Duma of the Russian Federation supported the draft resolution "On the State Duma appeal 'To the President of the Russian Federation Vladimir Putin on the necessity to recognize the Donetsk People's Republic and Luhansk People's Republic.'" In particular, the resolution states that the Duma deputies consider recognition of the self-proclaimed Donetsk and Luhansk "people's republics," or the DPR and LPR, "to be legally justified and morally sound." Although during a press conference that same day with German Chancellor Scholz, Vladimir Putin did not support recognition of these units on Ukraine's non-controlled territory, the many reservations in his speech suggest that the "people's republics" card will continue to be played.

It is important to note that after the disruption of the gradual quieting down in the Donbas in the winter of 2020–2021, a group promoting the idea that the self-proclaimed republics should develop as "Russian national states" has become increasingly important in Moscow since those entities could eventually become part of the supranational organization the Union State of Russia and Belarus.[272] The fact that President Putin did not support the Duma's appeal on February 15, mentioning only his "hope ... that the Minsk agreements would be implemented," does not mean that the Kremlin will not continue to support the existence and development of the DPR and LPR until it can recognize them, as was done in the case of Georgia's two breakaway units, Abkhazia and South Ossetia.

---

[271] A shorter version of this column has previously been published as: Minakov, M. (2022). LPR and DPR Threaten Ukrainian Sovereignty as Russia Tries to Broaden Its Union State. *Focus Ukraine*, February 17, https://www.wilsoncenter.org/blog-post/lpr-and-dpr-threaten-ukrainian-sovereignty-russia-tries-broaden-its-union-state.

[272] Проект Доктрины "Русский Донбасс" (from Russian: Draft Doctrine "Russian Donbass"). *Russkii Centr*, 2021, https://russian-center.ru/8315-2/.

It is clear that recognition of the self-proclaimed Donbas republics would cost Russia dearly in the current context. In response to such a move, Western governments would impose new and tougher sanctions, undermining Russia's socioeconomic stability, while Ukraine would get a legitimate chance to abandon the Minsk agreements and emerge with new opportunities in international politics. Recognition would intensify the antagonism between Russia and the West, something the Kremlin does not appear to be planning right now.

Secession, or the separation of part of a state's population and territory from the parent state with the aim of creating an independent state, is a rare but not unprecedented political event. Sometimes secession leads to recognition of the sovereignty and independence of the separated parts, such as the North American colonies of Britain, which became the United States of America, or the republics of the USSR, which became recognized independent states.

Quite often, however, secession is the result of external intervention rather than of the desire of the population to live separately. Some examples are Abkhazia in Georgia, Transnistria in Moldova, the Turkish Republic of Northern Cyprus, and, potentially, the LHR and DPR. In such a case, a "secession triangle" emerges, a complex, conflict-prone relationship between the parent state, the sponsor state, and the self-proclaimed statelet.

In this triangle, the parent state finds itself in a state of "damaged sovereignty" whereby the government is unable to regain control of its citizens and its internationally recognized territory and cannot fully implement its constitution with respect to citizens living in the non-controlled territory. Damaged sovereignty of the parent state means that it partially fails to fulfill the basic functions of the state as defined by the 1933 Montevideo Convention on the Rights and Duties of States.[273] Thus the parent state: (1) is not fully capable of defending its territory against other states, (2) is not fully capable of ensuring the supremacy of power and a monopoly on

---

273 Minakov, M. (2021). Post-Soviet Sovereignty and Ukraine's Political Development. *Ukraine Analytica*, 2 (24): 26-34, https://ukraine-analytica.org/post-soviet-sovereignty-and-ukraines-political-development/.

the legitimate use of violence against its population, (3) has a government that provides unique public services, but not to all citizens, and (4) enters into relations with other states from a weakened position.

Ukraine, Georgia, and Moldova are examples of states whose sovereignty is systematically violated by the presence of self-proclaimed republics on their internationally recognized territories. To compensate in part for the damage to the parent states, international law provides for sanctions against secessionists and support for parent states in their claims to reintegrate illegally seceded communities. A recent example of such support is found in the US response to Russian security claims, namely, that Russia withdraws from the territories of Georgia, Moldova, and Ukraine.[274]

A self-proclaimed statelet (or de facto state, or parastate) is only partially capable of performing the functions of the state. Being in existential conflict with the parent state, the parastate is mired in a military-political conflict ("hot" or "frozen") on its unstable borders, is constantly competing for the loyalty of its population, and is able to provide only low-quality government services. Furthermore, it remains outside interstate relations. The de facto state is flawed both in terms of its efficacy and in terms of unrecognized sovereignty. The situation in the LPR and DPR is quite consistent with this picture.

Parastates can exist for a long time only with the support of the sponsor state. This sponsorship may take the form of "supplementing sovereignty" (when the sponsor represents the parastate on the international scene), providing weapons and military advisers (to maintain the parastate's borders), and funding the parastate's budget. The Russian Federation performs all these functions with regard to the self-proclaimed Donbas republics.

Yet Russian sponsorship goes far beyond the Donbas. Since the early 1990s, the Kremlin has created a network of de facto states in Eastern Europe, which until 2014 included South Ossetia,

---

274 Forgery, Q. (2022). US Delivers Written Response to Russian Demands amid Ukraine Crisis. *Politico*, January 26, https://www.politico.com/news/2022/01/26/us-russia-ukraine-written-response-00002414.

Abkhazia, and Transnistria, with a population totaling up to one million people. By the beginning of the war in the Donbas, these parastates and the Russian Federation had created a military-political and socioeconomic model that allowed them to survive in the face of conflict with their parent states and international sanctions. This model has been applied to the de facto state-building on Ukrainian soil in the Donbas so that today, the parastate network overseen by Russia is populated by more than four million Eastern Europeans. The Kremlin's military, political, and financial investment in this network pays off in that the parent states find themselves strategically tied to intractable conflicts and limited in their ability to join alliances such as the EU or NATO.

The Russian State Duma's decision is an act that deepens the damage to Ukrainian sovereignty and increases the Kremlin's strategic options in conflict with Ukraine and the West. De-escalation on the Ukrainian-Russian border may be in the offing, but the systemic conflict in Eastern Europe continues to expand.

III. Leader

The start of the Russian war on Ukraine

February 2022[275]

On February 24, 2022, the Russian Federation launched a full-fledged war on Ukraine. This attack is the next stage of an aggressive course that first showed its colors in 2014. It also represents a continuation, more focused this time, of the same revanchist ideology that drove the earlier incidents with Moscow. An aging President Putin and his entourage are hurrying to revise the post–Cold War international order and reconfigure Russia's place in it.[276] They want Russia to be among the weightiest states geopolitically, yet their every step since 2013 has led to further isolation and a declining influence on the international scene: Russia is no longer a G8 member, its impact is waning in the post-Soviet space, and Central and Eastern European countries are receiving a growing number of NATO forces. Despite getting results opposite to its goals, the Kremlin continues adding to its snowballing mistakes and violations of international norms. Blindly pursuing its aims, Putin's regime has moved from the hybrid warfare it has waged against Ukraine in 2014–2021 to bad old ground warfare against its western neighbor starting February 24, 2022.

A shared destiny for Ukraine and the West

Putin's most recent actions show him to be engaged in a high-stakes test of how Westless the world is. If in February 2020 Westlessness was more a hypothesis,[277] today the Russian regime is trying to

---

[275] A shorter version of this column has previously been published as: Minakov, M. (2022). The War on Ukraine: The Beginning of the End of Putin's Russia. *Focus Ukraine*, February 28, https://www.wilsoncenter.org/blog-post/war-ukraine-beginning-end-putins-russia.

[276] Putin's Poker. *Project Syndicate*, January 27, 2022, https://www.project-syndicate.org/onpoint/putin-s-poker.

[277] Ludewig, A. (2021). Westlessness? Challenges for the EU's Soft Power Approach. *Australian and New Zealand Journal of European Studies*, 13(1), 23-33.

prove it empirically. And this exercise is something that the great powers of Asia are also attentively watching. China has increased its cooperation with Russia during the invasion of Ukraine. India has not reacted officially to the atrocities being committed against Ukraine, and Imran Khan, Prime Minister of Pakistan, while expressing his regret over the "conflict," met with President Putin on February 25. Make no mistake: the war in Ukraine is testing the geopolitical value of the West as much as it is the resilience of Ukrainians. Whether the United States and the EU are ready for that or not, the destiny of Ukraine and that of the West-led order are inseparable.

There are signs that the West is coming together with a single voice and will and presenting a united stance in the face of the Kremlin's new war. The decisions made last week—both in Moscow and in the West—have established a new Iron Curtain. But is it enough to stop the war against Ukraine?

A failed Blitzkrieg

The first four days of the war exploded the Kremlin's initial plan to mount a Blitzkrieg: General Valery Gerasimov was unable to deliver a swift victory for Putin. The focused military operations were aimed at a speedy takeover of Kyiv, southern Ukraine, and left-bank Ukraine. Even though Russian troops have reached the northern suburbs of Kyiv after gaining entry into the country through Belarus, the city is neither under siege nor in a panic. Diversionary forces were liquidated, while the local population is organizing itself into groups for territorial defense, equipped with arms recently delivered from NATO partners.

Despite some uncertainty in the West as to how he would perform under pressure, President Zelensky and his team have exhibited courage and the strong leadership needed by a country at war.[278] It seems likely that one of the primary goals of the Russian

---

278 As Russian Threat Looms, Ukraine's Government Is No Laughing Matter. *The New York Times*, December 25, 2021, https://www.nytimes.com/2021/12/25/world/europe/ukraine-russia.html; Ukraine's Zelensky asks citizens to resist

attack on Ukraine was to seize Zelensky and force him to sign a capitulation agreement. But from the moment of capture, the president would no longer lead the country; and if the president becomes unable to fulfill his or her duties, the Rada speaker, Ruslan Stefanchuk, is constitutionally next in line to lead the nation. The Kremlin would need to hunt for that person as well, and for others in the line of succession, but all its efforts would be for naught. Furthermore, the Ukrainian president—or his or her substitute—does not have the power to sign any sort of capitulation document without parliament's collective decision to that end. And the collective will in Ukraine is singularly focused on a diametrically opposite scenario: resist the attack, overcome the attackers, and win. No legally binding capitulation is possible.

The security situation in the East and South of the country is, however, grave. At the time of this writing, the Russian troops south of Kharkiv and armed insurgents in the self-proclaimed Luhansk People's Republic are moving toward each other to merge, despite the Ukrainian army's heroic fight. The Russian troops moving eastward from Crimea will try to join the guerrilla factions of the self-proclaimed Donetsk People's Republic and lay siege to Mariupol, the largest port and industrial city in the government-controlled Donbas. The Russian troops moving westward from Crimea besieged Kherson, and now move toward Mykolaiv. In all these zones the best Ukrainian army units are fighting so well that the plan for a speedy takeover of these cities with a significant Russophone population has pathetically failed. The citizens of these cities are putting their lives on the line to defend Ukraine and Ukrainian sovereignty, and to dismantle the revanchist hopes of the Kremlin.

Ukraine's resilience has improved significantly since 2014, and, despite the heavy blow delivered to the Ukrainian military infrastructure in the first days of the war, the defense system was able to derail the Kremlin's plan A, the Blitzkrieg.

---

and Europe to do more. *BBC*, February 25, 2022, https://www.bbc.com/news/world-europe-60527346.

Beginning of the end

The attack on Ukraine was not just an absolute crime (which never bothers autocrats), it was an irreparable mistake that put into motion the endgame for Putin's regime in Russia. The military campaign was not prepared for an operation of any duration. Already on the third day of fighting there were signs of personnel shortages among the assaulting troops, who cannot get control of the besieged but resisting Ukrainian cities. The Russian population was not mobilized to support this war (as it so shamefully was in 2014), and the antiwar movement in Russia is growing.[279] The Western sanctions are set to destroy Russia's economy at large and the economic security of households in particular.[280]

Nor are Russia's Asian partners its allies. They may feel no solidarity with the Ukrainians experiencing tragedy, but they also don't care to risk getting into a conflict with the West. Putin's geopolitical adventurism may speak to some Asian leaders' hidden hopes, but they keep those hopes close. Putin's Russia is alone in its war against Ukraine and its conflict with the West.

Understanding his failure, Vladimir Putin has had recourse to the ultima ratio—the last hope—of terrified dictators: the threat of deploying nuclear weapons.[281] Yet just as before, his means lead away from the desired end. They just hasten the end of his rule, which most probably will come about as a result not of external but of internal forces awakened by the autocrat's mistake.

---

[279] Compare data from: Volkov, D. (2015). How Authentic is Putin's Approval Rating? *CEIP*, July 27, https://2cm.es/LSP3; Events of the Month. *Levada-Center*, February 18, 2022, https://www.levada.ru/en/2022/02/18/events-of-the-month-4/; Dehn, C. (2022). Anti-War Protests in Russian Cities. *Deutsche Welle*, February 25, https://www.dw.com/en/anti-war-protests-across-russian-cities/g-60915712.

[280] Sorkin, A.R. et al. (2022). Sanctions and Consequences. The Ripple Effects of Russia's Invasion of Ukraine Are Coming into Focus. *The New York Times*, February 25, https://www.nytimes.com/2022/02/25/business/dealbook/russia-ukraine-sanctions-energy.html.

[281] Putin Puts Russia's Nuclear Deterrent Forces on Alert. *Politico*, February 27, 2022, https://shorturl.at/2GATD.

First attempts of Ukraine-Russia talks

April 2022[282]

The Russian war on Ukraine has gone on for almost fifty days. And negotiations between Kyiv and Moscow — on two tracks so far — started the day after the Russian invasion. Even as the parties' positions become clearer, no compromise seems to be on the horizon.

Two tracks and the people involved

The first track of negotiations is being handled by two consulting teams. Several in-person meetings of the Ukrainian and Russian teams, led by David Arakhamia on the Ukrainian side and Vladimir Medinsky for the Russians, took place in Belarus during the early weeks of the war.[283] Later, the teams working on this track began meeting more often to discuss enforcement of humanitarian corridors, POW exchanges, and, most important, the agenda for the meeting of the respective countries' foreign affairs ministers.[284]

The Ukrainian negotiating team includes representatives of President Zelensky's team: David Arakhamia, leader of the parliamentary faction Servant of the People party; Justice Minister Denys Malyuska, adviser to the presidential office Mykhailo Podolyak, Defense Minister Oleksii Reznikov, Deputy Foreign Affairs Minister Mykola Tochitsky, and three MPs, Andriy Kostin, Dmytro

---

[282] A shorter version of this column has previously been published as: Kusa, I., Minakov, M. (2022). Ukraine-Russia Negotiations: What's Possible? *Focus Ukraine*, April 11, 2022 https://www.wilsoncenter.org/blog-post/ukraine-russia-negotiations-whats-possible.
[283] See information from: Tayfur, N. A. (2022). Ukraine's President Forms Delegation for Talks with Russia. *AA TV*, April 5, https://shorturl.at/psGkx; Russia No Longer Requesting Ukraine Be 'Denazified' as Part of Ceasefire Talks. *Financial Times*, April 2, 2022, https://www.ft.com/content/7f14efe8-2f4c-47a2-aa6b-9a755a39b626; Johnston, R. A. (2022). The Only Russian Official Angrier Than Putin at How Things Are Going in Ukraine. *Slate*, March 8, https://shorturl.at/xYv7j; Babachanakh, D. (2022). Here's Why a Russia-Ukraine Deal Is Not on the Agenda. *OpenDemocracy*, March 15, https://www.opendemocracy.net/en/odr/russia-ukraine-deal-negotiations-war/.
[284] Russia, Ukraine Set to Resume Negotiations via Video Link Monday. *The Times of Israel*, March 14, 2022, https://rb.gy/vwkq39.

Lubinets, and Rustem Umerov. In April 2022 the team was officially enlarged with the addition of two seasoned experts, the international lawyer Alexander Malinovsky and Alexander Chaly, Ukraine's veteran diplomat. Most of the members of this group have direct access to President Zelensky and represent his administration.

The Russian delegation is headed by one of President Vladimir Putin's aides, Vladimir Medinsky, former minister of culture and chairman of the Russian Military Historical Society. The Russian delegation also includes Deputy Foreign Minister Andrei Rudenko, Russian Ambassador to Belarus Boris Gryzlov, Leonid Slutsky, head of the State Duma International Committee, and Deputy Defense Minister Alexander Fomin. The members of Russian team have less access to President Putin and are a group of experienced bureaucrats trusted to implement the president's wishes.

Another track of negotiations is ongoing at the foreign affairs ministerial level. Ukrainian foreign affairs minister Dmytro Kuleba and his Russian counterpart, Sergei Lavrov, have met twice, in Antalya, Turkey, on March 10 and again in Istanbul on March 28.[285] Talks on this track have led to highly important decisions, such as the withdrawal of Russian troops from three northern Ukrainian oblasts, and to the preparation of some sort of deal that might be agreed to at a future possible meeting of Presidents Zelensky and Putin. (This meeting is not yet in the works). However, this track appears to have reached a stalemate. On April 7, Lavrov issued a public statement claiming that Ukraine had presented him with a draft peace agreement that "deviated" from proposals both sides had previously agreed on "in writing."[286]

The MFA track has involved mediation by the Israeli and Turkish leadership and some other negotiators, including unofficial

---

285 Lavrov, Kuleba End First High-Level Talks Since Russian Invasion of Ukraine with No Progress on Cease-Fire. *RFE/RL*, March 10, 2022, https://www.rferl.org/a/ukraine-kuleba-lavrov-meeting-ceasefire/31746012.html; Russia-Ukraine Talks in Istanbul Mark Most Significant Progress Yet: Cavusoglu. *AlArabia News*, March 29, 2022, https://rb.gy/tv1ob6.

286 Russia's Lavrov Says Ukraine Presented 'Unacceptable' Draft Peace Deal. *AlArabia News*, April 7, 2022, https://rb.gy/wkhj5b.

ones such as Roman Abramovich.²⁸⁷ Also, many other powers from the West and East participate in this track.

Political issues related to resolving the principal disagreements between Russia and Ukraine in the longer-term perspective — including the status of the occupied territories, security guarantees for Ukraine, Ukraine's neutrality and non-nuclear status, and so forth — moved to the forefront of negotiations almost immediately, in parallel with discussions more directly related to the conflict itself, such as a permanent ceasefire, POW exchanges, evacuation efforts, and access by humanitarian aid organizations.

Positions of the parties

The positions of the parties — Ukraine and Russia, as well as the United States, the UK, the EU, and the Asian powers — can be sketched briefly in the following way.

Ukraine insists on a return to the prewar status quo, meaning that Russian troops are to withdraw at least to the positions held before February 24. President Zelensky and his aides have constantly emphasized that Russia should contribute financially to Ukraine's postwar reconstruction efforts and pay compensation to all war victims. Should Moscow refuse, sanctions are to be preserved even after a formal ceasefire agreement has been concluded.²⁸⁸ In addition, the Ukrainian authorities want the territories occupied in 2014 to remain subject to further negotiations. In the interim, Ukraine insists on the need for Moscow to withdraw its recognition of the self-proclaimed republics in the Donbas. It seems that Kyiv is ready to make concessions on its NATO membership

---

287 Russia Views Turkish, Israeli Mediation Efforts Favorably: Lavrov. *Daily Sabah*, March 16, 2022, https://rb.gy/s5m6hk; Russia-Ukraine War: Abramovich Spotted in Istanbul Peace Talks. *BBC*, March 29, 2022, https://www.bbc.com/news/world-europe-60912474.

288 Росія повинна щоденно платити за цю страшну війну: Зеленський очікує нових санкцій (from Ukrainian: Russia Must Pay for This Terrible War Every Day: Zelensky Expects New Sanctions). *UKRINFORM*, March 11, 2022, https://2cm.es/LSQl.

aspirations and is ready to talk about neutrality under strong foreign guarantees, including Russia's.[289]

The Russian position has evolved over the last fifty days. In the first weeks of the war Moscow's political demands included not only that Ukraine not join NATO or that Ukraine change its constitution to remain neutral, but also certain restrictions on the size of Ukraine's defense system, the number of military personnel, and the volume and types of arms imports. Culturally, Moscow demanded that Ukraine constitutionally include the Russian language as the second official language and ban far-right organizations. Finally, Moscow insisted on Ukraine's recognition of occupied Crimea as part of Russia and the so-called Donbas people's republics as independent states.

Currently, it seems that the Russian demands have been scaled down, especially after it became clear that Moscow couldn't take Kyiv and control Ukraine's northern regions. In recent weeks Moscow has shifted its military focus to eastern and southern Ukraine, where Russian ground forces have managed to make some progress. Russia's recent demands are mainly focused on Ukraine's neutral and non-nuclear status, dropping the NATO membership topic and nondeployment of foreign military bases or weapon systems. Moreover, while it seems that Russia is willing to withdraw from the territories occupied after February 24, it is unlikely to leave Ukraine's southern and eastern regions, where Russia has significant manpower deployed and has already started recruiting local politicians to establish new occupational authorities.

Today, for Russia, it seems imperative to have at least a minimum "victory kit" comprising the following: (1) control of the city of Mariupol, (2) expansion of the self-styled Donbas people's republics to the limits of their oblast administrative borders, (3) a

---

[289] Гарантії безпеки Україні дадуть змогу зафіксувати статус постійного нейтралітету — Олександр Чалий (from Ukrainian: Security Guarantees for Ukraine Will Allow to Fix the Status of Permanent Neutrality — Oleksandr Chaly). *Interfax*, March 29, 2022. https://interfax.com.ua/news/general/819049.html. Compare this information with the draft document published by The New York Times in 2024 at https://static01.nyt.com/newsgraphics/documenttools/a456d6dd8e27e830/e279a252-full.pdf.

permanent military presence in Kherson oblast sufficient to guarantee freshwater supplies to Crimea, and (4) preservation of the land bridge connecting the separatist-controlled territory in the Donbas with the occupied Crimean Peninsula by way of the Sea of Azov coast and Kherson oblast. This would be enough for the Russian government to declare victory.

The United States and the UK seem to by expecting a long-term proxy war against Russia through Ukraine.[290] Such an extended engagement would allow retention of the anti-Russian sanctions, a further consolidation of Western allies, and a weakening of Russia in the long term. These are some of the reasons why American and British officials were initially skeptical or guarded with respect to Ukraine-Russia peace talks.[291] For Washington and London, a quick peace settlement, however short-lived, would allow Russia to bounce back from its military venture and regroup, while some European partners would ease up on the sanctions regime and restore at least some trade ties with Moscow.

The European countries are clearly divided on the Russia-Ukraine war issue. While the EU member states seem to be consolidated on the need to respond to the Russian military invasion, they have their differences when it comes to burning bridges with Moscow, strengthening the sanctions pressure, or giving Ukraine more sophisticated weaponry. Germany, the Netherlands, Austria, France, Belgium, and other Western European countries want this war to end as soon as possible. A quick end would allow them to stabilize markets and commodity prices, make the threats to socio-economic stability manageable, and partially restore trade with Russia. On the other hand, Poland, Slovenia, Lithuania, Latvia, and Estonia are pushing for more sanctions against Russia, including a total energy embargo and a transport blockade, and for the delivery

---

[290] Winter-Levy, S. (2022). A Proxy War in Ukraine Is the Worst Possible Outcome—Except For All the Others. *War on the Rocks*, March 28, 2022, https://2cm.es/OdTZ.

[291] Cohen, Z. et al. (2022). US and NATO Officials Struggle to Decipher Status of Negotiations between Russia and Ukraine. *CNN*, March 20, https://edition.cnn.com/2022/03/20/politics/russia-ukraine-negotiations-us-nato/index.html.

of more sophisticated weaponry to Ukraine, including planes, tanks, and anti-aircraft systems.

Most countries in the global south, including such heavyweights as India, Pakistan, China, Indonesia, Malaysia, Uzbekistan, the UAE, Saudi Arabia, and Egypt, continue to insist on enhancing the West-Russia dialogue and achieving peace in Ukraine as soon as possible. However, several countries are also eyeing a potential role as a future guarantor of Ukraine's security, with China, Turkey, and Israel among them.

In a long-term perspective, Asian and African countries believe that the war in Ukraine should lead to the establishment of a new post-Cold War security architecture, one not dominated by Western institutions. For them, Russia seems to be a challenger to the West and a champion of such a geopolitical shift.

In this intersection of competing interests, it is too early to come up with a clear vision of what the framework for a possible peace deal might look like. It seems clear that the bulk of the negotiations will be dedicated to determining the lines along which the parties will have staked out their positions by the time a ceasefire agreement is reached. Territorial control will determine not only the future military and political balance between Russia and Ukraine but also the prospects for Ukraine to successfully recover economically.

Moreover, the status of Crimea and the Donbas is a key issue on the negotiators' agenda, owing to the enormous significance of the issue for the highly polarized domestic audiences of both Ukraine and Russia. Finally, the modality of Ukraine's neutral status will be of high interest to Moscow and Kyiv. Ukraine clearly wants to minimize any limitations on its sovereignty inscribed in any possible neutrality agreement, while Russia is expected to try to impose additional arms restrictions and weaken foreign security guarantees for Ukraine.

Still, it is too early to know what framework might emerge, especially as the war is continuing. The battle for Ukraine's East is likely to be crucial to the overall outcome of the war and the parties' negotiating positions. Meanwhile, atrocities and war crimes continue to take place in Ukraine.

Zelensky versus Putin: the personality factor in Russia's war on Ukraine

April 2022[292]

Russia's war on Ukraine is a historical event that impacts directly on the lives of Ukrainians and Russians, but also on the political geography of Europe and on international politics globally. The war marks the end of a period that could be termed "post-Soviet" in the region and the start of an as yet unnamed but so far tragic period for Europe and Eurasia.[293]

I have no doubt that the war was a product of numerous powerful systemic forces — from institutional and political to structural and economic — and their leaders' miscalculations. The war's first fifty days have illustrated the crucial role of personality in deciding the course of history: the figure of Ukraine's president Volodymyr Zelensky has proven to be a decisive factor in shaping the force of the Ukrainian resistance, while the figure of Russia's president Vladimir Putin has been a major factor in shaping Russia's military and political failures.

The Zelensky factor

In the first half of his term, Zelensky went through several stages of popularity. As a decisive winner in the 2019 presidential elections, he united Ukraine's East and West, city dwellers and rural inhabitants, rich and poor. However, in both January 2021 and January 2022 his approval ratings fell well below 30 percent, as most Ukrainians thought the country was going in the wrong direction.[294]

---

[292] A shorter version of this column has previously been published as: Minakov, M. (2022). Zelensky Versus Putin: The Personality Factor in Russia's War on Ukraine. *Focus Ukraine*, April 13, 2022 https://www.wilsoncenter.org/blog-post/zelensky-versus-putin-personality-factor-russias-war-ukraine.

[293] More on this era's end see: Minakov, M. (2024). *Post-Soviet Human*. Stuttgart: ibidem Verlag.

[294] Общественно-политические настроения: итоги 2021 (16-18 декабря 2021) (from Russian: Socio- Political Attitudes: Results of 2021 (16-18 December 2021)). *SGR*, December 21, 2021, https://n9.cl/k2ibt.

But while as a peacetime president, Zelensky exhibited strengths and weaknesses, as a wartime president, he came into his own. Zelensky has turned out to be a tough and courageous wartime leader, perfectly meeting the nation's needs for firm leadership. Despite his draft dogging from 2008–2015, he attained the right to call the people to arms.[295] Despite world leaders' numerous urgings, he has refused to leave Ukraine, both before and after the start of the Russian invasion.[296] He remained in the country, despite alleged assassination attempts, and has served as a model of resistance to the personal and national existential threat.[297] In numerous conversations, Ukrainian soldiers, activists, and businessmen have told me that they joined the defense because the president "did not flee." Whatever was happening in the past, since February 24, 2022, Volodymyr Zelensky inspired Ukrainians to unite around him and defend Ukraine.

Zelensky has also used his best leadership and performance abilities to unite the international community around the cause of defending Ukraine and restoring the international order. In his addresses to Western parliaments, international summits, and UN meetings, Zelensky has transformed Zoom from a pandemic-era utility into a tool to win the hearts and minds of global leaders and people of good will worldwide. Ukraine's unprecedented internal solidarity, as well as the growing military and humanitarian support from NATO, the United States, and the EU, are in many ways the personal achievement of Zelensky.[298]

---

295 Дмитрук, А. (2019). Зеленському 4 рази надсилали повістку до військкомату, він ігнорував — Міноборони (from Ukrainian: Zelensky Was Sent a Summons to the Military Commissariat 4 Times, He Ignored It — Defense Ministry). *Hromadske*, April 19, https://2cm.es/LSRd.
296 Atwood, K., Mattingly, P., Chance, M. (2022). Biden Administration Urged Zelensky Not to Leave Ukraine and Visit Munich. *CNN*, February 18, https://edition.cnn.com/2022/02/18/politics/biden-zelensky-ukraine-munich/index.html.
297 Lungariello, M. (2022). Ukraine President Volodymyr Zelensky Survives Three Assassination Attempts in the Last Week. *The New York Post*, March 3, https://nypost.com/2022/03/03/ukraine-president-zelensky-survived-three-assassination-attempts/.
298 See more on this Zelensky's factor in a later publication: Onuch, O., & Hale, H. E. (2022). *The Zelensky Effect*. London: Hurst.

It comes as no surprise, then, that his public approval rating in Ukraine and abroad has skyrocketed. Well over 90 percent of Ukrainians trust him, and he is now the most popular politician in the United States, with more than 70 percent of Americans surveyed expressing confidence in him.[299]

The Putin factor

A contrasting picture emerges from the failures of the Russian troops in the initial phase of the war against Ukraine, which in many ways stem from Putin's personal miscalculations. A mature politician and enduring autocratic ruler, Putin has enormous experience in politics and international relations. However, as an authoritarian figure who lives in a bubble and is isolated from Russian society and the rest of the world, he has become hostage to his own regime and ideological beliefs.

Putin's recent speeches and writings show the depth of the ideological trap in which he finds himself.[300] The illusion that "Russians and Ukrainians are one people" has clashed with the reality in Ukraine. It seems that the Kremlin's plan A was based on the expectation that the citizenry and political elites of Kyiv, Chernihiv, Sumy, Kharkiv, Mariupol, or Mykolaiv would welcome the invaders. The Kremlin expected Zelensky to flee or surrender. The strength of Ukraine's leadership, armed defense, and civilian resistance presented a stark challenge to the dictator's personal beliefs.

To Putin, his army's unprovoked invasion of another country is a "special military operation," not a war. The thousands of killed Ukrainians and the millions of those made refugees have not

---

[299] Smith, Z. S. (2022). More Americans Are Confident in Zelensky Than Biden, Study Finds. *Forbes*, March 30, https://n9.cl/gsuiz4; Общенациональный опрос: Украина в условиях войны (26-27 февраля 2022 года) (from Russian: Nationwide Poll: Ukraine at War (February 26-27, 2022)). *SGR*, February 27, 2022, https://n9.cl/2yyht.

[300] 'No other option': Excerpts of Putin's speech declaring war. *Aljazeera*, February 24, 2022, https://n9.cl/7d7et; Putin, V. (2022). On the Historical Unity of Russians and Ukrainians. *President of Russia Official Website*, https://www.prlib.ru/en/article-vladimir-putin-historical-unity-russians-and-ukrainians.

moved Putin to change his preferred vocabulary. The thousands of Russian protesters and the silent disapproval of hundreds of thousands more have not made him reconsider his beliefs. To help ensure that Putin's illusion prevails over reality, his regime has introduced legislation criminalizing the use of the word war and any disapproval of the war he has launched.[301]

When illusions do not match reality, people tend to respond with violence in an attempt to punish reality. If the person is a political leader with no institutional, legal, or moral constraints on his decisions and actions, the violence can reach unfathomable levels, damaging the lives of many people. This is likely the source of the ferocity and viciousness demonstrated by Russian troops in Mariupol, Bucha, and other Ukrainian locations they occupy. And this is definitely the source of Putin's complete denial of his own responsibility for the massacres in Ukraine.

As Putin's war against Ukraine and the international conflict it has produced evolve, both the structural factors and the personality factors involved in them will be tested. Zelensky's resilience will be tested in particular by the next stages of military action and by the economic hardships sustained by the Ukrainian people. A coming socioeconomic crisis and war losses will test Putin's abilities. There is reason to believe that the personality factor will be increasingly important to the future of Ukraine, Russia, and the world we live in.

The Kremlin's secessionist plans put Ukrainian statehood at risk

April 2022[302]

The Russian war against Ukraine constitutes an existential threat to Ukraine as a state and a country. This threat can be seen in the risks

---

301 Russia Bans Media Outlets from Using Words "War," "Invasion". *The Moscow Times*, February 26, 2022, https://n9.cl/12d0d.
302 A shorter version of this column has previously been published as: Minakov, M. (2022). Ukrainian Statehood at Risk: The Kremlin's Secessionist Plans. *Focus*

to life of noncombatants, as happened particularly in Mariupol and Bucha. Forced hunger and the shelling of critical civilian infrastructure underscore the lethal nature of such risks and the extent to which Moscow is willing to go. Yet the threat is also to the Ukrainian commonwealth — to Ukraine's statehood itself.

After the Kremlin's attempt to swiftly execute regime change in Kyiv failed and the battle for Kyiv was won by Ukraine, Russia seems to have redirected its efforts to taking over the eastern and southern regions. Judging from Kremlin official statements, Russian propaganda, and practices in the temporarily occupied territories in the Donbas and in Kharkiv, Zaporizhzhia, and Kherson oblasts, Russia is preparing to further undermine, even destroy, the territorial foundations of the Ukrainian state's sovereignty.

Russian-sponsored secessionism of post-Soviet quasi-republics

Creating and sponsoring post-Soviet de facto statelets is an old and tested policy of the Russian Federation. By supporting some irredentist or secessionist movements in newly independent states in the 1990s, Moscow managed to create structural obstacles for Georgia, Moldova, and Ukraine to integrate into the EU and NATO. After more than thirty years of existence, the post-Soviet de facto statelets have developed their own socioeconomic and political models providing the local elites and populations — which in six such statelets amounted to four million people at the beginning of 2022 — with opportunities to stably exist and avoid the imposition of sanctions by the parental states and the international community.

Also, Russia and its allies have started the process of legitimizing these quasi-republics. As a result of the Russo-Georgian war in 2008, Russia has recognized South Ossetia and Abkhazia as independent states. Prior to launching the major war on Ukraine, Russia recognized the independence of the self-proclaimed "people's

---

Ukraine, April 19, 2022 https://www.wilsoncenter.org/blog-post/ukrainian-statehood-risk-kremlins-secessionist-plans.

republics" of Donetsk and Luhansk on February 20, 2022.[303] The leadership of Transnistria, according to sources in Tiraspol, may also expect that quasi-republic to be recognized as a result of the Russian-Ukrainian war.

Along with this recognition by the Russian Federation, the elites of these quasi-republics are looking for closer integration with Russia. The ideology of "Russian national states," which was announced in January 2021 in Donetsk, envisaged the post-Soviet de facto states joining the Union State, which now consists of the Russian Federation and Belarus.[304] More recently the approach has shifted to organizing referenda on joining the Russian Federation itself. Voting on such a referendum has been promised by the insurrectionist authorities in South Ossetia and Luhansk.[305]

In each case, recognition of the post-Soviet quasi-republics has added to disorder and entropy of the security regime in Eastern Europe. Georgia, Moldova, and Ukraine face further threats to their statehood with the unilateral actions of their insurrectionist regions and Russia.

New separatist projects on Ukrainian soil

Some officials, journalists, as well as my informed collocutors from Kherson, Mariupol, and Henichesk — cities in the temporarily occupied Ukrainian regions — told me about the preparations the Russian authorities are undertaking in advance of declaring the "Kherson People's Republic" or merge it with Russia as its oblast.[306] If the project of such a factitious republic is chosen, its territory would consist of the areas of Kherson and Zaporizhzhia oblasts seized by Russian forces. To gin up a legitimate pretext for the creation of a

---

303 Russia Recognizes Independence of Ukraine Separatist Regions. *Deutsche Welle*, February 21, 2022, https://n9.cl/zzqbx.
304 Skorkin, K. (2021). Merge and Rule: What's in Store for the Donetsk and Luhansk Republics. *Carnegie Endowment for International Peace (CEIP)*, March 16, https://n9.cl/99qmm.
305 Georgia Says "Unacceptable" for Breakaway Region to Vote on Joining Russia. *Reuters*, March 31, 2022, https://n9.cl/rrbom; Ukrainian Rebel Region Luhansk May Vote to Join Russia. *Reuters*, March 27, 2022, https://n9.cl/scc2d.
306 Lohsen, A. (2022). Will Russia Create New "People's Republics" in Ukraine? *War on the Rocks*, March 25, https://n9.cl/ycn3x.

new "republic," Russian authorities may hold a referendum — an illusory ritual already carried out in Donetsk and Luhansk in 2014.[307] Despite low turnout and the illegality of such events, they were used by Russian propaganda to support the LPR's and DPR's "state-building" efforts.

The Russian plan may also include activities intended to sow distrust and encourage fragmentation in other regions. During the early days of the war, Moscow attempted to defreeze its Rusyn separatism in Transcarpathia.[308] More risks to Ukraine may, therefore, emerge from the Odesa oblast, which is near Transnistria and the Russian troops deployed there.

Obstacles to Russia's plans

The first problem that Russian forces have faced was the rejection by local elites and populations of the Kremlin's plans. Even at the risk of being killed, the citizens of many temporarily occupied towns have dared to participate publicly in peaceful acts of defiance against the invasion.[309]

The Russian defeat near Kyiv, the violence of the invading troops, and stronger support from the West for Ukraine have seemingly discouraged the local elites in southern Ukraine from cooperating with Moscow. Still, the longer this war goes on, the more incentives there will be for local leaders and communities to weaken their resistance and accept Russian authorities. In such a case, the Kremlin's plans to destroy the territorial integrity of Ukraine could come partly true.

---

307 Ukraine Rebels Hold Referendums in Donetsk and Luhansk. *BBC*, May 11, 2014, https://www.bbc.com/news/world-europe-27360146.
308 Обращение к Президенту РФ В. В. Путину от Русинов (from Russian: Appeal to the President of the Russian Federation V.V. Putin from the Rusyns). *International Center "Matitsa Rusynov"*, February 28, 2022, https://n9.cl/dtqbv.
309 Talmazan, Y, Melkozerova, V. (2022). Some in Ukraine's Russian-Occupied Southern Cities Take to the Streets in Show of Defiance. *NBC News*, March 13, https://n9.cl/n4y32.

The first two months of the big war in Ukraine

April 2022[310]

Two months have passed since the Russian Federation started a new phase of its invasion of Ukraine. This war may continue much longer, but a few interim conclusions can be drawn at this stage. Based on a thorough monitoring of the political and military processes in Ukraine, Russia, and Europe, I offer the following five conclusions.

Ukraine's resilience grows in the face of Russia's miscalculations

It is clear today that the Kremlin's initial plan for fast regime change in Ukraine has failed. The Ukrainian army, the government, and society have shown tremendous resilience in the face of the massive Russian attack. Over the course of the last sixty-three days, Ukraine has managed to survive the initial shock and adapt—militarily, economically, and administratively—to the war. Despite considerable losses, Ukraine has been able to inflict comparable damage on the Russian troops.[311] As a result, the Russian army has had to retreat from some areas, limit its on-the-ground activities, regroup, and declare it was starting "the second phase of the special operation"—a not so subtle acknowledgment that the initial plan had failed.

Ukraine's resilience will likely only strengthen in the near future, especially with the infusion of new military hardware from its Western allies.

---

310 A shorter version of this column has previously been published as: Minakov, M. (2022). Russia's War on Ukraine: The First Two Months. Focus Ukraine, April 27, 2022, https://www.wilsoncenter.org/blog-post/russias-war-ukraine-first-two-months.
311 Wasielewski, P. (2022). Appraising the War in Ukraine and Likely Outcomes. *Foreign Policy Research Institute*, April 8, https://www.fpri.org/article/2022/04/appraising-the-war-in-ukraine-and-likely-outcomes/.

The anti-Putin global coalition is growing

The Zelensky administration has managed to increase Ukraine's strategic cooperation with the United States, Japan, NATO, the EU, and individual EU member states. Kyiv has become the crux of Western politics. Ukrainian leaders meet almost daily with Western cabinet officials and politicians. The pilgrimage to Kyiv, even if it is indeed dangerous, was undertaken by, among many others, the US secretary of state Antony J. Blinken and secretary of defense Lloyd J. Austin, the prime ministers of Denmark and Spain, and the presidents of Poland, Lithuania, Latvia, and Estonia. President Zelensky is in constant communication with the leaders of Western and Eastern partner states: just in the past several days he spoke with the prime minister of Japan, the parliamentarians of Portugal, and the US president Joe Biden.

This political communication has led to a more resolute partnership between Ukraine and the Western powers. The United States, the UK, the EU, and NATO have all imposed multiple sanctions on Russia, which, despite some damage to those entities' economies, are expected to limit Russia's ability to continue the war and ultimately lead to a loss for Russia. Additionally, the NATO countries have considerably increased their military support for Ukraine,[312] now delivering on a daily basis heavy weapons and sophisticated air defense systems. With this support finally arriving, Ukrainian resilience will only grow.

Kyiv and northern Ukraine wrung out a hard-won victory

Somewhat confounding the Kremlin's and the West's expectations, Kyiv has fought back against the Russian attacks and remained free. If in March Russian troops were deployed in ten regions of Ukraine, by the end of April they had retreated from Kyiv, Chernihiv, Sumy, Dnipropetrovsk, and Mykolaiv oblasts. The ground

---

312 Hirsh, M. (2022). Why Russia's Economy Is Holding On. *Foreign Policy*, April 22, 2022, https://foreignpolicy.com/2022/04/22/russia-war-economy-sanctions-ruble/.

operations of the Ukrainian army have also seen some success in the areas around Kharkiv, Zaporizhzhia, and Kherson.

Though the geography of the Russian ground forces' deployment has narrowed to the eastern and southern regions of Ukraine, the number of missiles and the areas targeted in air attacks are both growing steadily. At this point, no Ukrainian city is safe from such an attack.

The "land bridge"

Kremlin managed to take over the territories that constitute the "land brigde" from Russian territories via Luhansk, Donetsk, Zaporizhzhia, and Kherson oblasts to Crimea. Russia's control over the areas it claims to control is far from stable. During the initial phase of the war, Russian troops succeeded in taking over Kherson oblast and approximately 70 percent of Zaporizhzhia oblast. Even if these actions made it possible to restart a supply of water to Crimea and to install pro-Russia administrations in local settlements, the land bridge between Russia and Crimea that Moscow so desires is not yet in place.

Despite Putin's claim of victory in Mariupol, the defense of the city is continuing at the time of writing.[313] A partisan movement has engaged in small-scale operations to thwart the efforts of the Russian military administrations and has blockaded railroads in Kherson and Zaporizhzhia oblasts. The Ukrainian army has also launched missiles strikes on this region, which makes the Crimean land bridge unsafe for passage of military vehicles.

The war shows a tendency to proliferate

Even though Moscow sought to limit warfare to Ukrainian soil only, this goal has not been met, and cannot be. Instead, the war has turned back on the Russian Federation: Russian infrastructure near the Russian-Ukrainian border was hit on several occasions in the past four weeks. Belarusian workers have engaged in sabotage of

---

313 Polityuk, P. (2022). Putin Claims Victory in Mariupol; Ukrainian Fighters Hold On. *Reuters*, April 22, https://n9.cl/csmi6.

rail lines used to resupply Russian troops from Belarusian territory. Several explosions in Transnistria, a Moscow-backed breakaway region of Moldova on the Ukrainian border and host to a large stockpile of Russian military matériel, may reignite the old conflict on Moldovan soil. Russia's war in Ukraine has shown a tendency to break the bounds of Moscow's expectations and contaminate neighboring countries, drawing hostile responses from an enlarging group of states.

The war goes on, bringing more and more pain and misery to the people of Ukraine literally every minute. But in this tragedy Ukrainians are not alone, and these interim conclusions demonstrate it.

Ukraine's government tries to balance military and socioeconomic needs

May 2022[314]

Russia's war against Ukraine has gone on for almost three months. During this period Russia's military campaign has shifted from a Blitzkrieg style of attack aimed at fast regime change in Kyiv to a longer-term war of attrition.[315] Ukraine's military strategy has undergone a similar evolution. The government's initial plan involved total and uncompromising defense at any cost on all fronts—including military, financial, information, and diplomatic. These strenuous efforts worked rather well: Ukraine demonstrated huge resilience in the face of the invasion, won the battle for Kyiv and for northern Ukraine, and inspired the West to provide the Ukrainian army with increasingly sophisticated weapons.

---

314 A shorter version of this column has previously been published as: Minakov, M. (2022). Ukraine's Wartime Governance Dilemma: Balancing Military and Socioeconomic Needs. *Focus Ukraine*, May 26, 2022, https://www.wilsoncenter.org/blog-post/ukraines-wartime-governance-dilemma-balancing-military-and-socioeconomic-needs.

315 May 2022 Monthly Forecast—Ukraine. *Security Council Report*, April 29, 2022, https://www.securitycouncilreport.org/monthly-forecast/2022-05/ukraine-4.php.

The context of the debate

Changes in the pacing and the theaters of the conflict have handed Ukraine's leadership another problem, adapting the government's military, political, and economic policies for a much longer war of attrition.

From a military point of view, the security and defense arm of the government has improved its strategic operations planning and increased arming and staffing of the army operating in key areas of the front. This has already brought results. In the south, the Russian Black Sea Fleet is considerably weakened, while Ukrainian forces in Odesa and Mykolaiv are growing stronger. In the northeast, Ukrainian forces won the battle for Kharkiv and strengthened the defensive infrastructure on the Russian border. The pace of Russian attacks in the northern Donbas has considerably slowed.

Politically, Ukraine has tremendously increased its cooperation with the G7 countries, the United States, the EU, NATO, and the UK. Kyiv has become a must-visit capital for Western leaders and delegations. Despite the ongoing conflict, President Zelensky and his team have managed to move forward with Ukraine's application for EU candidacy, establish an advanced dialogue with Western leaders and societies, and stick fast to the idea of integrating with—or even joining—NATO. Zelensky's government has shown the Kremlin that Ukrainians will fight to fashion a future settlement on Ukraine's terms, however close or distant that future might be.

Meanwhile, the government has sought to balance the armed forces' needs for matériel and munitions to increase the likelihood of a military victory in the distant future and the current pressing needs of the Ukrainian people. Even while engaged in a protracted war of attrition, official Kyiv needs to develop at least a medium-term socioeconomic policy that simultaneously enables the army's progress, the population's survival, and the country's development.

Immediately after the Russian invasion of Ukraine, the Ukrainian government declined to enforce tax collection on small businesses and citizens; offered relief to the country's crippled economy, operating under shelling and martial law; and eased the regulatory regime for job providers.[316] The National Bank of Ukraine froze the exchange rate, restricted cash withdrawals, and limited most cross-border transactions.

However, all these measures did not prevent inflation from rising over 13 percent (year-over-year) in March 2022. Ukraine's GDP will probably decrease by up to 45 percent by the end of this year.[317] The finance minister estimated the monthly losses of Ukraine's economy—with up to half of companies terminating their business, a decrease in metallurgical and agricultural exports, and depressed customs revenues—at around $5 billion (or 5 percent of GDP) monthly.[318] Since the beginning of the war, Ukrainians have lost 4.8 million jobs (out of 16 million jobs existing in January 2022, ILO data), which may push nine out of ten people in Ukraine into poverty or near poverty.[319]

Now that the tempo of the war has changed, the Ukrainian government has started working on a plan for socioeconomic development based on the assumption that the war may go on for another two to three years. If that happens, the kind of resilience that Ukrainians displayed in the first months of the war can be kept alive only if it is supported by a solid economic foundation. Serhiy Marchenko, Ukraine's minister of finance, has recently acknowledged that the accumulating economic issues are forcing the government to change its economic policies.[320] And this is exactly where the debate between the government and experts is joined.

---

316 Regarding Submission of the Property and Income Tax Declaration by Citizens. *State Tax Service of Ukraine*, March 11, 2022, https://tax.gov.ua/en/mass-media/news/576606.html; Ukraine Introduces Special Labour Regulation During Martial Law in Ukraine. *CMS Law Now Group*, March 25, 2022, https://n9.cl/ip2z9.
317 Russian Invasion to Shrink Ukraine Economy by 45 Percent this Year. *World Bank*, April 10, 2022, https://n9.cl/y302o7.
318 It Will Be Hard for Ukraine's Economy to Sustain a Long War. *Economist*, May 14, 2022, https://n9.cl/lzal1k.
319 War in Ukraine. *UNDP Ukraine*, April 2022, https://n9.cl/jjlem.
320 See the above article in the Economist.

How to develop socioeconomically during wartime?

One of the approaches to development during wartime is to create a "war economy" with a strong tax discipline and a big role for government. As Minister Marchenko said to the Economist journalists, a prolongation of the military conflict for more than three months would require painful measures, including a sharp increase in taxes, cuts in social spending, the possible nationalization of some sectors critical for defense, and the continuing financial support of Ukraine's allies.

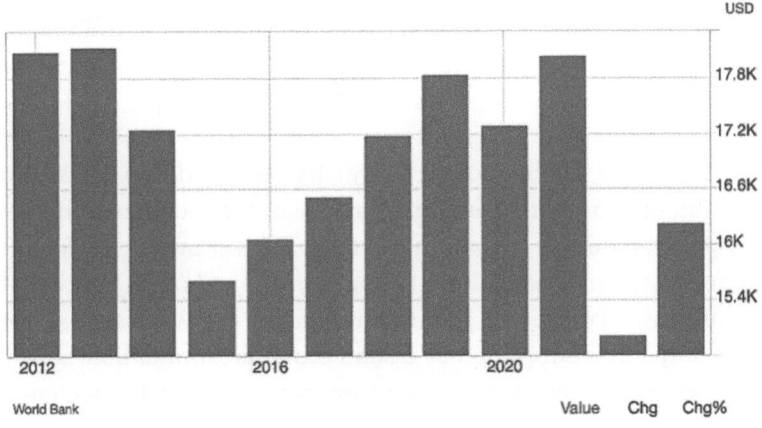

Other experts, not necessarily contradicting that position, call for active measures that would turn the growing numbers of unemployed Ukrainians, refugees, and internally displaced persons from a liability on the state's ledgers into an economic asset. As the country's reconstruction projects get under way, labor of all kinds will be needed, some part of which may be supplied by refugees and local populations, which would contribute to an economic rebound while providing financial security to participants. Such an ambitious national welfare program would depend on focused initiatives by the central government and regional administrations, with strong financial support from the Western powers.

Yet others, such as Pavlo Sheremeta, Ukraine's ex-minister of economic development and trade, use the momentum for development to propose a neoliberal reform of the economy along the lines of the Israel model.[321] According to this model, a country with limited resources can progress and provide its people with a social safety net during long periods of conflict if its economy is open to innovation, encourages entrepreneurship, and has financial support from the West.

These positions offer different solutions to the dilemma of economic development during wartime, but generally all agree on the need to start reconstruction early with the support of Ukraine's Western allies. In this debate, they try to influence the current cabinet's reconstruction planning.

A program for reconstruction

Already in April 2022, Prime Minister Denis Shmyhal announced a Marshall Plan style of "reconstruction planning" and talks with Western governments on creating a recovery fund.[322] That same month an international group of well-known economists offered its views on priorities for a reconstruction program in Ukraine, rightly stating that such a program should put in place emergency response measures, act rapidly to restore critical infrastructure and services, and lay the groundwork for future modernization.[323] The reconstruction program thus is evolving into a set of policies that would be responsive to the short-, intermediate-, and long-term goals of Ukraine.

The reconstruction program is still far from being agreed upon. But debate around it widens. Under discussion are not only the different policy approaches outlined above but also how the

---

321 Шеремета, П. (2022). Фізична війна перейде у війну економічну. Її теж треба буде вигравати (from Ukrainian: The Physical War Will Turn into an Economic War. It Will Also Have to Be Won). *Ukrainska Pravda*, May 16, 2022, h ttps://www.pravda.com.ua/columns/2022/05/16/7346585/.
322 Ukraine's Prime Minister Says Reconstruction Planning Must Start Now. *Economist*, April 30, 2022, https://n9.cl/ltgla1.
323 Weder di Mauro, B. et al. (2022). A Blueprint for the Reconstruction of Ukraine. *CEPR Office*, April 7, https://cepr.org/voxeu/columns/blueprint-reconstruction-ukraine.

program is to be funded and which agency should control the program.

Currently, the European Commission and the governments of the EU member states are discussing allocating around €15 billion to the program. The United States and the G7 have pledged up to $24 billion additionally. However, European politicians estimate that up to €500 billion will be needed, with no clear answer as to the sources of such funding emerging so far.[324]

In addition, there are divergent views on the timing of such a program: while the experts would like to get started on an urgent basis with reconstruction of critical infrastructure, Ukraine's Western partners see reconstruction starting after the end of hostilities.[325]

Finally, governance of the reconstruction program would need to be crafted in such a way as to satisfy both President Zelensky's team, whose authority in a time of war has been unquestioned, and Western donors. Concerns over the appropriate control of future funding supplied to help Ukraine rebuild have already been voiced in the US Senate.[326] My sources in the cabinet say that Ukrainian officials, having learned from past mistakes,[327] are preparing a serious program implementation and budget oversight model that would ensure the public's and donors' trust in the program.

The vital consequences of the war in Ukraine are measured in lives lost and thrown off course both by military actions and by the numerous socioeconomic implications of a war that has affected every person in Ukraine. Ukraine's leadership must find the wisdom to resolve the dilemma and achieve both military victory and progress on the socioeconomic front as it looks forward to rebuilding.

---

324 Tamma, P. (2022). Ukraine Needs €500B to €600B for Reconstruction: Commission's Dombrovskis. *Politico*, May 11, https://n9.cl/jsxmr.
325 Jones, M. (2022). Top EU Official Backs Multi-Trillion Plan to Rebuild Ukraine. *Reuters*, May 12, https://n9.cl/z4ts26.
326 US Senator Delays $40 bn Ukraine Aid Package. *Aljazeera*, May 13, 2022, https://www.aljazeera.com/news/2022/5/13/us-senator-blocks-40bn-ukraine-aid-package.
327 Rapoza, K. (2022). Ukraine 2021: The Crisis Continues. *Forbes*, April 21, https://n9.cl/7g3dt.

Ukraine becomes EU member candidate

June 2022[328]

On June 24, 2022, the EU leadership granted Ukraine candidate membership status. At the same meeting, Moldova was also granted candidate status. The accession of both to the bloc is contingent on the implementation of successful reforms.

The decision came after uneasy discussions among European politicians during the EU summit in Brussels. Under different conditions, this resolution would be an extremely hopeful and meaningful event for me personally. For many years I promoted the European choice as a strategy for Ukraine's development toward greater freedom, stricter adherence to the rule of law, and greater social responsibility. But I find little joy in the news. Leaks from the summit deliberations indicate that the EU bestowed candidate status on Ukraine as an advance against the future of a nation at war. As a country at war, however, Ukraine needs first to vanquish the enemy, conclude hostilities, rebuild the country, and execute the reforms needed to meet the Maastricht economic convergence criteria. After that we can celebrate.

Long path to candidate status

For Ukraine, EU candidate status is an interim result on a long path to full membership. The first steps on this path were taken back in the 1990s, when Europeanization moved to the center of development strategies: a newly independent nation planned its future as a part of the European family of states, economies, and societies.

In 2002, EU commissioner Günter Verheugen publicly announced for the first time that Ukraine indeed had "the European perspective."[329] This position was supported by the European

---

[328] A shorter version of this column has previously been published as: Minakov, M. (2022). Ukraine, EU Member Candidate. *Focus Ukraine*, June 28, https://www.wilsoncenter.org/blog-post/ukraine-eu-member-candidate.

[329] Mahoney, H. (2002). Ukraine's Ideas of EU Membership Spurned. *EU Observer*, September 18, https://euobserver.com/news/7594.

Parliament in 2005.[330] Later, Ukraine and the EU began moving closer together with respect to a free trade agreement, the Bologna Process (to ensure comparability of standards in higher education), the Eastern Partnership (a joint initiative of the EU and six post-Soviet states to promote stability and cooperation on such matters as trade, economic strategy, and travel agreements), and preparations to join the association. This effort resulted in the signing and ratification of the EU-Ukraine Association Agreement in 2014–2017.

Every step on this path was fraught with risks for Ukraine-Russia relations. Those risks were realized in Russia's annexation of Crimea and at the start of the war in the Donbas in 2014. Yet neither the events of 2014 nor the Russian invasion in 2022 changed Ukraine's dedication to the common European cause.

Ukraine's candidate status won't necessarily lead to the start of accession negotiations. However, it does open up a clear set of opportunities for and obligations incumbent on the Ukrainian government in preparing for a future accession. This is one way for the EU to ensure that the candidate state respects the common values of the member states.

Opportunities for Ukraine

The opportunities for Ukraine from achieving candidate status are many, ranging from political to financial ones. I highlight two here, both critical for a nation trying to survive a war.

First, EU candidate status sets clear goals for state- and economy-building connected with the EU accession criteria (also known as the Copenhagen criteria of 1993). That means that Ukraine's postwar reconstruction will be directed toward three targets: (1) building stable institutions guaranteeing democracy, the rule of law, human rights, and respect for and protection of minorities; (2) putting in place a functioning market economy and the capacity to cope with competition and market forces; and (3) developing the administrative capacity to implement the obligations of EU

---

330 European Parliament Resolution on the Results of the Ukraine Elections. *European Parliament Official Website*, January 13, 2005, https://www.europarl.europa.eu/doceo/document/TA-6-2005-0009_EN.html.

membership. With such clear goals in mind, Ukraine can proceed without the usual hesitations about development priorities, which so often stymied efforts over the past thirty years.

Second, Ukraine can now get access to funding that can help the wounded country prepare for EU accession. This funding is available through the Instrument for Pre-accession Assistance (IPA), which for 2021–2027 has a budget of over €14 billion. The funding will cover Ukraine's efforts to put in place standards equal to those enjoyed by the citizens of the EU in respect to peace, the rule of law, a functioning democracy, and social stability, as well as a sustainable economic situation.

Ukraine's obligations

EU candidate status comes with obligations. Candidate status means that Ukraine, despite the existential threat of the current war, must commit to using the opportunities afforded candidates and make an effort to develop even as the people's hearts and minds are absorbed in defense and resistance needs.

These are some of the immediate tasks that Kyiv must address in the near future:

- Continue judicial reform to provide Ukrainian citizens with accessible justice in a reasonable time span.
- Reform the Constitutional Court to make it more effective in defending Ukraine's constitution and citizens' civil rights.
- Continue fighting corruption, which can be demonstrated by the appointment of a new director of the National Bank of Ukraine and a special anti-corruption prosecutor.
- Enforce and start implementing the anti-oligarch legislation, to prevent massive media and political influence.
- Accept the anti-money laundering legislation.
- Accept the media law introducing the norms of the EU audiovisual media services directive into Ukrainian legislation.
- Reform the system to protect national minorities.

How successful Ukraine is in fulfilling this first set of tasks will be indicative of the strength of the European agenda for a wartime government.

Reactions to the European Council's decision

The European Council's decision has been tremendously inspiring for Ukrainians, more than 90 percent of whom support EU accession.[331] Ukrainians' dedication to the European choice has also prompted other Europeans—up to 65 percent—to value their own EU membership more.[332]

Ukrainian politicians were united in their positive response to EU candidacy. President Zelensky called the decision "a victory" and "a unique and historic moment." Former president Petro Poroshenko, one of today's opposition leaders, supported the decision, saying that it united Ukrainians and added yet more motivation to resist Russia's attacks. The leaders of the EU member nations also greeted Ukraine's EU candidacy favorably.

More mixed reactions came from the leadership of Georgia (which did not receive the same status as Ukraine and Moldova) and from the Balkan nations that had already received candidate status but have not yet converted to membership.

The Russian war against Ukraine has hugely narrowed Ukraine's future. The EU summit's decision has partly undone this limitation and has broadened the choice for Ukraine once again. Now it is up to Ukraine to make this future come to pass.

---

331 Support for Ukraine's EU Accession Hits Historic High of 91% amid Russian Invasion – Poll. *Euromaidan Press*, April 8, 2022, https://2cm.es/LSTE.
332 EU-Wide Survey: In Face of Ukraine War, Citizens Close Ranks in Support of EU. *The European Sting*, June 23, 2022, https://2cm.es/OdXe.

Ukraine's wartime political struggle continues with a new twist

July 2022[333]

Political processes change dramatically during a time of war. In the early stages of the war, the usual competition between the ruling group and the opposition is dampened, while society becomes more disciplined and united around the government. But the longer the war goes on, the more politics adapts: either it further organizes around the leader of the nation at war or the usual competition returns, but posing an unusual threat to national security.

Ukraine seems to be entering the second phase. After four months of the undisputed unity of all political groups around national defense, July offers some early signs of a much more multifaceted politics in Kyiv. Two highly visible political processes are noteworthy: a return to the deoligarchizing agenda and the redistribution of roles on the presidential team.

Deoligarchization

Among the many impacts of the Russian war on Ukraine, there is one that concerns the role of the oligarchs in Ukrainian politics. Russian shelling of numerous industrial plants and the energy infrastructure across Ukraine has destroyed the economic foundations of the resources used by oligarchs to influence politicians in Kyiv. In conjunction with President Zelensky's prewar deoligarchization policy, this situation creates momentum for uprooting the oligarchy in Ukraine.

Zelensky's prewar agenda for 2022 included deoligarchization as one of its key elements. In 2021, Act 5599, the "Anti-Oligarch Act," was approved stipulating the creation of a special institution to identify individual oligarchs through an assets test and to limit

---

[333] A shorter version of this column has previously been published as: Minakov, M. (2022). Ukraine's Wartime Politics Takes a New Turn. *Focus Ukraine*, July 19, https://www.wilsoncenter.org/blog-post/ukraines-wartime-politics-takes-new-turn.

their influence on society, political groups, and government. The Ministry of Justice planned to implement the twenty-step plan to uproot the oligarchs. But this policy was postponed when the Russian invasion of Ukraine changed everyone's priorities.

Despite the change in priorities, however, deoligarchization is moving ahead—in more ways than one. The Russian destruction of plants such as the Azovstal iron and steel works in Mariupol or the oil refining plant in Kremenchug was certainly a considerable blow to Rinat Akhmetov and Ihor Kolomoysky. However, the anti-oligarchic legislation of 2021 hits the oligarchs even more: it requires them to leave politics and sell their media holdings as soon as possible. Just recently Vadym Novynsky relinquished his MP mandate, while Rinat Akhmetov exited his media business.[334] These steps now vacate the legal grounds—having an undue influence on politics and the mass media—that would have put them on the official registry of oligarchs.

Changes on the Zelensky team

On Sunday evening, July 17, President Zelensky addressed the nation, announcing changes in the leadership of the General Prosecutor's Office (GPO) and the Security Service of Ukraine (SSU). The president suspended General Prosecutor Iryna Venedyktova and SSU head Ivan Bakanov. Both decisions are explained by the fact that members of the presidential team must take responsibility for traitors in the ranks of their institutes. Venedyktova and Bakanov themselves were trusted members of the team and are not directly accused of wrongdoing.

This decision was not an easy one for Zelensky to make. Bakanov, the president's childhood friend and lifelong companion, joined the SSU right after Zelensky's and his party's electoral victory in 2019. Bakanov led an uneasy process of SSU reform and a reduction of the oligarchs' influence on the service. Venedyktova

---

334 See: Sheremet, A. (2022). Vadym Novinsky Decided to Draw Up the Credentials of a Member of Parliament. *Babel*, July 6, https://2cm.es/LSU2; Akhmetov Exits Media Business, Says Doesn't Want to Be Labeled Oligarch. *The Kyiv Independent*, July 11, 2022, https://2cm.es/OdXB.

continued the GPO reform, begun by Ruslan Ryaboshapka, in 2020. Both were key figures on the ruling team and safeguarded its stable growth of power as Zelensky's presidency matured.

Both officials are suspended, not fired. To fire them, the president would need parliamentary approval, even during a time of war. To avoid a longer process, the president chose a faster process, which would help ensure stability in both offices during the change of leadership. The newly appointed acting heads of both organizations are the former first deputies — Oleksiy Symonenko in the GPO and Vasyl Malyuk in the SSU — so that the organizations can continue operating with maximum efficiency. Neither is from the old cadre of Zelensky's business partners; both have earned the president's trust over the past two years.

Many trace the president's decision not only to the results of an investigation into the actions of some prosecutors and SSU officers during the early days of the war but also to the growing pressure on Andriy Yermak, chief of Zelensky's staff. On July 8, US congresswoman Victoria Spartz sent a letter to President Joe Biden raising issues with Yermak's work in his official position and in his contacts with the US administration.[335] On July 11 the congresswoman stated that Yermak should resign because he had been an ineffective public administrator during the war, and for organizing a smear campaign against her.[336]

These appeals fell on receptive government ears not only in D.C. but also in Kyiv. Since both acting heads — Symonenko and Malyuk — seem to be not only professionals loyal to Ukraine but also loyal members of the presidential team, the decision can be seen as reinforcing Zelensky's positions after the attack on his chief of staff.

It is too early to say in which direction Ukrainian political development will turn with the phase-out of the oligarchs and a reshuffling of the president's team. But politics are definitely

---

335 See this letter at https://2cm.es/OdXJ.
336 Spartz: Kyiv Should Better Support its Heroic Army and Mr. Yermak Should Resign. *The Congressmember Official Website*, July 11, 2022, https://2cm.es/OdXM.

changing in Kyiv, and this change may affect Ukrainians' resilience in the ongoing war.

The Russian annexation of Southeastern Ukraine

July 2022[337]

After five months of all-out war, the Kremlin appears to have refined its plans for the future of the temporarily occupied territories in southeastern Ukraine.

Currently Russian forces control about 20 percent of this Ukrainian territory, once populated by over eight million people. Today those parts of Donetsk, Luhansk, Kharkiv, Kherson, and Zaporizhzhia oblasts that are under Russian military control are only thinly populated: local people have fled the battles and missile strikes, going either to Ukrainian government-controlled regions, to Europe, or to Russia.

For those who remain, the Kremlin has a new plan: annexation instead of secession. Annexation would ensure Moscow's control over the local population and extend its "nuclear umbrella" onto the newly conquered land.

Annexing lands

As I wrote three months ago, Kremlin planned to hold local referenda on secession of the Russian-controlled territories of southeastern Ukraine. However, it seems that the Kremlin's plans have changed: the referenda now aim at creating quasi-legal grounds for annexing this land.

For example, on July 23, 2022, Yevgeny Balitsky, the Russian-appointed "head of the temporary administration of Zaporizhzhia oblast" (operating on the territory occupied by Russian troops), signed a decree to create an election commission as the first step to

---

[337] A shorter version of this column has previously been published as: Minakov, M. (2022). The Kremlin's Plans to Annex Southeastern Ukraine Go into Effect. *Focus Ukraine*, July 26, https://www.wilsoncenter.org/blog-post/kremlins-plans-annex-southeastern-ukraine-go-effect.

holding a referendum on Zaporizhzhia oblast becoming part of Russia. The referendum may be held in the first half of September 2022.

That same day a decree with the same language was signed by the deputy head of the Kherson regional administration, Yekaterina Gubareva. Should the battles in Donbas taper off or end, the Russian proxy-controlled governments of the self-proclaimed Donetsk People's Republic (DPR) and Luhansk People's Republic (LPR) most likely will sign off on similar decrees.

The Kremlin's choice of annexation — making these lands just a regular part of the Russian Federation — is evidently connected to Moscow's declining trust in the local elites and the subjugated communities. Russian-installed governors and mayors of Ukrainian origin — Yevgeny Balitsky in the occupied parts of Zaporizhzhia oblast, Vladimir Saldo in Kherson oblast, Galina Danilchenko in Melitopol, Konstantin Ivashchenko in Mariupol — have neither local support nor the administrative know-how sufficient to satisfy their new masters.

Which is why the Russian authorities have recently appointed so-called "heads of the regional executive bodies" from among Russian bureaucrats. At the beginning of July Anton Koltsov, former first vice-governor of Vologda oblast in northern Russia, became head of the government of Zaporizhzhia oblast, while Sergey Eliseyev, ex-deputy head of the Kaliningrad government, became chairman of the government of Kherson oblast. The role of Russian officials is also growing in the DPR and LPR.

This marks a sea change in Russia's approach to the conquered territories. For about thirty years, Moscow supported self-proclaimed republics on the territories of Georgia (South Ossetia and Abkhazia) and Moldova (Transnistria), and subsequently in Ukraine (the DPR and LPR). But despite having fully Kremlin-loyal "presidents," the de facto statelets in Georgia and Moldova and their populations still had some level of agency that forced Russia to constantly bargain with them through kuratory, the Kremlin special appointees for these issues. In a war situation, however, the controlled communities are not allowed any agency. They must obey the new authorities without question.

At this point, moreover, the Russian government seems ready to raise the stakes in the war. After the annexation of Ukraine's southeastern territories by referendum goes through this fall, Moscow can claim that the shelling of these regions would constitute an attack on Russia, which would allow the Kremlin to respond with nuclear weapons, as prescribed in the Russian Federation's National Security Strategy.

Annexing minds

Along with land, the Kremlin plans to annex local communities' hearts, minds, and wallets. Moscow is speeding up the linkage of conquered communities with communities in Russia, constructing a new tax system compatible with the Russian system, and establishing new educational curricula in the conquered Ukrainian territories to integrate youth into the Russian educational system.

Last May the first deputy head of the Russian presidential administration, Sergei Kiriyenko, declared that the reconstruction of cities and transport infrastructure in the conquered territories would follow the Crimean model. After Russia's annexation of Crimea in 2014, sixteen Russian regions were assigned to different cities and districts of the peninsula to help them survive sanctions and integrate into the Russian Federation.

Now the Russian Federation regions are to take Ukrainian territories under their "guardianship." By the end of July 2022, more than thirty Russian regions will have assumed patronage of various cities and districts in southeastern Ukraine. For example, pro-Russia officials and mayoral offices are preparing St. Petersburg and Mariupol for a partnership that will allow local authorities to start reconstructing the destroyed city. These partnerships are controlled by Russian Deputy Prime Minister Marat Khusnullin and the RF Ministry of Construction.

Simultaneously, the pro-Russia local administrations are developing an increasingly extensive tax collection system. According to an edict of the Russian military-civil authorities, all individuals and companies must register as taxpayers in the occupied lands by August 1, 2022. This nullification of Ukrainian taxation authority goes hand in hand with Russian "passportization": the local population is forced to accept Russian citizenship in order to access basic services in their communities.

The process is moving rather slowly, however. For example, in Berdyansk, a pleasant Azov seaside city with over 100,000 population before the war, only 800 local residents have received Russian citizenship, though as many as 4,500 have applied for it. Moreover, Ukrainian populations on the temporarily occupied territories are discouraged from acquiring Russian citizenship by Kyiv, which is preparing an act to criminalize such behavior.

The occupying administrations are also building a new secondary education system, appointing new loyal school principals and getting teachers from Russia involved. As of September 1, schoolchildren in the occupied territories of Ukraine will study according to "Russian standards." Officials are hurriedly looking for principals and teachers. So far about 250 teachers from thirty-one Russian regions have applied to teach in southeastern Ukraine. They are promised salaries ranging from 7,000 to 8,600 rubles ($120–$150) per day.

Insecurity of the pro-Russia collaborators

With more long-range arms delivered by the West to Ukraine, the shelling of critical targets in Berdyansk, Donetsk, Luhansk, and Kherson has stepped up. For example, Ukrainian forces recently hit Russian-controlled bridges in the Kherson oblast to slow the advance of Russian troops and munitions. Russian anti-aircraft and anti-missile systems are not sufficient for the occupiers to defend military and civilian infrastructure on the occupied land.

This situation led Russian foreign minister Sergei Lavrov to declare on July 20 that Moscow's military "tasks" in Ukraine had gone beyond the eastern Donbas region: the Kremlin plans to grab more land to ensure that its aims in Crimea and the Donbas can be secured.

The security of pro-Russia officials and Russian servicemen in the occupied territories is not assured at all. Despite the newly created system of militarized police — comprising Russian soldiers, the

DPR and LPR militias, and other local collaborators—the number of attacks on Russian officials and military staff by local pro-Ukrainian resistance groups is growing.

So far the Russian military administrations have not managed to establish order on the occupied territories. To prevent annexation by Russia, the Ukrainian army is preparing a counteroffensive aimed at liberating the conquered lands and communities. This is the only real way to stop the new Kremlin policy from going into effect.

The war changes the Ukrainian oligarchy

August 2022[338]

Vladimir Putin's February 2022 decision to launch an assault on Ukraine has killed civilians and soldiers and destroyed countless structures across Ukraine. But it has also ended some of the processes and phenomena associated with the post-Soviet way of life. The institution of oligarchy may very well become one of them.

A short history of post-Soviet oligarchy

The Ukrainian oligarchy is rooted in the 1990s, when Ukraine—as well as other countries in Eastern Europe, the Southern Caucasus, and Central Asia—allowed some individuals and their clans to get an iron grip simultaneously on the Soviet industrial legacy, the administration of the new state, the state budget, and public opinion.

The post-Soviet oligarchy was based on the inseparability of economic wealth, political influence, and personal networks. It united public administrators, the police, judges, parliamentarians, and politicians in stable clans and patronal pyramids, vertical

---

[338] A shorter version of this column has previously been published as: Minakov, M. (2022). The War and the Future of Ukraine's Oligarchy. *Focus Ukraine*, August 3, https://www.wilsoncenter.org/blog-post/war-and-future-ukraines-oligarchy

chains of personal relations that connected a clan to many subordinate social groups.[339]

In Ukraine, oligarchy prohibited the separation of public and private spheres. (It did so in other post-Soviet states as well, such as Russia, Georgia, and Kazakhstan.) It created systems of "grand corruption" — a phenomenon that the European Court of Auditors defines as "the abuse of high-level power that benefits the few at the expense of the many."[340]

The post-Soviet oligarchy is an ambiguous phenomenon. On the one hand, oligarchy and grand corruption prevent democracies from effectively applying the rule of law, providing access to justice in the court system, or assuring the inviolability of private property. Oligarchy, then, can be an obstacle for liberal democracies.

On the other hand, because oligarchy exists in the form of many competing clans, it creates systemic obstacles for those with autocratic leanings. Clan competition for control of the centers of power gives citizens some degree of freedom and leads to less predictable election results.

Oligarchy emerged with the post-Soviet states, and in many ways the destiny of the oligarchic clans was inseparable from the destiny of these states. Some postcommunist states underwent some version of the deoligarchization process. This process could lead to one of two diametrically opposed results. For example, if the 1990s saw attempts at building oligarchic clans in Poland and Lithuania, the internal forces of democracy and the external norms endorsed by the EU forced would-be oligarchs to settle for being "just" captains of industry. This meant that liberal democracy and a market economy could develop without patronal pyramids and grand corruption.

In Russia, the process was different and produced a different result. Between 2002 and 2004 Putin, whose regime had just taken an authoritarian turn, forced Russian oligarchs and their clans into

---

[339] Magyar, B., & Madlovics, B. (2020). *The Anatomy of Post-Communist Regimes.* Budapest: CEU Press.

[340] ECA (2021). Reducing Grand Corruption in Ukraine: Several EU Initiatives, But Still Insufficient Results. *European Court of Auditors,* March, https://op.europa.eu/webpub/eca/special-reports/ukraine-23-2021/en/.

a single patronal pyramid, which he himself headed. The legal proceedings against former Yukos chairman Mikhail Khodorkovsky and the many criminal prosecutions of regional oligarchic figures showed the clans what they could expect if they did not fall in line. Oligarchs as an independent political force seized to exist. At the same time, corruption on a grand scale was becoming part of the real political system, as formal and informal institutions served the interests of the ruling elite.

By 2021, the 30th anniversary of the dissolution of the USSR, only a handful of post-Soviet countries had more or less independent oligarchic clans. Ukraine was one of them, along with Armenia, Georgia, Kyrgyzstan, and Moldova.

Evolution and decline of the oligarchy in Ukraine

In Ukraine, contention between oligarchic groups caused several deep political crises that put the state on the verge of collapse. These crises occurred in 1993, resulting in early elections of the president and parliament; in 2004, resulting in the fall of the Kuchma regime; and in 2014, leading to the fall of the Yanukovych regime. In each case, oligarchic groups supported both sides, and the victory of protesters meant that some clans were deposed while other clans had a clearer path to power.

Thus in 1994, following the 1993 political crisis, the Dnipropetrovsk clans came to power in Kyiv. By the end of 2005, following the 2004 Orange Revolution, the clans from Sumy, Kharkiv, Dnipropetrovsk, and Donetsk had returned to power. In 2014, following Euromaidan, some oligarchic groups managed to survive around Petro Poroshenko and Arseny Yatsenyuk and to bring outsized influence to bear on substantial parts of the government again.[341]

The rotating fates of the clans, however, were only one face of the coin. The Euromaidan also kicked off stronger institutional integration with Western institutions. This convergence prompted

---

[341] Jarábik, B., & Bila, Y. (2015). And Then There Were Five: The Plight of Ukraine's Oligarchs. *CEIP,* June 15, https://n9.cl/md11t.

the creation of a set of new state anti-corruption agencies: the National Agency for the Prevention of Corruption, the Special Anti-corruption Prosecutor, the National Anti-Corruption Bureau, the State Bureau of Investigations, and the High Anti-Corruption Court.

This suite of institutions did not have enough teeth to limit corruption during Petro Poroshenko's presidency,[342] but its force gradually grew. And in 2021, when President Volodymyr Zelensky's team dared to approve several anti-oligarchic acts, the anti-corruption institutions and new legislation provided grounds for expectations of real deoligarchization in 2022.

War's impact on oligarchy

The ongoing war in Ukraine has delayed but not canceled the deoligarchization process, as I wrote in previous chapters. The destruction of Ukrainian industry, economic hardships, and the mobilization of many workers have weakened the economic might of the oligarchs. According to Forbes data for the US and Ukraine, the wealth of the following individuals has dropped considerably from January to July 2022:[343]

> Rinat Akhmetov: from $13.7 billion to $4.4 billion
> Victor Pinchuk: from $2.6 billion to $2 billion
> Vadym Novinsky: from $3.5 billion to $1.4 billion
> Genadiy Boholyubov: from $2 billion to $1.1 billion
> Ihor Kolomoisky: from $1.8 billion to $1 billion
> Petro Poroshenko: from $1.6 billion to $0.7 billion

Most of these individuals are doing their best to vacate the legal grounds that would mean inclusion on the registry of oligarchs

---

342 See the OCCRP multiple reports on this issue at https://www.occrp.org/en/people/petro-poroshenko.

343 Forbes (2022). The World's Real-Time Billionaire. *Forbes*, n.d., https://www.forbes.com/real-time-billionaires/#1f5a25a83d78; Ланда, В. (2022). Порошенко та Гереги втратили статус мільярдерів. А що зі статками Ахметова та Пінчука? Forbes оновив рейтинг з початку війни (from Ukrainian: Poroshenko and Gerega Have Lost Their Billionaire Status. What About Akhmetov and Pinchuk's wealth? Forbes Has Updated Its Rating Since the Beginning of the War). *Forbes Ukraine*, March 14, https://n9.cl/r3b1r.

introduced by President Zelensky last June. According to the Ukraine's National Security and Defense Council, there are 86 people who could be legally recognized as oligarchs in Ukraine.[344]

To avoid qualifying as an oligarch, Novinsky gave up his seat in parliament. Akhmetov, founder of System Capital Management Group, divested his media businesses and said he would transfer those licenses to the Ukrainian state.[345] It looks like the end of the oligarchic era as well for Kolomoisky, founder of PrivatBank, who has allegedly been stripped of Ukrainian citizenship.[346]

Only Petro Poroshenko, among the six, remains active in politics. He is one of the leaders of a parliamentary opposition group and a tireless critic of the Zelensky administration. The accusations of high treason lodged against him seem not to have been investigated actively in recent months, but the mass media channels once associated with him have been shut down.[347]

So the Russian war against Ukraine, Zelensky's deoligarchization policies, and Ukraine's anticorruption system together might finally put an end to oligarchy. The question is: will Ukraine take advantage of this chance? If it does, will the deoligarchization push Ukraine toward democracy or autocracy? Or will this post-Soviet dilemma simply disappear, along with the entire epoch?

---

344 Данілов уточнив свою заяву про 86 потенційних олігархів: підпадають під один з критеріїв (from Ukrainian: Danilov Clarified His Statement about 86 Potential Oligarchs: They Fall under One of the Criteria). *Ekonomichna Pravda*, July 22, 2022, https://www.epravda.com.ua/news/2022/07/22/689493/.

345 Balmforth, T. (2022). Ukraine's Richest Man Announces His Holding's Exit from Media Business. *Reuters*, July 11, https://2cm.es/LSVQ.

346 Kossov, I., Sorokin, O. (2022). Rumors of Zelensky Stripping Top Oligarch Kolomoisky's Citizenship Gain Ground. *The Kyiv Independent*, July 23, https://n9.cl/phls1.

347 Herszenhorn, D. M. (2022). Zelenskiy's Office Accuses Poroshenko of Fleeing Treason Charges. *Politico*, January 14, https://www.politico.eu/article/volodymyr-zelenskiy-office-accuses-petro-poroshenko-treason-ukraine/; The Channels from Poroshenko's Pool Were Shut Down Because of His Narcissism – Podolyak. *Instytut masovoi informatsii*, May 30, 2022, https://n9.cl/zxoc8.

Violent referendum in occupied territories of Southeastern Ukraine

September 2022[348]

Ukrainian citizens in the temporarily occupied areas of Luhansk, Donetsk, Zaporizhzhia, and Kherson oblasts have been put into yet another situation of survival and humiliation—this time, by the September 24–27 forced referenda on joining Russia. Under military occupation by a foreign power, with the everyday risk of being killed, in the absence of free media and other means of reasonable discussion of key political issues, the citizens of Ukraine are requested to answer the question: do they want their communities to join Russia and to become Russia's citizens?

Under the wartime circumstances, the referendum—one of the core democratic procedures—has neither legitimacy nor legality. On the contrary, this question is an act of violence against people living under Russian occupation.

What is a referendum?

A referendum is an act of political decision-making made directly by citizens. This decision usually is of an extraordinary nature. For this reason, it is not representatives or political leadership that makes it, but the citizens themselves. Only after the citizens vote can a government implement the nation's decision.

The democratic quality of a referendum comes from two factors that make the citizens' decision legal and legitimate. First, for a referendum to be legal, there should be a law (or several laws) that prescribes how to initiate a referendum, how to define the question(s) on the ballot, how to prepare the polling places, counting commissions, and observers' oversight over the voting and

---

[348] A shorter version of this column has previously been published as: Minakov, M. (2022). Referendum as Violence and Humiliation in Southeastern Ukraine. *Focus Ukraine*, September 29, 2022 https://www.wilsoncenter.org/blog-post/referendum-violence-and-humiliation-southeastern-ukraine.

ballot counting, and how to translate the citizens' decision into legal and political acts afterwards.

The second factor, legitimacy, is even more important. If a referendum is to be legitimate — to conform with justice, constitutional logic, and fundamental political norms — it must make sense as justified. This justification stems from the need for citizens to make informed decisions in a secure environment. A free media and open debates within a reasonable time frame are needed. The questions for a referendum should be simply and clearly phrased. In such cases the referendum process is a deliberative and direct democratic act of free citizens in their republic.

When citizens come to their polling stations, there must be no legal or legitimate objections from society, branches of power, or constitutional guardians. Only then is a referendum one of the fundamental acts of a functioning democracy.

Illegality and illegitimacy of the Russia-imposed referenda in southeastern Ukraine

The referenda in southeastern Ukraine this week should be recognized as illegal and illegitimate. From the legal point of view, these questions take place outside any national legal framework, be it Ukraine or Russia. The decisions on referenda were made by illegal administrations installed in the occupied territories of two Ukrainian oblasts (Zaporizhzhia and Kherson) and of two contested territories (controlled by the self-proclaimed governments of DNR and LNR). Neither Ukrainian, nor Russian legislation could be applied to these initiatives. From the outset, all four referenda do not have any legality behind them.

Since the occupants' administrations cannot provide voters with secure voting, the casting of ballots is done not so much at the polling stations, but via voting at home. And the observers — local and foreign — who should guarantee the democratic quality of the process and the results come from organizations and governments that have no reliable record of proper oversight of voting; their list adds suspicions to the referenda rather than diminishes them.

There is also no legitimacy behind the referenda. The four of them were conducted without any discussion among citizens with regard to the legal reasons and consequences of the referendum results. All four decisions were made hurriedly, under pressure on Russian authorities by the Ukrainian forces' victory in the Kharkiv oblast.[349] There were neither reasonable time frames for discussion nor reliable means to transmit information necessary for Ukrainian citizens to make up their minds regarding the forced referendum question.

The language of the referendum's question is highly dubious. For example, the ballot for the occupied territories of my native Zaporizhzhia oblast states in two languages (Russian and Ukrainian) the following:

> Are you in favor of the withdrawal of Zaporizhzhia oblast from Ukraine, the formation of Zaporizhzhia oblast as an independent state and its incorporation into the Russian Federation as a subject of the Russian Federation?[350]

As everyone can see, this formulation has basically three questions for which only one response — yes or no — is offered. This dodgy trick can hardly be regarded as a clear and fair definition of a question in the referendum.

It is not only formulation that is dubious, though. At the time I am writing this, the Russian army controls about 65 percent of Zaporizhzhia oblast, which is inhabited by not more than 25 percent of the oblast's population. Such a small portion of the population cannot make any legitimate decision for the entire oblast.

In Kherson oblast, the question — and the context — is similar to the Zaporizhzhia one.

In the case of the self-proclaimed "Donetsk and Luhansk People's Republics," the formulation includes just one question since

---

349 Russia Signals Annexation of Parts of Ukraine, Raising Stakes in Fighting. *The New York Times*, September 20, 2022, https://n9.cl/hhjmt.
350 Дегтярев, А. (2022). Опубликован бюллетень для референдума в Запорожской области (from Russian: The Ballot for the Referendum in Zaporizhzhya Region Was Published). *Vzglyad*, September 22, https://vz.ru/news/2022/9/22/1178869.html.

the first two questions have already been responded to in equally illegal and illegitimate referenda of 2014.[351]

In any case, even if the language of the question is better in the last two cases, in all four cases, the decision is being made by a minority of the population forced to participate in the voting by local administrations, Russian forces, and local militia.

Finally, the figures that Russian official sources reported on the process and results of the referenda show their non-realistic quality. According to these sources, in the war-torn lands the turnout in Luhansk oblast was 92.6 percent of the oblast's population; in Zaporizhzhia oblast, it was 85.4 percent; in Kherson oblast, it was 76.86 percent, and in the Donetsk oblast the turnout was 97.51 percent.[352] These ghost participants gave the positive response to the tricky question of the referenda organizers: the accession to Russia was allegedly supported by 98.69 percent of voters in Donetsk oblast, by 97.93 percent of those in Luhansk oblast, by 97.81 percent of those in Zaporizhzhia region, and by 96.75 percent of the voters in Kherson oblast. Both sets of data are highly unrealistic: there is no such level of population on the lands under Russian control, while the people remaining on these lands has no such unanimity.

Under all these conditions, neither legality nor legitimacy can be given to the process and the results of such forced referenda.

Referenda as raising the stakes and creating "new Russians"

If the referenda in southeastern Ukraine of 2022 clearly have no legal and legitimate grounds, why hold them? Indeed, even for Vladimir Putin's KGB-style legalism, these referenda break any reasonable standard.[353] In my opinion, there are two reasons behind it. The

---

351 Ukraine Rebels Hold Referendums in Donetsk and Luhansk. *BBC*, May 11, 2014, https://www.bbc.com/news/world-europe-27360146.
352 Опубликованы результаты референдумов по ДНР, ЛНР, Запорожской и Херсонской областям (from Russian: Results of Referendums on DNR, LNR, Zaporizhzhya and Kherson Regions Published). *TASS*, September 27, 2022, https://n9.cl/4twoh.
353 Engelhart, K. (2014). Putin's Legalism. *Foreign Policy*, March 24, https://foreignpolicy.com/2014/03/24/putins-legalism/.

first has to do with raising the stakes in the deepening conflict between Russia, on one side, and Ukraine and the West, on the other.

The second reason for such referenda is to start some sort of specific post-war nation-building. It is quite common among the post-Soviet power elites to see their populations as a kind of "biomass" from which they can form loyal subjects. In my many past conversations with the representatives of these elites, the issue of "biomass" was often brought up and justified by the example of Chechnya. Indeed, once a symbol of resistance to the Kremlin's colonialism, today's leadership of Chechnya is one of the biggest supporters of Putinism in Russia. It took less than 20 years to change mutineers into militant supporters of Kremlin imperialism. Later, this method was repeated in post-2014 Crimea, where super-loyalty was demonstrated in recent Russian elections, referenda, and the current mobilization into the Russian army.[354] So the more violent, humiliating, illogical, and illegitimate are the referenda, the stronger the impulse to form new, loyal subjects out of the southeastern Ukrainian population.

The ongoing war, if not won by Ukraine and its Western allies, will close the prospect of political liberty and civic freedom for the peoples of Eastern Europe, Russia included, for another several generations.

Ukraine in center of the militarist remapping of Europe and Northern Eurasia

November 2022[355]

The year 2022 has witnessed an avalanche of conflicts in Europe and northern Eurasia triggered by Putin's decision to launch a

---

354 Chenoweth, E., Lasota, I. (2022). From Chechnya to Crimea, Putin Saw Green Light for His Assault on the World Order. *Just Security*, March 18, https://n9.cl/mzzi0; Vitkine, B. (2022). Putin Changes Course With Mobilization of 300,000 Reservists and Nuclear Blackmail. *Le Monde*, September 21, https://n9.cl/iifb2.

355 A shorter version of this column has previously been published as: Minakov, M. (2022). The Militarist Remapping of Europe and Northern Eurasia. *Focus Ukraine*, November 3, 2022 https://www.wilsoncenter.org/blog-post/militarist-remapping-europe-and-northern-eurasia.

large-scale war against Ukraine. Many old and recent conflicts, most not addressed by the project of Greater Europe, which was supposed to stretch from Lisbon and Dublin to Vladivostok, have returned to change the life of European societies and of the nations that aspire to be European.[356] The chain reaction set off by the invasion has destroyed the system of deterrence of international and internal political conflicts—and so, as 2022 draws to a close, we see the continuing fragmentation and militarization of the space that was expected to be "Greater Europe," a region of peace and cooperation.

Triggered by Russia's invasion of Ukraine, militarism—a way of thinking and acting that understands military ends and means as the political and socioeconomic norm[357]—seems to be becoming the Zeitgeist redefining the Old World's understanding of its geography and recent history. This war started in 2014, and the massive Russian invasion was just the next step in the almost nine-year-long military conflict. But with this step, Ukraine's war zone has become the epicenter of the region's reconfiguration.

As we approach the end of 2022, it is crystal clear that Europe is caught within at least three rings of militarization. In the first, local ring, the war unleashed against Ukraine has proliferated into neighboring countries. In the second ring, frozen conflicts melt while simmering conflicts flare up with renewed vigor. And in the third ring, which spans northern Eurasia, countries that react to or participate in the deepening and protracted Russia-West antagonism are encountering new political and socioeconomic realities with new risks and struggles.

Three rings around Ukraine

In the first ring are Belarus and Russia's southwestern regions. The Belarusian government has allowed the Kremlin to use its terrain

---

356 Sakwa, R. (2021). Sad Delusions: The Decline and Rise of Greater Europe. *Journal of Eurasian Studies*, 12(1), 5-18.

357 Bucholz, A., Lalgee, R. (2008). Militarism. *Encyclopedia of Violence, Peace, & Conflict*, 1218-1227, https://www.sciencedirect.com/science/article/abs/pii/B9780123739858001057.

to launch attacks on Ukraine since February 2022.[358] In recent months, Minsk has increased its army units and invited more Russian troops onto Belarusian soil.[359] On October 20, 2022, because of growing military incidents on Russian soil, President Putin was forced to increase the alert levels nationwide. A "basic readiness level" is in effect for all Russia, a "high readiness level" for the central and southern federal districts, and a "medium response regime" in all Russian regions bordering Ukraine. Here the militarism is directly connected to the war in Ukraine and its cross-border spread.

The second ring includes countries with their own conflicts that have the potential to restart. It might be Moldova, on whose soil Russian missiles fell, the frozen conflict in Transnistria has never been resolved.[360] The Azerbaijan-Armenia conflict has expanded beyond Karabakh and spread deeper into Armenia this year.[361] Clashes in Central Asia have taken increasingly more lives in 2022.[362] The old Balkan conflicts definitely feel the injection of a new militarist inspiration.[363] The militarist spirit nurtures old wounds in that limbo of Europe and northern Eurasia.

In the third ring around Ukraine's war zone, we find the rest of European and northern Eurasian societies. Militarism changed the political preferences of European societies and in some cases, such as Italy and Sweden, swept far-right political parties into leadership positions.[364] The instability of many European governments

---

358 Belarus' Role in the Russian Military Aggression of Ukraine. *European Council*, March 2, 2022, https://n9.cl/9ngad.
359 Slunkin, P. (2022). Putin's Last Ally: Why the Belarusian Army Cannot Help Russia in Ukraine. *ECFR*, October 27, https://ecfr.eu/article/putins-last-ally-why-the-belarusian-army-cannot-help-russia-in-ukraine/.
360 Varenikova, M., Pronczuk, M. (2022). Moldova Condemns Russian Strikes after Missile Debris Lands in its Territory. *The New York Times*, October 31, https://2cm.es/Oe39.
361 Carafano, J. J. (2022). Armenia-Azerbaijan War Of 2022: What Should America Do? *Heritage Foundation*, September 22, https://2cm.es/LSZt.
362 Davys, A. (2022). Kyrgyzstan-Tajikistan Border Clashes Claim Nearly 100 Lives. *BBC*, September 19, https://www.bbc.com/news/world-asia-62950787.
363 The Effects of the War in Ukraine on the Western Balkans. *The International Institute for Strategic Studies*, August 2022, https://2cm.es/Oe3h.
364 Public Opinion on the War in Ukraine. *DG COMM's Public Opinion Monitoring Unit*, September 29, 2022, https://2cm.es/Oe3m; Balfour, R. (2022). How a Far-

was linked to the war in Ukraine, making the government turmoil in the UK only one of the most striking examples.[365]

Another militarist influence can be seen in the competition in the EU as to which country will have the biggest European army, Poland, France, or Germany.[366] The European and Eurasian economies have been hard-hit by the Russian war in Ukraine and by the anti-Russian sanctions.[367] The launch of the war has also reverberated in the Russian regions that are far from the war zone as they enter the waters of deeper social conflicts and political polarization, leading to the view that Putin's regime is destabilizing the economy and society.

Reframing a future Europe

The ongoing war has deeply changed how we understand peace, war, and the political geography of the world we live in. The former geopolitical periphery is more and more central, while the ex-core follows the trends set by newly emboldened nations.

The current crisis surrounding the idea of Europe shows that we indeed became deeply integrated in the last thirty years. It also teaches us lessons. One of them is that the future project of a united Europe will have to seriously address the sources of inter- and

---

Right Victory in Italy Might Ripple Through the EU. *Carnegie Endowment - Europe*, September 29, https://2cm.es/Oe3q; Sweden's Right-Wing Announces New Government with Far-Right Backing. *Le Monde*, October 14, 2022, https://2cm.es/Oe3t.

365 Borrell, J. (2022). The War in Ukraine and Its Implications for the EU. *EU External Action*, March 14, https://www.eeas.europa.eu/eeas/war-ukraine-and-its-implications-eu_en.

366 See: Poland Dreams of Building Europe's Largest Army, Against Backdrop of Russia's War Against Ukraine. *The Conversation*, October 26, 2022, https://2cm.es/Oe3w; France Promises to Increase Military and Humanitarian Aid to Ukraine. *Reuters*, April 30, 2022, https://2cm.es/Oe3y; Germany to Have Largest NATO Army in Europe: Scholz. *First Channel*, May 31, 2022, https://2cm.es/Oe3A.

367 Bobasu, A., De Santis, R.A. (2022). The Impact of the Russian Invasion of Ukraine on Euro Area Activity via the Uncertainty Channel. *European Central Bank*, Issue 4/2022, https://2cm.es/LS-0; The War in Ukraine and Its Wider Impact on the Eurasia Region. *The International Institute for Strategic Studies*, May 19, 2022, https://2cm.es/LS-2.

intranational conflicts and build institutions able to resolve or prevent them in a timely manner.

Future Europe will thrive only if it looks not only to successful urban communities, such as those found in Lisbon, Dublin, or Vladivostok, but also to places of ongoing troubles. Thus the new Greater Europe must be the region from Belfast, which risks falling back into dark days, to Magadan, once the capital of Stalin's gulag system. Future Europe must be a place of vigilant peace and a seasoned, robust liberal democracy.

Further problems for Ukrainian oligarchs

November 2022[368]

The Russian invasion of Ukraine profoundly changed the political regime and social order in the country. However, the commitment of President Zelensky's administration to deoligarchization not only survived the start of the large-scale war, but it also increased — in part because of wartime policies.

By May 2022, the Ukrainian government had adapted to the war situation and endorsed a multidimensional approach, simultaneously pursuing deoligarchization and anticorruption policies while mounting an all-out rebuttal to the Russian invasion. Deoligarchization and a continuation of anticorruption efforts were critical for preserving the trust of Ukraine's Western allies, which were providing Ukraine with increased military, political, and financial support.

The Zelensky administration also started preparing the country for the possibility of a long war, and for the future reconstruction of Ukraine. The fight against the oligarchs and corruption is central to both efforts. And the martial law situation has provided the president and his team with more opportunities to crack down on the oligarchy.

---

368 A shorter version of this column has previously been published as: Minakov, M. (2022). The War Has Helped Ukraine Rein in the Oligarchs. *Focus Ukraine*, November 15, 2022 https://www.wilsoncenter.org/blog-post/war-has-helped-ukraine-rein-oligarchs.

Declining asset values and the anti-oligarch law have hit billionaires

In August 2022, I wrote about how the administration's struggle with the oligarchy had forced Rinat Akhmetov to exit his media business and Vadym Novynsky to relinquish his MP mandate; how the pursuit of deoligarchization had resulted in rolling the investigations of ex-president Petro Poroshenko and pro-Russia oligarch Viktor Medvedchuk into one criminal investigation; and how the war was making an impact on the Ukrainian oligarchy by physically destroying the oligarch-owned industrial complexes. I also reported on the speed with which the oligarchs' net value fell. But oligarchs' problems grew even more, and it is worth to look at this issue again.

Using same data—Forbes magazine data on the real-time value of billionaires' assets and data from Forbes Ukraine magazine on the market values of Ukrainian oligarchs' holdings before the war (both expert teams used the same methods for data collection), it is possible to compare the change in the value of their assets by these days. Based on these data, the wealth of the following individuals dropped considerably from January 15 to November 14, 2022, and continues to fall daily:

> Rinat Akhmetov: from $13.7 billion to $4.3 billion;
> Victor Pinchuk: from $2.6 billion to $2 billion;
> Vadym Novinsky: from $3.5 billion to $1.3 billion;
> Genadiy Boholyubov: from $2 billion to $1.1 billion;
> Ihor Kolomoisky: from $1.8 billion to less than $1 billion;
> Petro Poroshenko: from $1.6 billion to $0.7 billion.

The Zelensky administration has also moved forward with implementing the Anti-Oligarch Law, which envisages the creation of an oligarchs' registry. Last week the Security Council's secretary Oleksiy Danylov said that the registry is under construction while his team investigates the legal grounds for declaring eighty-six citizens oligarchs. In October 2022 the Security Council announced a tender for the creation of the registry's software.³⁶⁹ Moving ahead with plans for the registry has already had a noticeable impact on the oligarchs' activities, though the registry itself does not yet exist.

The Zelensky administration has also continued depriving some oligarchs of Ukrainian citizenship. So far the best-known of those who have lost citizenship are Ihor Kolomoisky, Hennady Korban, and Vadim Rabinovich.³⁷⁰ Rescinding the citizenship of these prominent figures has added to the general pressure on all oligarchs.

The oligarchs lose shares in industries critical to the war effort

The next critical step in deoligarchization was taken on November 6, 2022, when the National Commission for Securities and the Stock Market implemented the decision of the headquarters of the supreme commander-in-chief to seize the shares of major industrial companies owned by the oligarchs.³⁷¹ This was done, in part, because of the importance of these companies to the war effort and in accordance with the Law of Ukraine "On the transfer, forced alienation or seizure of property under the conditions of the legal regime of war or state of emergency," which calls for "forcefully alienat[ing] into state property" the shares of strategically important enterprises. The takeover affected, among others, five big oligarch-owned industrial companies:

> Ukrnafta (42% of shares belonged to Kolomoisky);
> Ukrtatnafta (60% of shares belonged to Kolomoisky and Henadiy Bogolyubov);

---

369 РНБО хоче заплатити мільйони за реєстр з кількома олігархами (from Ukrainian: NSDC Wants to Pay Millions for a Register with Several Oligarchs). *Dzerkalo Tyzhnya*, October 13, 2022, https://zn.ua/ukr/ECONOMICS/rnbo-kh oche-zaplatiti-miljoni-za-rejestr-z-kilkoma-oliharkhami.html.
370 Liphshiz, C. (2022). Zelensky Said to Strip 3 Jewish Oligarchs of Ccitizenship. *The Times of Israel*, July 28, https://www.timesofisrael.com/zelensky-reportedl y-strips-3-jewish-oligarchs-of-ukrainian-citizenship/.
371 The Commission Approved a Decision on Changes to the Depository Accounting System. *National Securities and Stock Market Commission*, November 7, 2022, https://2cm.es/LS-i.

Motor Sich (56% of the shares were almost sold to Chinese investors by Vyacheslav Bohuslaev, but the deal was stopped by the Antimonopoly Committee, and Bohuslaev himself is under arrest);
AvtoKrAZ (owned by Kostyantyn Zhevago); and
Zaporozhtransformator (owned by Konstantin Hrygoryshyn).

The confiscated shares now are considered military property and are managed by the Ministry of Defense of Ukraine. At the end of martial law, in accordance with the law, either these shares will be returned to the owners, or the owners will be reimbursed their value.

All the above-mentioned steps of the Zelensky administration show that deoligarchization not only is back on track during the war, but it is also now a much more radical process, changing the established political economy in Ukraine. The ongoing war and imposition of martial law have provided the government with the opportunity to destroy the existing oligarchic clans.

Fighting corruption in wartime Ukraine

February 2023[372]

Even when the country is at war, the Ukrainian political calendar proceeds according to routine: a new political year starts in the last week of January. In 2023, the start of the election cycle coincided with a wave of political and legal actions connected with the fight against corruption, accompanied by a broader public discussion of this issue.

On January 21, the influential newspaper Dzerkalo Tyzhnia (Weekly Mirror) published an article by investigative journalist Yuriy Nikolov on the Ministry of Defense's (MOD) purchases of food for the Ukrainian military.[373] In the article, the ministry was

---

372 A shorter version of this column has previously been published as: Minakov, M. (2023). Fighting Corruption in Wartime Ukraine. *Focus Ukraine*, February 13, https://www.wilsoncenter.org/blog-post/fighting-corruption-wartime-ukraine.
373 Nikolov, Y. (2023). Тилові пацюки Міноборони під час війни «пиляють» на харчах для ЗСУ більше, ніж за мирного життя (from Ukrainian: Rear Rats of the Ministry of Defence 'Cut' More on Food for the Armed Forces During the War Than in Peaceful Life). *Dzerkalo Tyzhnya*, January 21, https://2cm.es/LS-n.

accused of purchasing food at prices well above the usual retail prices. The investigation resulted in the resignation of Deputy Minister of Defense Vyacheslav Shapovalov, who was responsible for logistics for the army, and the firing of Bohdan Khmelnytsky, the MOD official who had signed the contract with the supplier. The MOD has continued to deny any involvement in excessive payments.[374]

Why should allegations of misuse of funds have garnered such a fast and firm response from the administration? Two reasons appear most prominent. The Ukrainian Army is among the country's most important institutions and is well supported by the citizenry; during war it has an existential significance for the survival of the nation. Any taint of misuse of funds threatens its vital role. And external institutional support for Ukraine, such as by the IMF and EU agencies, is linked to continued anticorruption efforts.

Zelensky's immediate reaction to the growing suspicions of corrupt behavior was thus directed to two different audiences, showing both Ukrainian society and the country's allies and partners that lapses in good governance would not be tolerated.

Anticorruption campaign

Starting on January 22 and culminating on February 1, 2023, an avalanche of law enforcement activities took place that was directed at investigating the corruption cases that had piled up in 2022. On February 1 alone, tens of searches took place, along with the issuing of notices of official suspicion. I will name just a few of them.

The Security Service of Ukraine and the Economic Security Bureau (ESB) searched the home of Ukrainian businessman Ihor Kolomoysky on February 1, 2023. The searches were connected to the investigation of alleged tax avoidance by the companies Ukrtatnafta and Ukrnafta, of which Kolomoyskyy is a major shareholder.

---

374 Скандал в міноборони. Що кажуть у відомстві на звинувачення у завищенні цін (from Ukrainian: Scandal in the Ministry of Defence. What the Ministry Says about Accusations of Price Gouging). *BBC*, January 22, 2023, https ://www.bbc.com/ukrainian/news-64361225.

The State Bureau of Investigation (SBI) searched the offices of the acting head of the Kyiv tax service and the deputy head of the Main Department of the State Tax Service in Kyiv. Later these officials were suspended from their positions.

The SSU and the SBI conducted searches of the property of Arsen Avakov, former minister of internal affairs of Ukraine. The searches were connected to a contract signed several years ago with the French company Airbus and may have been prompted by the January 18 helicopter crash in which several senior members of the Ministry of Internal Affairs die.

The SBI has served a notice of suspicion to a former minister of the Ministry of Energy and Coal Industry of Ukraine, whose negligence allegedly led to public budget losses of almost 40 million USD in favor of oligarch-owned companies.

At around the same time, counterintelligence units and investigators from the SSU revealed new information concerning the alleged criminal activities of Vyacheslav Bohuslaiev, ex-president of the Ukrainian aircraft engine company Motor Sich, who was already suspected of providing funding and support to Russian proxies and terrorists in the so-called Donetsk People's Republic.

Also on February 1, 2023, the SSU conducted searches at the home of Vadym Stolar, a Kyiv developer and MP. According to the law enforcers, his construction companies were involved in the legalization of funds of Viktor Medvedchuk, Taras Kozak, and other persons sanctioned by Ukraine and Western states.

That same day, the prosecutor general's office served notices of suspicion to two officials from the MOD and Volodymyr Tereshchenko, former deputy director of the state-owned enterprise Promoboronexport (an entity engaged in the export and import of military goods and equipment).

In a separate action, SSU officers exposed an unnamed official from the MOD's Department of Public Procurement and Supply for allegedly embezzling public funds.

In addition to these high-profile cases, numerous other operations were carried out around Ukraine by the NABU, the SAPO, the police, and other law enforcement and anticorruption agencies.

Domestic results of the latest anticorruption efforts

Together with the wave of law enforcement operations, the presidential team underwent some painful changes.

In a major move, President Zelensky accepted the resignation of Kyrylo Tymoshenko, deputy head of the presidential administration, and dismissed four governors who were regarded as belonging to the "Tymoshenko group." Tymoshenko was an important member of the president's team who provided some informal power checks and balances in the office of the president.

There followed a wave of dismissals that affected not only the administration but also the prosecutor general's office, the cabinet of ministers, the Tax Administration, the Customs Service, the MOD, and the military administrations in several oblasts.[375]

The MOD has reshuffled its upper ranks. Following the scandal over purchases of food for the army at inflated prices, Defense Minister Oleksiy Reznikov, who seems to have survived the reshuffle so far, saw his position weakened; he has promised to ensure stronger control over procurements for the army.[376]

These changes are expected to continue in February 2023 with President Zelensky's announcement of new rounds of dismissals of "those in the system who do not meet the fundamental requirements of the state and society." The reshuffle has resulted in the presidential team appearing more united under Andriy Yermak, the head of the presidential administration, whose political power has grown. Another result is the evidently greater involvement of the SSU in the fight against corruption. The anticorruption agencies created after the Euromaidan were less visible in the most recent campaign.

---

375 Ukraine Fires Officials Amid Corruption Scandal, as Allies Watch Closely. *The New York Times*, January 24, 2023, https://www.nytimes.com/2023/01/24/world/europe/ukraine-corruption-firing-western-aid.html.

376 Roshchina, O. (2023). Резніков обіцяє повернути громадський контроль над частиною закупівель (from Ukrainian: Reznikov Promises to Return Public Control over Part of Procurement). *Ukrainska Pravda*, January 31, https://www.pravda.com.ua/news/2023/01/31/7387364/.

International resonance

Western politicians have largely assessed these developments as an indication of the Ukrainian government's firm intention to adhere to principles of good governance and a commitment—and ability—to fight corruption.

For example, on January 24, 2023, Democratic and Republican US lawmakers praised Ukraine's government for taking swift action against corruption and insisted that US military and humanitarian aid to President Zelensky's government should continue.[377] On January 26, 2023, Celeste Wallander, the US assistant secretary of defense for international security affairs, said at a House hearing that the Biden administration "has not seen credible evidence of any diversion of US-provided weapons outside of Ukraine."[378] On January 31 a US Treasury Department representative said the department "had no indication that US funds had been misused in Ukraine" and that it would continue to work closely with Ukrainian authorities to ensure appropriate safeguards were in place to prevent diversion of funds.[379] Finally, on February 3, during the EU-Ukraine summit in Kyiv, EU leader Ursula von der Leyen stated that she is "comforted" to see that Ukraine's "anti-corruption bodies are on alert and effective in detecting corruption cases."[380]

Western trust in Ukraine was also supported by the work of a monitoring mission. On January 27, 2023, Bridget A. Brink, the US ambassador to Ukraine, posted a photograph of herself with visiting inspectors from the US State and Defense Departments and USAID in Kyiv. As she wrote, the visitors were in Kyiv "to advance their independent oversight of US assistance to Ukraine."[381]

---

[377] Zengerle, P. (2023). US Lawmakers Praise Zelenskiy for Fighting Corruption, Back Continued Aid. *Reuters*, January 24, https://2cm.es/LS-J.

[378] US Officials Overseeing Aid Say Ukrainian Leaders Are Tackling Corruption. *The New York Times*, January 27, 2023, https://www.nytimes.com/2023/01/27/us/politics/ukraine-corruption-scandal.html.

[379] Shalal, A. (2023). US Funds Not Misused in Ukraine, US Treasury Says Amid Corruption Crackdown. *Reuters*, January 31, https://2cm.es/LS-N.

[380] EU, Ukraine Leaders Meet to Discuss Weapons, Corruption, EU Accession. *RFI*, February 3, 2023, https://2cm.es/Oe4t.

[381] See the message at https://x.com/usambkyiv/status/1618906385521180673?s=46&t=oJam75tjOO6rhCj4R_eg6w.

The endless struggle

The struggle with corruption goes on in Ukraine. Somewhat overshadowed by the public attention devoted to high-profile incidents were several unflashy but important achievements in the country's efforts to combat corruption. For example, in January 2023, NABU and SAPO completed the second part of a sprawling investigation into fifteen persons suspected of operationalizing the so-called "Rotterdam Plus" formula, a legacy of former president Petro Poroshenko. Under the terms of the formula, electricity consumers overpaid oligarch-controlled companies more than 400 million USD in 2018–2019. Among those suspected of putting the formula into practice are two former heads and seven members of the National Energy and Utilities Regulatory Commission.

Or another example, this one a positive development: the National Agency on Corruption Prevention has prepared the State Anti-Corruption Program for 2023–2025, a plan that further advances a system supporting transparency in governance. It expected the cabinet of ministers will approve it in the coming days.

Both cases show that progress is being made, slowly but surely. The Ukrainian government is gradually increasing its capacity to prevent corruption in the public sector and to undertake corrective actions when corruption is uncovered.

But measurable progress lags, undoubtedly hampered by Ukraine's all-out fight against Russia's war of aggression and a cadre of pro-Russia sympathizers and oligarchs used to the old ways prepared to take advantage of the difficult situation. Transparency International's recently published index of corruption perception for 2022 shows that Ukraine, despite some improvement, is still perceived as Europe's most corrupt country and is in thirty-third position worldwide, in a space shared with Algeria, El Salvador, and Zambia.

Recent actions in Ukraine underscore a certain contrariness. On the one hand, corruption in the public sector remains, despite martial law being in effect and huge social sensitivity on this issue. On the other hand, the Zelensky administration has shown it has the political will to fight corruption. And this will is backed by the system of anticorruption institutions, which can turn rhetoric into reality.

Ukrainian society and Ukraine's Western allies trust the leadership of the country, which is engaged in a fight on two fronts, against the Russian Federation and against internal corruption. And this trust nurtures Ukrainians' hope for improvement on both fronts.

Further steps with Ukraine's EU membership goals in 2023

February 2023[382]

Right after a politically stormy January in Ukraine, when some officials were sacked and others suspected of corruption, President Zelensky seized the opportunity thus created to promote Ukraine's EU agenda in February. The anticorruption wave has cleared the way for Kyiv to increase pressure on Brussels to provide more support in the face of Russia's new military campaign and to start negotiations on Ukraine's EU membership.

The EU-Ukraine summit-2023 in Kyiv

The EU-Ukraine summit held in Kyiv on February 3, 2023, was the first summit since Russia's full-scale invasion. Despite all the dangers, European Commission president Ursula von der Leyen along with fifteen of the twenty-seven EU commissioners arrived in the capital of Ukraine to meet with the Ukrainian government and discuss five key strategic issues: (1) Ukraine's EU accession process, (2) the EU's support for Ukraine in the latter's fight against Russia's war of aggression, (3) Kyiv's initiatives for a just peace and accountability, (4) reconstruction and economic cooperation, and (5) global

---

382 A shorter version of this column has previously been published as: Minakov, M. (2023). Political Will or Procedure? Assessing Ukraine's EU Membership Goals in 2023. *Focus Ukraine*, February 13, https://www.wilsoncenter.org/blog-post/political-will-or-procedure-assessing-ukraines-eu-membership-goals-2023.

food security. All these issues are important, but for Kyiv the two first items are of primary importance.

The major unanswered question hanging over the proceedings was, how fast can Ukraine become an EU member? The Brussels delegation clearly expects to follow the usual procedure: a candidate country should meet the Copenhagen criteria and receive an official decision from the European Commission on how well it has done on that objective; based on the commission's positive assessment, the EU Council can start negotiations with a country on membership. However, Kyiv is trying to insert political will as a factor that might speed up the process and secure a positive evaluation from the commission quickly.

As President Zelensky and his team made clear during the summit, Ukraine wants to become an EU member as soon as possible. This position is supported by the demonstration of the administration's political will to accomplish this task, bureaucratic obstacles notwithstanding. Accordingly, representatives of the Ukrainian government stated that 77 percent of the obligations under the Association Agreement had been met, including 90 percent in the area of justice.[383] These numbers were accepted by the EU participants and experts at the summit, though with some reservations.

The EU's official position on how well Ukraine complied with the integration plan is as yet unknown: Kyiv expects that the European Commission will publish a written document in March 2023. In this document it will be clear which factor came out ahead in the current talks, procedure or will. During a joint press conference following the EU-Ukraine summit in Kyiv, President Zelensky stressed that the main task of his government was to start accession negotiations with the EU in 2023.[384]

---

[383] Olha Stefanishyna: Ukraine Has Fulfilled 72% of Its Obligations under the Association Agreement with the EU. *Ukrainian Government Portal*, February 3, 2023, https://2cm.es/LT00.

[384] Ukraine Should Start EU Entry Talks "this year", Zelensky says. *France 24*, February 2, 2023, https://2cm.es/LT01.

Zelensky's lightning visits to London, Paris, and Brussels

As several participants of the summit in Kyiv shared with me, President Zelensky's team has achieved all tasks relevant to issues 3, 4, and 5 at the summit, however, success on the tasks needed for a favorable outcome on issues 1 and 2, Ukraine's EU accession process and EU support in the war against Russia, was less certain. The summit resulted in no promises about Ukraine's EU membership negotiations in 2023, and talks about airplanes and intermediate-range missiles for Ukraine to end the war this year did not conclude with clear commitments.

With respect to the second issue, Ukraine was assured that the EU will continue to provide political and military support to Ukraine for as long as necessary. The support includes military aid of about €3.6 billion in the framework of the European Peace Facility and the EU Military Assistance Mission to train 30,000 Ukrainian soldiers in 2023. Together with military support provided by individual EU member states, total EU military assistance to Ukraine is estimated at nearly €12 billion in 2023. Still, this form of military support, while needed and welcomed, was not responsive to the issue of jets and missiles.

The Zelensky administration therefore organized lightning visits of the president to major European capitals to ensure that the necessary weapons would reach Ukraine soon and that EU membership negotiations would start this year.

On February 8 and 9, 2023, President Zelensky visited London, Paris, and Brussels. His public speeches and the responses of his British, French, German, and EU partners showed that some progress is being made on weaponry. Prime Minister Sunak said that the UK "is assessing the possibility" of providing Ukraine with fighter jets.[385] President Macron did not "rule out" fighter jets, and promised greater military support soon.[386] Also, Ukraine's

---

[385] UK's Sunak Is Assessing Possibility of Sending Jets to Ukraine. *Bloomberg*, February 8, 2023, https://2cm.es/LT04.
[386] Harmash, O. (2023). Russia Hits Ukraine Power Grid and Gains Ground in East. *Reuters*, February 11, https://2cm.es/Oe4K.

European allies started considering providing missiles after the US decision to provide Ukraine with longer-range bombs.[387] Moreover, all three capitals openly support Zelensky's ten-step peace plan.

Yet the membership issue continues to be discussed between Ukrainian and EU leaders, as indicated by deliberations at the Special European Council meeting in Brussels on February 9, 2023. Despite a warm welcome for Ukraine from the commissioners and a round of applause from the European parliamentarians, Brussels did not change its procedure-oriented response. As the official document states,

> The European Council acknowledged the considerable efforts that Ukraine has made to meet the objectives required for its EU candidate status and welcomed the country's reform efforts in such difficult times. EU leaders encouraged Ukraine to fulfil the conditions specified in the Commission's opinion on its membership application in order to advance towards future EU membership.[388]

Thus the first task of the Zelensky administration at the summit, to start the EU-Ukraine membership negotiations in 2023, has not been achieved. Not yet.

Political will or the usual membership procedure?

In June 2022, Ukraine became an EU candidate. This decision was made by the EU Council based on the European Commission's statement:

> The European Commission has found that Ukraine overall is well advanced in reaching the stability of institutions guaranteeing democracy, the rule of law, human rights and respect for and protection of minorities; has continued its strong macro-economic record, demonstrating a noteworthy resilience with macroeconomic and financial stability, while needing to continue ambitious structural economic reforms; and has gradually approximated to substantial elements of the EU acquis in many areas.[389]

---

387 US to Send Ukraine Longer-Range Bombs in Newest Package. *PBS News*, February 2, 2023, https://2cm.es/LT07.
388 See official document at https://www.consilium.europa.eu/en/meetings/european-council/2023/02/09/.
389 See the document at https://ec.europa.eu/commission/presscorner/detail/en/ip_22_3790.

This statement was made about a country under enormous, relentless attack by the Russian Federation, with its government and society living under wartime conditions, including martial law, economic hardships, and mass migration. In the European Commission's statement—and in the decision made by the European Council based on the arguments therein—one can see both references to facts and a very visible political will to support Ukraine in its aspiration to become formally a part of Europe.

The political will factor does speak to Ukraine's leadership and people. The Zelensky administration wants to lean into it further to ensure that EU membership negotiations start this year. Several days ago, I spoke to two Ukrainian diplomats, who made an argument for launching negotiations very clearly. After the Russian invasion of Ukraine, international relations have fewer and fewer rules working. If the guarantees of the Budapest Memorandum do not work, if the norms of the Ukraine-Russia Friendship Agreement are violated, if WTO rules and procedures have less and less value in the multidimensional antagonism with Russia, why should Articles 6 and 49 of the EU Treaty (Accession criteria, otherwise known as the Copenhagen criteria) remain so inflexible? The Ukrainian government has demonstrated the political will to join the EU, and Kyiv expects that the same will be demonstrated by the European Commission.

My interlocutors also pointed out that political will was demonstrated by a united Europe (at that time it was the European Community) in the case of Greece: the country was in a difficult sociopolitical and economic situation, but the will of France's and Western Germany's leadership made Greece's membership possible.

My colleagues in Brussels also say that the internal EC debate around Ukraine's membership special case goes on. As Zelensky says, in this war Ukrainians are demonstrating the will to defend themselves and Europe at the same time—and the EU leadership understands this. But the EU is an alliance based on values, norms, and rules: to value will above norms speaks against its foundational idea. Also, the commissioners must take into account that there is a queue of countries working hard to meet all EU accession requirements before the start of negotiations. So the internal debates in Brussels are over a decision that adequately takes into account all aspects of the situation.

This leaves the answer to the all-important question hanging. Will Kyiv achieve its goal on issue 1 and start negotiations on EU membership in 2023 or will the procedural norms prevail, which would likely result in delay?

Ukraine's historical moment a year after the start of the war

February 2023[390]

February 24 marks the one-year anniversary of Russia launching a full-scale offensive against Ukraine. The events of the past twelve months have given many of us, observers and participants alike, the harrowing experience of watching the war — and the profound changes it wrought — in real time, of witnessing a historical moment that vastly overshadows our usual daily concerns.

In this piece, which is a result of my conversations with family, friends, colleagues, and students, both inside and outside of Ukraine, I focus on the results of the war to date for Ukraine, Russia, and the West writ large — the three parties most comprehensively involved in the conflict. All three have responded to the challenges of this moment in ways that stand to change them for good.

Ukraine's endurance

In arguably the most extraordinary and least expected turn of events, Ukraine met Russia's attack with powerful resistance, and to date has outlasted and outstrategized the Russian forces. Trained by the grueling experience of the drawn-out hostilities in the Donbas, Ukraine's diverse citizenry has built capacity to resist military violence and bear up under a wartime economy.

---

[390] A shorter version of this column has previously been published as: Minakov, M. (2023). Ukraine's Historical Moment. *Focus Ukraine*, February 21, 2023 https://www.wilsoncenter.org/blog-post/ukraines-historical-moment.

Political scientists have asserted for decades that warmaking is state-building. But since 2014, Ukraine has demonstrated how warmaking becomes nation-building. While the core state institutions of Ukraine were arguably not fully prepared to fight the aggressor back in February 2022, Ukrainian society was. Its unshakable resistance has provided Kyiv, Washington, and Brussels with the time necessary to prepare Ukraine's military for success in liberating some of the territory seized in the first weeks of the war.

Ukraine's endurance is notable because it achieved far more than simply survival (though that is an achievement in and of itself). Ukrainians have exhibited honor and courage in coping with the challenges of war and defending their country. Their response to lethal aggression from a much bigger country with one of the strongest armies in the world has commanded attention and respect across the globe.

Ukrainian citizens have developed tremendous solidarity and resilience, which show up in everyday interactions. For example, when Ukrainians ask how you are, it is not just a formulaic greeting: they really want to know how you are feeling today, and whether you need any help. Many Ukrainians say they have developed some "emotional calluses" and do not react to the wartime tragedies with the kind of sensitivity they would exhibit in peacetime. But when a neighbor asks for help, a response comes quickly.

Mass participation in the resistance has forced many Ukrainians to radically change their lifestyles. Sometimes they ask each other, who were you before the war? It takes an effort to remember, since their wartime roles are all-consuming and a return to civilian occupations is unimaginable right now.

Putin's Russia in moral shock

Russian elites and the Russian population are in a deepening moral shock. For Putin's clique, whose corruption destroyed the efficacy of Russia's intelligence services and the strength of the Russian army, the shock comes from its own inability to compete with Ukrainian forces or to undermine the Western alliance around Ukraine's cause. The oligarchic clans, who ceded their political role to the Kremlin in the early 2000s but continued enjoying the luxury-filled lives of tycoons, were dealt a blow by the Western sanctions and the necessity to assume a humbler existence, now as global outcasts.

The Russian power elites have lost the ground on which their regime was built. Putin's social contract envisaged an exchange of civil and political liberties for the socioeconomic security of Russian households.[391] Today the Kremlin can offer neither security to current (and future) military recruits and their families nor a stable income to families. The only future Putin can offer is a war that ends in defeat, an international tribunal, lasting poverty, and political destabilization.

The Russian populace has passed from a state of denial (or ignorance: many consume only the propagandistic news stories of state-owned media) to a deep moral and psychological shock comparable to that of the Soviet population during Gorbachev's perestroika when it learned of the crimes of Bolshevism and Stalinism. In the 1980s, this moral shock induced a kind of self-destruction of Soviet society.[392]

In 2022, the moral and legal groundlessness of Russia's attack on Ukraine forced Russians to take a hard look once again at what had happened to them, their federation, and their economy. Internal debates on the causes of the war and any protest against it are deemed criminal behavior. Now the most sanctioned country in the world, and militarizing its rather undeveloped economy, Russia has turned away from what arguably could have been the most economically rewarding period in its history. From being a major migrant-receiving nation, Russia has become a nation of emigrants. Russia — the state, the society, and the economy — is on the path of self-destruction once again.

---

391 Hodge, N. (2022). Putin's Draft Could Upend the Deal That Kept Him in Power. *CNN*, September 27, https://edition.cnn.com/2022/09/27/europe/putin-draft-analysis-intl/index.html.
392 Kampfner, J. (2023). State of Denial. *The New European*, February 16, https://www.theneweuropean.co.uk/putins-state-of-denial/.

The reshaping of the West

During the Russian invasion of Ukrainian Crimea and the Donbas in 2014, the West dithered over an appropriate response, proving ineffective in contending with Russia's aggression. In the pre-pandemic year, Western leaders, some under the influence of hard-right Ukrainian nationalism or its spokespersons, stood by as the global trend toward "Westlessness" picked up steam. In the fight against the pandemic, Western nations often looked inward for solutions to a global catastrophe. But Russian aggression in 2022 awakened Western nations and their leaders.

During 2022, the West exhibited more solidarity than at any time in recent decades. The cooperation of the United States, the EU, NATO, and the G-7 countries around the agenda of supporting Ukraine and containing Russia coalesced with unprecedented speed and effectiveness. NATO was reinvented as a major security provider to the central and western European countries, with several new candidate countries reevaluating their previously neutral status and seeking admission to the organization. The EU governing bodies demonstrated salutary efficiency in supporting Ukrainian refugees and the Ukrainian government. The new Western solidarity is so intense that it has markedly compressed the space for the traditional neutrality of some European nations.

This solidarity is probably what has forced the West to reevaluate and be more open about its regional identity. The Borrell's politically unsavory metaphor counterposing the Western "garden" to the global "jungles" nonetheless expresses well the fragmentation of a global order once helmed by the West.[393] After the start of Putin's revolt against the rules-based international order, the West has become more united in some ways but geopolitically smaller and less globally influential in the matters of the "Global Majority." This reshaping happened quickly and efficiently, and both the West and the Kremlin must face the results.

---

393 Majumdar, R. (2022). EU Top Diplomat Denies "Jungle" Remark Was Racist. *Deutsche Welle*, October 19, https://www.dw.com/en/eu-top-diplomat-denies-jungle-remark-was-racist/a-63484246.

History does not stop here. It is hard to predict which outcomes will be in the headlines a year from now. However, I hope that in February 2024 the major topics of discussion will be the first steps in Ukraine's reconstruction, the postwar reordering of eastern Europe, and the workings of the war crimes tribunal. Let's see how realistic this dream is.

The wartime constitutional process

March 2023[394]

The day Ukraine was invaded by the Russian Federation, President Zelensky issued a decree to declare martial law. The parliament approved the measure, and martial law has remained in force since then.

The war and the adoption of martial law have created changes in the Ukraine's constitutional process. For one thing, martial law has restricted some constitutional rights and freedoms. In addition, although Article 157 of the Constitution asserts that the Constitution may not be amended "in the conditions of martial law or a state of emergency," the Constitutional Court has continued its work during the war, though on a limited basis. In particular, the granting of an EU candidate status to Ukraine has incentivized the administration to embark on a new set of reforms to meet the European Commission's expectations, one of which is ensuring an independent judiciary. Also, the question of the legality of eliminating the immunity of MPs, which harks back to prewar days and entangled the court for almost three years, has been resolved.

---

[394] A shorter version of this column has previously been published as: Minakov, M. (2023). The Constitutional Process in Wartime Ukraine. *Focus Ukraine*, March 14, https://www.wilsoncenter.org/blog-post/constitutional-process-wartime-ukraine.

Voiding MP immunity

The voiding of MP immunity — a thorny issue almost since the start of Zelensky's presidency — is one agenda item that through its sheer chronic nature has kept the constitutional process alive in Ukraine.

In 2019, when the new presidential team launched a wave of constitutional reforms in Ukraine, the newly elected pro-Zelensky parliament lifted some of the MP immunity provisions enshrined in Article 80 of the Constitution. This move, doing away with decades of privilege, did not go unopposed. In January 2020 a group of oppositional MPs asked the Constitutional Court to rule on the constitutionality of the process used to amend Article 80. On November 1, 2022, the court ruled that the process was indeed constitutional, ending a three-year-long internal dispute over the issue.[395]

That was not the end of the affair, however. The Venice Commission — the Council of Europe's constitutional law advisory body — mildly criticized the Ukrainian court's decision, suggesting that it was inconsistent with previous interpretations of Ukraine's Constitution and advising that inconsistency can "undermine legal certainty and constitutional stability."[396] The Constitutional Court has yet to respond to this criticism.

Ukraine's EU prospects linked to further reforms of the Constitutional Court

Russia's aggression and the West-led coalition in support of Ukraine have increased Ukraine's chances of joining the EU,

---

395 Конституційну процедуру розгляду, ухвалення та набрання чинності Закону України „Про внесення змін до статті 80 Конституції України (щодо недоторканності народних депутатів України) не було порушено", - Рішення КСУ (from Ukrainian: Constitutional Procedure for Consideration, Adoption and Entry into Force of the Law of Ukraine 'On Amendments to Article 80 of the Constitution of Ukraine (Regarding Immunity of People's Deputies of Ukraine)' Was Not Violated — CCU Decision). *Constitutional Court of Ukraine*, November 2, 2022, https://2cm.es/LT0G.

396 Amicus Curiae Brief on The Limits of Subsequent (a posteriori) Review of Constitutional Amendments by The Constitutional Court. *The Venice Commission*, June 17-18, 2022, p. 10, https://www.venice.coe.int/webforms/documents/?pdf=CDL-AD(2022)012-e.

opening up new prospects for constitutional reform. On June 23, 2022, the European Council granted Ukraine candidate status and invited the European Commission (EC) to monitor the implementation of reforms required for Ukraine to meet the necessary conditions for the membership application to proceed.

One of the seven major issues that the EC identified as critical for Ukraine to access the EU is further reform of the Constitutional Court. The commission stated that the court needed to introduce "a credible and transparent selection procedure for appointments of judges" to the court, "including an integrity check."[397]

Indeed, as the Ukrainian political system adapted to wartime conditions, the debates around reforming the Constitutional Court, inspired by EU membership prospect, came back to life. As a result, after much discussion by Ukrainian politicians and legal experts, as well as Venice Commission members, the government updated the mechanism of selecting the court's judges. But this law created tensions between the Ukrainian government, on the one hand, and the EC and the Venice Commission on the other.

The law, which the Verkhovna Rada adopted on December 13 and President Zelensky signed on December 20, 2022, stipulates that the appointment of candidates to the Constitutional Court is to be executed with the participation of an Advisory Group consisting of six members, three of whom are to be appointed by the president, the Verkhovna Rada, and the Congress of Judges (one each). Three other members are to be chosen by the National Academy of Legal Sciences, the congress of representatives of law schools and research institutions, and representatives of public associations active in the field of constitutional reform, the rule of law, and human rights protection over the past five years. However, during first six years these last three members will come from the ranks of international legal experts.

In November 2022, the Venice Commission issued an urgent opinion in support of this version of the act and its final opinion before the Verkhovna Rada took a final vote on the law in

---

397 Commission Opinion on Ukraine's Application for Membership of the European Union. *European Commission*, June 17, 2022, p. 5, https://2cm.es/Oe5s.

December 2022.[398] This time the Venice Commission was dissatisfied with the selection procedure described in the draft law and made two new recommendations. The first recommendation was that the Advisory Group add a seventh member, appointed by the international legal community, to reduce political influence on judge selection (points 60 and 72-78). The second recommendation was that parliament add to the law a provision that those candidates whom the Advisory Group rejected could not be accepted as candidates for a Constitutional Court judgeship (points 60 and 72-76).

The Verkhovna Rada approved the law without following these recommendations, prompting Ana Pisonero, the EC spokesperson, to issue a statement on December 23 expressing the hope that the Ukrainian authorities would fully take into account the Venice Commission's recommendations in formulating its Constitutional Court law.[399] This hope was not realized in 2022, and the tensions that emerged between Kyiv and Brussels remain on the agenda to be resolved for 2023.

The Constitutional Court's wartime functioning

In 2022, the Constitutional Court continued to function, though with decreasing efficiency. If in 2020–2021, the court's subpar functioning was connected to conflict with the president and his administration, in 2022, the court had to work under the constant threat of Russian attacks, in the absence of a chairperson, and with a

---

398 Urgent Opinion on the Draft Law "On Amendments to Certain Legislative Acts of Ukraine on Improving the Procedure for the Selection of Candidates for the position of Judge of the Constitutional Court of Ukraine on a Competitive Basis." *The Venice Commission*, November 23, 2022, https://www.venice.coe.int/webforms/documents/?pdf=CDL-PI(2022)046-e; Opinion on the draft law "On Amendments to Certain Legislative Acts of Ukraine on improving the procedure for the selection of candidates for the position of judge of the Constitutional Court of Ukraine on a Competitive Basis." *The Venice Commission*, December 16-17, 2022, https://www.venice.coe.int/webforms/documents/?pdf=CDL-AD(2022)054-e.

399 European Commission expects Ukraine to follow Venice Commission recommendations on Constitutional Court bill. *The Kyiv Independent*, December 23, 2022, https://2cm.es/LT0P.

minimal number of judges. The institutional conflict between the court and the presidency, however, died down.

Oleksandr Tupytsky's term as chairperson and a member of the court expired in May 2022; moreover, he had left Ukraine at the start of the war. Several more judges resigned during the year, leaving the court with only thirteen out of eighteen members. With its ranks reduced and in the political environment created by the state of war, the court became much more open to cooperating with the presidential team. But the number of judges now barely suffices to carry out normal court duties and elect the court's chairperson. For most of the year, the acting chairperson of the court was Judge Serhiy Holovaty. Even though the conflict between the presidency and the Constitutional Court has finally petered out, the Court can provide only limited constitutional oversight.

Perspectives and the To-Do List, war or no war

After the end of the war, Ukraine will face several pressing tasks, including repatriating millions of refugees and IDPs and reconstructing its economy. No less important will be reconstructing its political, constitutional, and legal systems in response to postwar issues. As President Zelensky pointed out in his address to parliament in December 2022, the postwar reconstruction will encompass all sectors and will be done with an eye toward accessing the EU.[400] Also in December Oleksandr Kornienko, parliamentary vice-chairperson and the president's close ally, told a gathering of civil society organizations that the presidential team envisaged significant constitutional reform after the war.[401]

Despite the uncertainty of the war and the lack of clarity on how and when it might end, it is now more clear what steps the government needs to take in 2023. The EU membership prospect requires that Ukraine make the Constitutional Court a stronger and

---

[400] President of Ukraine Delivered the Annual Message to the Verkhovna Rada and Presented State Awards to Ukrainian Defenders. *The President of Ukraine Official Website*, December 28, 2022, https://2cm.es/LT15.

[401] Конституція України буде змінена після війни – Корнієнко (from Ukrainian: Constitution of Ukraine Will Be Changed after the War – Kornienko). *Sudovo-Yurydychna Gazeta*, December 12, 2022, https://2cm.es/LT10.

more independent institution. Ukraine is expected to appoint all court judges — a process that will test the new selection procedure. It is also expected to follow the Venice Commission's recommendations to amend the law on the selection of judges and that the new selection process will enhance the court's ability to guarantee proper constitutional oversight.

Political struggle in the first half of 2023

March 2023[402]

Ukraine continues manifesting its hardiness under the least favorable conditions. War entered the country first with the shock of 2014, with the revolutionary change of government, Russian illegal annexation of Crimea, and the start of the Donbas war. Then came the Minsk Agreements, reforms, and the establishment of ideological monopoly since 2015, followed by "normalization" of wartime politics in 2016–2017 and the growth of internal competition and Putin's menace in 2018. There was hope for new leadership in 2019, and then the quest for survival under the war and pandemic conditions from 2020 to 2021. There has been firm social and economic resilience in the face of the Russian invasion in 2022.

War is usually hostile to democracy. However, Ukraine also demonstrates resilience on that front: despite the bombing, the chances for competitive politics remain high despite martial law's limitations.

Competing groups

The parliamentary elections — under normal conditions, scheduled for October 2023 — will probably be postponed until after the war, and for good reason. The mass media sector has numerous issues and needs time to prepare for a national debate. Hundreds of

---

[402] A shorter version of this column has previously been published as: Minakov, M. (2023). Political Competition in Wartime Ukraine. *Focus Ukraine*, March 27, https://www.wilsoncenter.org/blog-post/political-competition-wartime-ukraine.

thousands of Ukrainians are on the front, and over 13 million have left their homes as either internally displaced people or refugees to countries abroad. Local self-government is now civil-military administration. Political competition would seem unlikely under such conditions.

But the Ukrainian political system seems to be alive and kicking. Some old cleavages have survived the war: the struggle between the Zelensky and the Poroshenko camps is still in place. The rift between the presidential office and the "mayor's party," headed by Kyiv's mayor Klitschko, comes to the surface from time to time.

But recent polls show that there could be more groups on the current political map than just these. Probably the most telling is the poll that the Razumkov Center conducted recently (February 22–March 1, 2023).[403] While measuring Ukrainians' assessment of the situation in their country, the pollsters could see which leaders—from institutions, individuals, and parties—the public trusts today. Among the most trusted public institutions are the army (96 percent of respondents trust it), volunteer organizations (88 percent), the president (83 percent), the church (70 percent), NGOs (66 percent), Ukrainian media (65 percent), heads of local administrations (62 percent), ombudspersons (52 percent), and the government (50 percent). The least trusted include officials (64 percent do not trust them), political parties (63 percent), courts (59 percent), and the Verkhovna Rada of Ukraine (51 percent).

Poll respondents were split on the question of whether corruption has changed since the start of the Russian invasion: 33 percent believe that the level of corruption grew, 30 percent believe it did not change, and 21 percent think it decreased (the rest abstained).

In terms of politicians and public figures, the respondents most often expressed trust in Volodymyr Zelensky (85 percent trust him), ex-comedian and current popular volunteer Serhiy Prytula (65 percent), presidential aide Mykhailo Podoliak (59.5 percent), Vitaly Klitschko (58 percent), security council secretary Oleksiy

---

[403] Citizens' Assessment of the Situation in the Country and Government Actions, Trust in Social Institutions (February – March 2023). *Razumkov Center*, March 15, 2023, https://2cm.es/Oe5Q.

Danilov (55 percent), Prime Minister Denys Shmyhal (52 percent), and Minister of Defense Oleksiy Reznikov (51 percent). The least trusted figures include Yuri Boyko (82 percent do not trust him), Yuliya Tymoshenko (76 percent), Petro Poroshenko (65 percent), and Oleksiy Arestovych (59 percent).

This poll omitted General Valery Zaluzhny, but he must also be included among the key political figures, since he was named in January 2023, by popular vote, the second "most popular politician" of 2022.[404] Oleksiy Arestovych can be included in the mix too, since businessmen and experts around him may turn into a new political force.

This poll shows some leaders who may oppose Zelensky and his party in future presidential and parliamentary elections. Among them are Zaluzhny and Prytula who enjoy vast national trust. Some growth in political weight has also been demonstrated by Klitschko. If General Zaluzhny is a professional soldier who, so far, has stayed away from politics, Prytula and Klitschko both are involved in their political parties in a way that could be important for future elections.

Setting the framework for future competition

Political diversity is currently limited by the war and by national wartime consensus, which is expressed in minimal criticism towards the president and commander in chief. So, the major competition is about chances to win in the future. The framework of these elections is being currently debated around three draft laws that prescribe the role of the military, the freedom of mass media, and the spectrum of parties allowed in the country.

The debate on the role of the military concerns a draft law on the strengthening of democratic civilian control over the Armed Forces of Ukraine (Law no. 4210). This draft was conceived in 2020 and approved in the first reading just before the invasion, on February 16, 2022. Among other measures, it proposes giving control

---

[404] Politics in 2022 (December 2022 – January 2023). *Razumkov Center*, January 12, 2023, https://2cm.es/LT1i.

of the army's commander to the minister of defense. In the current context, this draft law has become politicized, an issue for debate between those who support and those who oppose a greater role for the military in the political system.

The quality of future elections will depend on how free mass media is. In December 2022, a new law on mass media was approved in Ukraine and immediately sparked debates.[405] The law prescribes new rules for broadcasting, on-demand media services, video-sharing platforms, print and online media, and electronic communications operators—rules for the period of armed aggression, and up to five years thereafter. The current debate focuses on the harmony between this law's norms with the norms of the EU and the Council of Europe, which ensure the media freedom necessary for functional democracy.

Yet in May 2022, the Ukrainian government banned all pro-Russian parties.[406] In March 2023, a number of the MPs from the Servant of People and the Voice parties proposed an "anti-Kremlin lustration" act, which envisions a ban on participation in elections for all those who were members of parliament or on local councils representing the prohibited (pro-Russian) parties (Art. I-3). This initiative has launched a debate which will define who gets to participate in future political campaigns in Ukraine.

War stopped neither public debate nor political competition in Ukraine. The results of the ongoing debates will define the framework of future elections and Ukrainian democracy in the postwar period. Ultimately, they will also define the speed of Ukraine's European and Euro-Atlantic integration.

---

405 Discussion About New Ukrainian Media Law. *Eurotopics*, December 19, 2022, https://www.eurotopics.net/en/293628/discussion-about-new-ukrainian-media-law.
406 Zelenskiy Signs Law Banning Pro-Russian Political Parties in Ukraine. *RFE/RL*, May 14, 2022, https://www.rferl.org/a/ukraine-law-bans-pro-russia-parties-zelenskiy-signs/31849737.html.

The paradox of deoligarchization in post-Soviet Ukraine

June 2023[407]

Despite the ongoing war, the Ukrainian government remains committed to fighting oligarchy in Ukraine, as I wrote in the previous chapters. This commitment stems not only from President Zelensky's long history of struggling with the oligarchs but also from the strategic aim of developing Ukraine as a functioning democracy and a country able to achieve membership in the European Union and NATO.

Zelensky's fight against the oligarchs

As I wrote above, in 2020–2021, Zelensky's team chose the path of defanging the Ukrainian oligarchy by fighting individual oligarchs. In 2021, with the Anti-Oligarch Act, President Zelensky started creating a special institution within the National Security and Defense Council that would identify individual oligarchs through their assets (types and value) and a political influence test, enroll them in an official registry of oligarchs, and limit their influence on society, political groups, and government. Furthermore, during the first year of the war, the Ukrainian government took several steps to nationalize oligarchs' shares of major industrial companies. Zelensky stripped several oligarchs of Ukrainian citizenship. The Russian hits on Ukrainian industry have considerably diminished the market value of many Ukrainian oligarchs' assets. Currently the oligarchs are under unprecedented multilevel pressure. In a way, deoligarchization has proceeded far in Ukraine.

Still, with one exception, the expected start of the registry of oligarchs had not yet taken place by June 2023. In part, this delay is connected with the fact that the fight against the oligarchs is now not only an issue of internal politics but also part of the EU

---

[407] A shorter version of this column has previously been published as: Minakov, M. (2023). The Paradox of De-oligarchization. Focus Ukraine, June 27, https://www.wilsoncenter.org/blog-post/paradox-de-oligarchization.

membership agenda. This means that deoligarchization should be carried out in accordance with EU standards of democracy and the rule of law.

Deoligarchization in the European fashion

In June 2022, in its opinion on the EU membership application by Ukraine, the European Commission not only supported Ukraine as a country worthy of accessing the EU but also recommended implementing the Anti-Oligarch Act "in a legally sound manner, taking into account the forthcoming opinion of the Venice Commission on the relevant legislation."[408] Legality and a critical imbalance between two normative approaches in this act were indeed an issue (and one raised many times by Ukrainian and European lawyers in 2021–2022).

These drawbacks were highlighted in the opinion of the European Commission for Democracy through Law (the Venice Commission), which was finally published on June 13, 2023.[409] The commission has clearly indicated that the norms of the act stem from two approaches to fighting grand corruption: systemic and personal (Art. 17-21). The systemic approach "involves the adoption and strengthening of legal tools in many fields of law, such as legislation relating to media, anti-monopoly, political parties, elections, taxation, anti-corruption and anti-money laundering (etc.) with a view to preventing the destructive influence of oligarchy in a comprehensive and coordinated manner." It has a long-term preventative effect and increases the efficacy of liberal democracy in every country.

The personal approach "seeks to identify the persons who are considered to wield this negative influence on the state through

---

[408] The European Commission Recommends to Council Confirming Ukraine, Moldova and Georgia's Perspective to Become Members of the EU and Provides Its Opinion on Granting Them Candidate Status. *The European Commission*, June 17, 2022, https://ec.europa.eu/commission/presscorner/detail/en/IP_22_3790.

[409] Opinion on the Law on the Prevention of Threats to National Security, Associated with Excessive Influence of Persons Having Significant Economic or Political Weight in Public Life (Oligarchs). *The Venice Commission*, June 9-10, 2023, https://www.venice.coe.int/webforms/documents/?pdf=CDL-AD(2023)018-e.

specific criteria, such as wealth, media ownership, etc." Persons who are regarded by the government as "having significant economic or political weight in public life" are to be registered as "oligarchs." Such registration leads to punitive measures that may include "exclusion from the financing of political parties or activities, exclusion from privatizations of public property, and the strict obligation for public officials to report on the content of exchanges with them or their representatives."

The Venice Commission decided that the mixture of the two normative approaches was imbalanced and could lead to the use of legal instruments that threatened to turn deoligarchization into a process that "undermines democracy and rule of law" (Art. 28, 63). Such a conclusion comes from the fact that the "personal approach" in the law overweighs the "systemic approach" (Art. 61) and offers too "radical solutions," which in exceptional cases can be used as supplementary and additional, but not as the core ones (Art. 26). Also, in these exceptional cases the personal decisions that involve such punitive measures, as prescribed in the Anti-Oligarch Act, "would necessarily require clear legal criteria and strong guarantees of an independent decision-making body and due process, with notions defined in such a way that they can be proven, and—as a consequence—judicially controlled" (Art. 27).

The commission recommended that the Ukrainian government take several concrete steps in updating the act so that it would prepare Ukraine for EU membership (Art. 29-41, 64). First of all, Ukraine should defer implementation of the act. The government would then need to analyze why existing institutions do not limit oligarchs from their destructive influence, and define how to improve existing anti-corruption organizations to be more effective in fulfilling their duties. Also, the commission recommends that the Ukrainian taxation system be revised to eliminate oligarchic structures from tax benefits and exemptions. Altogether, the systemic response to the threat of the oligarchy should base on building bridges "between various fields of law and the institutions that implement them (through the specific lens of tackling oligarchization)," as well as closer cooperation with the EU and international organizations fighting corruption. Finally, after the war, the government of Ukraine should reassess the danger of the oligarchs and establish a preventive system compatible with European standards of human rights, democracy, and the rule of law.

The representatives of the Ukrainian government have so far reacted to this decision with some contempt.[410]

The deoligarchization paradox

The Venice Commission's opinion document is an example of contemporary European legal thought applied to the politico-economic realities of post-Soviet European states, such as Ukraine, Georgia, and Moldova (the last two countries are frequently mentioned in the commission's response). All three countries aspire to membership in the EU and try to fight corruption at home. Each faces the issue of which strategic path to choose. As I formulated in one of the previous chapters on Ukrainian deoligarchization, the choice is whether to fight oligarchy or the oligarchs.

The authors of the Venice Commission's opinion went further and formulated the paradox of deoligarchization (Art. 27):

> If the administration and the judiciary are strong and independent enough to support the implementation of 'personal measures'..., then such measures are no longer needed because the preconditions are met to deploy a much more systemic and effective strategy. If conversely the administration and judiciary are 'captured' by the interests that the 'personal measures' intend to fight, then such measures are either ineffective or — having to be adopted through executive acts that are not fully subject to effective judicial control — profoundly dangerous for human rights, democracy and the rule of law.

Indeed, deoligarchization, especially in the realities of the fragile Eastern European democracies, is a tricky process that does not allow simple solutions.

---

410 Venice Commission Recommends Ukraine Postpone Anti-Oligarchy Law Until War Is Over. *Evropeiska Pravda*, June 9, 2023, https://www.pravda.com.ua/eng/news/2023/06/9/7406146/.

Ukraine and the rise of the middle powers in the global interstate system

July 2023[411]

The current situation in Europe has been called a new Cold War.[412] Indeed, after Russia's attack on Ukraine, the common European space was divided between antagonistic blocs, which see each other as an increasingly existential threat. NATO's ranks are growing, as is solidarity among NATO countries.[413] Military solutions are increasingly seen as an acceptable instrument in countries' toolkits for managing international relations. Security has again become one of the guiding principles for structuring domestic politics.[414] And ideologically, the pan-European conflict is characterized as democracies against autocracies.[415] Thus there are many reasons to refer to the current European situation as a new Cold War.

Behind all those similarities, however, lie novelties as well. One of these novelties is the changing role of the middle powers in international relations.[416] Since February 2022, states that until recently were on the periphery and in the shadow of the global core are now playing a much bigger role and enjoying a much stronger influence in international relations. The change in Ukraine's

---

411 A shorter version of this column has previously been published as: Minakov, M. (2023). Ukraine and the Rise of the Middle Powers. Focus Ukraine, July 31, https://www.wilsoncenter.org/blog-post/ukraine-and-rise-middle-powers.
412 Diamantopoulou, A. (2022). The Three Challenges for the West in the New Cold War. *ECFR*, September 20, 2022, https://ecfr.eu/article/the-three-challenges-for-the-west-in-the-new-cold-war/.
413 Turkey Clears the Way for Sweden's Entry to NATO on the Eve of Summit. *The New York Times*, July 10, 2023, https://www.nytimes.com/2023/07/10/us/politics/nato-biden-ukraine.html.
414 Tardy, T. (2023). The New European Defence and Security Agenda. *European Liberal Forum*, Policy Biref #5, May, https://2cm.es/LT1G.
415 Smeltzer, M. (2023). Europe and Eurasia, the Democracy-Autocracy Gap is Widening. *Freedom House*, May 25, https://freedomhouse.org/article/europe-and-eurasia-democracy-autocracy-gap-widening.
416 Krastev, I. (2022). Middle Powers Are Reshaping Geopolitics. *Financial Times*, November 18, https://www.ft.com/content/0129492d-ac7f-4807-8050-2760a09e9ccc.

international influence after the Russian invasion may be the most striking example of such a trend.

Usual roles of the great, middle, and small powers

Even though all states in today's global system are formally regarded as equal, realists have rightly pointed out the different abilities of states to pursue their interests.[417] Indeed, the relationships among states are asymmetrical.[418] Those powers that can influence the governments of other nations and set the general principles of international relations are regarded as great. As Gen. Mark A. Milley famously said, today there are three great powers: the United States, China, and Russia.[419]

States that are objects of the latter states' influence and that must accept and adapt to the international rules defined by others are considered to be small. In between those two state types are the middle powers: the political entities that are weaker than the superpowers but that can still shape international events and influence the decisions of the stronger parties.

The size of a state can be measured by (1) its GDP, population, or military spending; (2) its ability to influence international politics; and (3) its foreign policy posture.[420] Together these three metrics determine the unequal abilities of states to influence each other politically, economically, militarily, and even culturally.

---

417 Simpson, A. W. (2018). Realism, Small States and Neutrality. *E-International Relations*, February 5, https://www.e-ir.info/2018/02/05/realism-small-states-and-neutrality/.
418 Long, T. (2017). Small States, Great Power? Gaining Influence Through Intrinsic, Derivative, and Collective Power. *International Studies Review*, 19(2), 185-205.
419 Clark, J. (2023). Milley Says Graduates Will Confront New Security Challenges. *The US Department of Defence*, June 9, https://www.defense.gov/News/News-Stories/Article/Article/3422571/.
420 Wegge, N. (2018). Small States vs. Middle Powers—What's the Difference? *Center for International Policy Studies*, July 15, https://www.cips-cepi.ca/2018/07/15/small-states-vs-middle-powers-whats-the-difference/.

The rise of the middle powers

In extended periods of peace and cooperation, the non-great states have little chance to shape the global or regional political agenda. However, when the great powers enter into antagonistic relations, the middle powers gain a footing to amplify their sovereign stature and influence relations between the states in their region or, sporadically, globally.

The current conflict among the United States, China, and Russia created an environment conducive to the growth of the middle powers' new role.[421] The most salient examples of it are Narendra Modi's India, Recep Tayyip Erdoğan's Turkey, and Andrzej Duda's Poland. The celebratory reception of Prime Minster Modi by the United States last June demonstrated how fast India has become an influential player in the Indo-Pacific region, and how remarkably profitable that role can be. Since the start of Russia's war against Ukraine, President Erdoğan has vastly increased Turkey's influence with NATO, Russia, Ukraine, and the United States. Poland has also dramatically increased its geopolitical weight over the past two years while becoming the logistical manager of NATO assistance to Ukraine and a new pole of influence in the EU.

Perhaps unwillingly, the great powers are adapting to the new situation and accepting the middle powers' vastly increased sovereign authority. This can be seen, for example, in the United States' and Russia's acceptance of Turkey's new weight and the need to strike compromises with that country's leader.

Resilient Ukraine as international influencer

But the most striking example of a middle state with markedly greater influence is Ukraine. Paradoxically, even though Ukraine's population and economy have declined as the war has dragged on, the country's international status has grown to equal that of the

---

[421] Biden - Harris Administration's National Security Strategy. *White House*, October 2022, https://2cm.es/LT1O; Sweijs, T., Mazarr, M. J. (2023). Mind the Middle Powers. *War on the Rocks*, April 4, https://warontherocks.com/2023/04/mind-the-middle-powers/.

powers that define global and regional agendas. And the United States, China, and Russia have had to adapt to it.

Consider: Ukraine has turned out to be at the center of a new, nonformalized but effective alliance — defined in defensive, political, and economic terms — that supports its efforts in defense of its people and statehood. Ukraine received EU candidate status in June 2022, a goal that seemed out of reach even in January 2022. Kyiv is exhibiting a growing influence on the NATO and G7 agendas. Ukraine is in dialogue not only with the West but also with the global South. In the war with Russia, Ukraine has not just American and European support but also the sympathies of most of the peoples around the world (see data for 2022 and 2023).[422]

Even though Ukraine's new international influence has systemic features, it is also undeniably connected to the personality of President Volodymyr Zelensky. From a middling president of COVID-era Ukraine, he has become an inspiring and globally admired leader in Ukraine's anti-Russian resistance movement. But more than that, he has turned into a skillful manager of the middle state's global influence. Ukraine's new status in the global system can be attributed not only to Zelensky's personal omnipresence at major political meetings and social gatherings but also thanks to Kyiv's skillful diplomacy vis-à-vis the US, EU, or G7 leadership. Zelensky's role was central to the profound changes that have occurred in the long-standing policies toward Russia of such states as Germany, Japan, and Italy.

Such middle-state behavior — whether as institutionalized policy or personal conduct — sooner or later can irritate the great powers' leadership. For example, Zelensky's pushy style has sparked some negative reactions on the part of the great powers' leaders, as during the NATO summit in Vilnius.[423] But even the irritation of

---

[422] One Year In, Global Public Opinion about the War in Ukraine Has Remained Remarkably Stable. *Ipsos*, January 20, 2023, https://www.ipsos.com/en/war-in-ukraine-january-2023; Fagan, M., Poushter, J., Gubbala, S. (2023). Large Shares See Russia and Putin in Negative Light, While Views of Zelenskyy More Mixed. *The Pew Research* Center, July 10, https://2cm.es/Oe6D.

[423] Olorunnipa, T., Rauhala, E., Kornfield, M., Birnbaum, M. (2023). Zelensky Slams NATO for Omitting a Timeline for Ukraine to Join. *The Washington Post*, July 11, https://2cm.es/Oe6H.

politicians can bring its results and deliver the Western support necessary for Ukraine's defense.

It is probably correct to say that global politics was and is still unfolding in the shadow of Ukraine. That is because Ukraine has demonstrated unexpected resilience in the face of the war with Russia, which is still regarded as a great power. Kyiv has ridden the wave—the "ninth wave" of the international storm—and laid down a kind of new model of behavior for medium-sized states. The question remains: how long can it stay afloat?

What comes after the storm?

The effect of resilient Ukraine—or of the middle powers in general—on international relations is most likely a result of the global political order surviving the storm. The political tempest that has affected the world may end in the future, with the middle powers returning to their customary peripheral position. The great powers—those that will survive the current geopolitical shift—will demand renewed acknowledgment of their supremacy from the upstart middles. But history is happening right now, redefining greatness, smallness, and the distribution of roles and status in the interstate system. And the experience gained from the current change in asymmetrical relations among states may help redefine the rules of greatness for the future international order.

Russian local "elections" in the occupied Ukrainian territories

September 2023[424]

Russia continues to illegally occupy Crimea and parts of four southeastern oblasts of Ukraine. On September 1–4 and September 8–10, 2023, the remaining population of these areas went through a new

---

[424] A shorter version of this column has previously been published as: Minakov, M. (2023). Local "Elections" in the Occupied Ukrainian Territories. Focus Ukraine, September 18, https://www.wilsoncenter.org/blog-post/local-electi ons-occupied-ukrainian-territories.

humiliating experience—local elections. This was the first electoral campaign run by Moscow in the occupied parts of Donetsk, Luhansk, Kherson, and Zaporizhzhia oblasts. The "elected" members of the "regional legislatures" will soon appoint executive bodies in these territories and in Crimea, if no changes occur on the front line.

From the 1990s through the early 2000s, elections functioned as a rather democratic institution in Russia. But with the rise of Vladimir Putin's autocratization, elections were reinvented as an exercise in bargaining among federal, regional, and local elites and communities with the government for the distribution of resources.[425] Additionally, regional and local elections were the period when local elites demonstrated to the federal "center" their ability to get the best electoral results, ones that would serve well for the next presidential elections, in which Putin must achieve ever-growing, clear, popular support.

It is in this context that the Ukrainian citizens who remain in the regions captured by the Russian army find themselves. In these elections, they learn how to survive under illegal Russian occupation. Simultaneously, the local elites learn how to integrate themselves into the Russian patronal pyramid.[426] The results of this learning process are quite murky. For example, it is close to impossible to state what percentage of inhabitants in the occupied lands of Ukraine indeed voted. In Russia, approximately 25 percent of the participants voted remotely, with the use of electronic devices. But in the occupied Ukrainian territories, this estimate was probably inflated for security reasons.

During the prolonged voting days, many electoral stations were closed because of shelling or drone attacks. The electoral commissions were leaving for shelters on many occasions on the last voting day, September 10. I talked to several people still living in Berdiansk, Donetsk, Henichesk, and Luhansk, and their common

---

425 White, S., & Feklyunina, V. (2014). Russia's Authoritarian Elections: The View from Below. In White, S., & Feklyunina, V. (eds). *Russia's Authoritarian Elections*. London: Routledge, 49-72.
426 Hale, H. E. (2017). Russian Patronal Politics beyond Putin. *Daedalus*, 146(2), 30-40.

line was that the stations were empty when they saw them. But they also reported that the "mobile electoral commissions" were going around streets and blocks to get votes on the spot for all 10 days before September 10, 2023.

In general, the United Russia Party (URP), the classical post-Soviet "power party" consisting of central and local power elite groups and bureaucrats, demonstrated two things in this campaign, across 85 Russian regions and localities. First, it is still the most popular (popular in a very specific authoritarian context) political organization. And second, it remains the best electoral structure for Putin to use for the March 2024 presidential elections. But it is worth paying attention to the fact that the candidates (whether from the URP or the other parties) who presented themselves as the biggest supporters of Russia's war against Ukraine did not achieve electoral victories in most Russian regions.

However, according to the regional electoral commissions (which function illegally, according to Ukrainian legislation), the pro-war and most anti-Ukrainian figures—like Denis Pushilin, Leonid Pasechnik, Yevgeny Balitsky, and Vladimir Saldo, the Kremlin-appointed temporary governors of the captured regions—were ascribed the biggest portion of votes in the occupied territory. This result is defined by Russian occupying authorities, not by the inhabitants of the war-torn settlements in southeastern Ukraine. By asserting it, the Kremlin plans to keep full control of newly created "regional legislatures" (or else "legislative assemblies") that will consist of 90 deputies in Donetsk oblast, 36 members in Kherson oblast, 50 deputies in Luhansk oblast, and 40 deputies in Zaporizhzhia oblast. These assemblies will appoint the "regional governments" by the end of October.

Election results that do not match the reality of voting constituencies can be witnessed in other instances. For example, the Russian media report the commissions' claims that 72 percent of the Luhansk oblast voters, 68 percent of Zaporizhzhia oblast voters, 65 percent of Kherson oblast voters, and 76 percent of Donetsk oblast voters participated in these elections.[427] These are definitely false claims, as so many voters have left these regions. My assessment is that the remaining population in these four oblasts is well below 30 percent of the 2021 population, so the "elected" members of the new "regional legislatures" can neither claim to be elected by a serious number of voters nor pretend to be representative of these constituencies.

Also, the electoral commissions ascribed victory to the URP in all four "regional legislatures." For example, in Kherson the votes were ascribed this way: URP, 74.86 percent (which translates into 28 seats); Communist Party of the Russian Federation, 10.56 percent (four seats); Liberal Democratic Party of Russia, 8.27 percent (3 seats); and the Just Russia — For Truth Party, 5.03 percent (one seat). And in the captured districts of Zaporizhzhia oblast, the URP was ascribed 83 percent of the vote (34 seats), while the CPRF was allocated 5.02 percent (two seats), the "Fair Russia" party was given 5.13 percent (two seats), and the LDPR received 5.82 percent (two seats). The "winner" of these elections has been assigned with no connection to the remaining population's will.

But it is important to see where the electoral result leads. The URP has won the majority of seats in the four "regional legislatures," setting up the structure for future presidential elections and further integration with the Ukrainian population which remains in the occupied areas. If the front line remains unchanged in southeastern Ukraine, the local "authorities" will provide the Kremlin with the same result in the March 2024 presidential elections as they did in Crimea in the 2020 campaign.[428] According to the latter, Putin claimed 92 percent of Crimeans' votes; in Russia, his average was 76 percent.

There is no doubt that the local elections in the captured Ukrainian territory are a prologue to the fraudulent presidential

---

427 Грищенко, Н., Ионова, Л. (2023). Как в ДНР, ЛНР, Херсонской и Запорожской областях прошли выборы депутатов (from Russian: How the Elections of Deputies Were Held in the DNR, LNR, Kherson and Zaporizhzhya Regions. *Rossiiskaya Gazeta*, September 13, https://2cm.es/LT2n.

428 Urcosta, R. B. (2018). The Crimean Factor in the 2018 Russian Presidential Election. *Eurasia Daily Monitor*, 39(15), 1-7, https://2cm.es/Oe6W.

elections in 2024. The results will also be used to appoint regional governments that Moscow will promote as legitimate authorities in the illegally occupied territories of Ukraine. There are very good reasons for the fact that the results of these elections were recognized neither by the US and G7, nor by the UN, nor by the EU.

Pros and cons of elections in wartime Ukraine

January 2024[429]

President Volodymyr Zelensky and the current Ukrainian parliament are approaching the hour when their formal legitimacy, their mandate, comes to an end. Under normal conditions, elections to the Verkhovna Rada would have been held October 2023, while candidates for the presidency would have started preparing for elections scheduled for the last Sunday in March of 2024.

But the country is consumed by war, and elections are probably not an option. Or are they? President Zelensky is considering the answer to this question.[430]

I should state at the outset that I find the idea of organizing elections, whether presidential only or both presidential and parliamentary, during wartime is a very bad idea. At the same time, I also disagree with those who think the matter of postponing elections can be settled purely by having recourse to existing laws. In this chapter I show that the ruling group could, if it chose, adopt some legal maneuvering that would formally respect the constitution and the nation's laws (though violating their spirit), and that these maneuvers have been tested several times in Ukraine since 2014. But such formally legal if doubtfully legitimate elections could also pose unjustifiably high sociopolitical risks for a state at war, and this creates a dilemma for the nation.

---

[429] A shorter version of this column has previously been published as: Minakov, M. (2024). Elections in Wartime Ukraine Would Test Ukraine's Legal-Political Flexibility. *Kennan Cable*, January 2024 https://www.wilsoncenter.org/publication/kennan-cable-no-85-elections-wartime-ukraine-would-test-ukraines-legal-political.

[430] President Zelenskyy Weighing Up Spring Presidential Elections. *Sky News*, November 3, 2023, https://2cm.es/LT2v.

Defining the wartime electoral dilemma

Currently, the Zelensky administration is under pressure to organize parliamentary and presidential elections soon. The first source of the pressure is the West.[431] Behind the scenes, Ukraine's allies are allegedly demanding that Kyiv renew its government's legitimacy, despite the ongoing war and the mass dislocation of citizens.

Ukraine's allies know well the constitutional limitations on wartime elections in Ukraine. They also know that the current legal regime is "flexible" enough to find legal ways of organizing elections. After all, they point out, the war started in 2014, and thereafter two presidents and two parliaments were elected. Also, some opposition-minded groups in the United States and Europe are casting doubt on the democratic nature of Ukraine's government as a reason to reduce the military and financial support being provided to Ukraine.[432] Elections would help the Western pro-Ukrainian governments overcome these objections at home in the upcoming budgetary debates.

A second source of pressure to hold elections is the domestic political situation. After a very uneven, challenging, and tragic five-year governing effort that had to deal with the "Green Wave" of radical reforms, the COVID-19 pandemic, growing clashes with opposition groups, and Russia's full-fledged invasion, President Zelensky and his party need to renew their mandate. For the sake of political stability, they must demonstrate their democratic legitimacy to the nation, the opposition, and, especially, the army. Whatever future awaits Ukraine, whether protracted war or peace negotiations, the government must be regarded as fully legitimate and must be trusted by its constituencies and the military to cope with upcoming challenges.

---

431 Stern, D. L., Belton, C., Hudson, J. (2023). Western Officials Press Ukraine to Hold Elections. *The Washington Post*, September 24, https://www.washingtonpost.com/world/2023/09/24/ukraine-elections-war-russia-west/.

432 Zelensky Showing "Authoritarian Traits", Says Swiss Intelligence Report. *Swissinfo*, July 9, 2023, https://2cm.es/Oe7d; Enten, H. (2023). How Republicans Have Grown More Skeptical of Zelensky and Ukraine. *CNN*, September 21, https://2cm.es/LT2z.

Under such circumstances, Volodymyr Zelensky and his closest associates must resolve the dilemma: to hold elections or not to hold elections. Each choice has pros and cons.

Reasons to defer elections. Russia's war of attrition goes on and demands all the government's attention and all the nation's resources. There are also many constitutional, legal, and political reasons for not holding elections.[433] To organize meaningful, free, and fair elections, Kyiv would need to lift the many political restrictions that were put in place to create national solidary and a singular national focus on achieving victory. This means that the government would need to revise electoral legislation, create new tools to enable the vast number of displaced citizens to vote, allow a more capacious writ and greater ideological diversity of the media, and restart political competition.

Reasons not to defer elections. On the other hand, without the essential democratic legitimacy conferred by free and fair elections, it may soon be impossible to govern a nation embroiled in a war for freedom. Even more, if elections were organized, they would need to be conducted in a way that citizens — whether serving at the front or working in the rear or living in the occupied territories — fully recognized that the campaign and ballot count were honest.

Ukrainians have a record of revolts provoked by a suspicious electoral process and results. The wartime legal, administrative, socioeconomic, and demographic problems could influence any elections in a big way and so rattle the political order and divert the government's attention from the needs of the front.

Legal-political flexibility as Ukraine's answer to a long war

Despite pressures for — and expert voices against — holding the elections in wartime, Zelensky's team is taking into account Ukraine's recent experience in living under conditions of war. The war in Ukraine started de facto with Russia's first acts of aggression, in

---

[433] Aivazovska, O. (2023). Opinion: Elections and War Are Incompatible. *The Kyiv Independent*, November 1, https://kyivindependent.com/opinion-elections-and-war-are-incompatible/.

2014, and has now spread throughout the country with Russia's full-scale invasion in 2022. However, de jure, the war between Russia and Ukraine has seen three different legal regimes during the past nine years.

First, between April 15, 2014, and April 30, 2018, Ukraine existed in the regime of the Anti-Terrorist Operation (ATO), which was a set of military and legal measures adopted by Ukrainian law enforcement agencies and aimed at countering Russian and pro-Russian armed groups in the war in eastern Ukraine. This regime limited some civil rights in some territories, but it was not martial law.[434] So both presidential and parliamentary elections could be conducted in 2014 in all regions not directly affected by war.

Both presidential and parliamentary elections were internationally recognized as free and fair, despite military actions in some oblasts and the inability of voters to participate in elections in Crimea and some districts of the Donbas.[435] The legal regime flexibly mixed elements of martial law and peacetime politics.

Second, between April 30, 2018, and February 24, 2022, the regime of the Joint Forces Operation was in effect which continued the logic of the ATO in slightly different military and administrative terms. Again, this flexible legal-political regime allowed free and fair presidential and parliamentary elections to be held in 2019, despite the ongoing war in the Donbas and the annexed Crimea.[436] Even though President Petro Poroshenko attempted to impose martial law and postpone the elections of 2019, the Verkhovna Rada resisted his efforts and saved the elections in a form characteristic

---

434 On Temporary Measures for the Period of the Anti-Terrorist Operation. *The VRU Official Website*, June 2, 2023, https://zakon.rada.gov.ua/laws/show/1669-18#Text.
435 Despite Violence and Threats in East, Ukraine Election Characterized by High Turnout and Resolve to Guarantee Fundamental Freedoms, International Observers Say. *OSCE*, May 26, 2014, https://www.osce.org/odihr/elections/119081; Ukraine, Early Parliamentary Elections, 26 October 2014: Final Report. *OSCE*, December 19, 2014, https://www.osce.org/odihr/elections/ukraine/13255.
436 Presidential Election, 31 March and 21 April 2019. *OSCE*, April 2019, https://www.osce.org/odihr/elections/ukraine/407660; Early Parliamentary Elections, 21 July 2019. OSCE, July 2019, https://www.osce.org/odihr/elections/ukraine/422585.

of peacetime.[437] The same legal flexibility allowed Zelensky to use military elements of the legal regime and to start using the Security Council as a core instrument in his fight with the oligarchs in 2020–2021.[438]

The third legal regime started with Russia's full-fledged invasion on February 24, 2022. It was thought that this time, Ukraine's legal-political flexibility would not be up to the task. But again, some legal-political flexibility remained: martial law (*voiennyi stan*) was imposed without declaration of a state of war (*stan viiny*) and war on Russia.

Indeed, de jure, martial law was initiated by Volodymyr Zelensky and approved by the Rada on February 24, 2022.[439] Since then the process has been repeated regularly, with martial law being continued for several months ahead at each approval.[440] This time, the legal order of war was additionally defined by the Law on the Use of the Armed Forces and other military formations to defend the country.[441] Military-civil administrations started governing all regions of Ukraine, and civilian associations, mass media

---

437 Prokip, A. (2018). Ukraine's State of Martial Law: A Surprise, with Political Undertones. *Focus Ukraine*, November 29, 2018, https://2cm.es/Oe7n.
438 Minakov, M. (2023). War, De-Oligarchization, and the Possibility of Anti-Patronal Transformation in Ukraine. In Madlovics, B., Magyar, B. (eds.). *Ukraine's Patronal Democracy and the Russian Invasion: The Russia-Ukraine War, Volume One* Central European University Press, 141–166.
439 Проект Закону про затвердження Указу Президента України "Про введення воєнного стану в Україні" (from Ukrainian: Draft Law on Approval of the Decree of the President of Ukraine "On the Introduction of Martial Law in Ukraine"). *The VRU Official Website*, March 24, 2022, https://itd.rada.gov.ua/billInfo/Bills/Card/39147.
440 Про продовження строку дії воєнного стану в Україні (from Ukrainian: On the extension of martial law in Ukraine). *The VRU Official Website*, August 17, 2023, https://zakon.rada.gov.ua/laws/show/451/2023#Text.
441 Проект Закону про схвалення Указу Президента України "Про використання Збройних Сил України та інших військових формувань" (from Ukrainian: Draft Law on Approval of the Decree of the President of Ukraine "On the Use of the Armed Forces of Ukraine and Other Military Formations"). *The VRU Official Website*, March 3, 2022, https://itd.rada.gov.ua/billInfo/Bills/Card/39151.

outlets, and political parties began functioning under wartime restrictions.442

According to the laws on the legal regime of martial law and on defense, martial law was introduced to avert the threat to the nation and to repel armed aggression in all regions of Ukraine.443 The laws on martial law and on defense provide state authorities, the military command, military administrations, and local self-government bodies with special powers necessary to fight the enemy. Also, as allowed by the constitution's Article 64, certain temporary restrictions on many civil rights and freedoms were imposed. Altogether, the various ramifications of the legal regime of martial law have directly affected domestic political processes.

At the same time, the Ukrainian government did not announce a state of war and did not declare war on Russia. Volodymyr Zelensky submitted to parliament a draft law on the declaration of a state of war, but it was never considered by parliament (and only the web archive has actually preserved some traces of this step).444 Even though a state of war regime is mentioned in the Ukrainian constitution, it has never been defined.

Where does the concept of a "state of war" come from, particularly with reference to Ukraine and its political-legal flexibility? In a nutshell, the concept stems from international agreements such as the Third Hague Convention on the Opening of Hostilities (1907) or the UN General Assembly Resolution 3314 (1974), both of which introduce the concepts of war and aggression (Ukraine is a signatory to both). They define the norm according to which one state may not initiate military action against another state absent a

---

442 Tarasov, S. (2023). The Role of Civil-Military Cooperation in the Protection of Civilians: The Ukraine Experience. *Center for Civilians in Conflict*, October 2023, https://2cm.es/LT2S.
443 Про оборону України (from Ukrainian: Law "On the Defense of Ukraine"). *The VRU Official Website*, April 15, 2023, https://zakon.rada.gov.ua/laws/s'ho w/1932-12#n138; Про правовий режим воєнного стану (from Ukrainian: Law "On the Legal Regime of Martial Law"). *The VRU Official Website*, October 19, 2023, https://zakon.rada.gov.ua/laws/show/389-19#n5.
444 Проект Закону «Про проголошення стану війни» (from Ukrainian: Draft Law on Declaring a State of War). *The VRU Official Website*, February 24, 2022, https://2cm.es/Oe7X.

declaration of war or an ultimatum. They also stipulate that the use of armed force by one state is sufficient evidence of an act of aggression against another state.

By not announcing war on Russia and not introducing a state of war, the Ukrainian government has some flexibility, for example, in continuing to transit Russian gas to the EU.[445] So, even after announcing martial law, the government of Ukraine has preserved some element of legal-political flexibility by not declaring war on Russia.

All three legal-political regimes have allowed and prepared Ukrainians to adapt their political and legal systems, as well as their communal life and economy, to the conditions of a temporally protracted and spatially enlarging war. This adaptability has immersed Ukrainian institutions in a state of legal, political, security, and even military affairs that has proved rather flexible in merging de jure and de facto situations.

For example, it has allowed the nation to survive when some of its territory was occupied by Russia or Russia-backed separatists—yet there are front-line areas with vast Ukrainian military operations. There are also the rear regions where, prior to the current state of conflict, Ukrainians continued to live and work. And before 2022, but during wartime, they enjoyed competitive elections, the division of power, functional courts, and active participation in international relations. This flexibility, whose roots survived even after 2022, may be used by the ruling group to organize yet another wartime election. And Western allies know it well.

Does the current legal regime allow elections in Ukraine?

Usually, elections are not conducted in countries at war. However, if the war is protracted, elections might be needed to reestablish the domestic and international legitimacy of the government. The Ukrainian constitution and its laws do not provide a clear answer

---

445 Russian Gas Transit through Ukraine. *Center on Global Energy Policy*, October 3, 2023, https://www.energypolicy.columbia.edu/qa-russian-gas-transit-through-ukraine/.

to this question, and this ambiguity is one of the sources of wartime Ukraine's legal-political flexibility.

Indeed, the constitution's Article 83 states that if the term of service of the Verkhovna Rada expires when the country is under martial law, its authority is extended until a new parliament is elected. This and other constitutional provisions cannot be changed while martial law is in effect (Article 157). However, the constitution does not prohibit either presidential or local elections from being held.

The restrictions on presidential and local elections are provided for in the Law on Martial Law and the Electoral Code's Articles 20 and 280.[446] These stipulations, however, can be changed by parliament and approved by the president, if there is political will to do so. Thus, if the Ukrainian political class agrees, presidential elections can be conducted under martial law next year.

Even more, if the president and the Rada agree, they could stop continuing the regime of martial law, despite ongoing military actions on the soil of Ukraine. That way even parliamentary elections could be legally held. However, in such a case the legality and the legitimacy of the decisions would openly contradict each other.

In sum, the existing legal-political flexibility indeed provides an opportunity for elections. But it neither resolves the question of the essential democratic legitimacy of elections held during a de facto war nor decreases the risk of desolidarization of society during competitive elections.

Security risks around wartime elections

Despite all the legal workarounds and some benefits that flexibility can bring, elections pose an existential risk for a nation at war. Ukraine has nonetheless held elections in the face of this risk after 2014, but with the current war of vastly greater scale than earlier

---

446 Про правовий режим воєнного стану (from Ukrainian: On the Legal Regime of the State of War). *The VRU Official Website*, October 19, 2023, https://zakon.rada.gov.ua/laws/show/389-19#Text; Electoral Code of Ukraine (official translation in English). *The VRU Official Website*, July 16, 2020, https://cvk.gov.ua/wp-content/uploads/2020/09/Election-Code-of-Ukraine.pdf.

stages of the conflict and having an incalculably greater influence on Ukrainian society, economy, and political institutions, the former success may not be repeatable. If elections are attempted in 2024, they may lead to disaster for Ukraine.

Ukrainian experts who publicly oppose the decision to hold elections in 2024 typically adduce two arguments. The first is that the constitution and laws prohibit elections when the country is under martial law. This argument has its weak side: there are ways to get around such prohibitions, as discussed above.

The second argument is stronger: the sociopolitical order will face overwhelming challenges to its stability if elections are conducted during wartime. The reasoning here usually refers to the unjustifiably high costs of elections and the fact that they would undermine national unity during war. Wartime elections would indeed drag a hugely sensitized society into debates that might still be constrained by the needs of war and into voting that might not be well attended by so many displaced citizens, reducing representation.

Here is the major contradiction that makes wartime elections so potentially destructive. If the aim is to uphold and reinforce by democratic means the legitimacy of the government, elections must be free, honest, based on open debate and competition, and accessible to all voters. If some element on this list is missing, the aim of elections will not be achieved. Also, if some element on this list is missing, the sensitized Ukrainian society, which already trusts military institutions more than it trusts civilian, democratic ones, might protest *en masse*. The picture is even more contradictory: if resources are so scarce as to hamper the country's defense efforts, and if international support is slowing, then diverting resources away from defense and toward some other purpose is counterproductive.

Indeed, allocating human, administrative, and financial resources to elections during a war of attrition is an unjustifiable luxury. Over 47 percent of the Ukrainian budget for 2024 is planned to come from external sources.⁴⁴⁷ And these sources, as the current debates in the US Congress demonstrate, may not be as generous as in 2022–2023.

Every public and economic sector in Ukraine reports a growing deficit in human resources.⁴⁴⁸ Well over six million Ukrainians have left the country, and many of them—over a million, at a minimum—live on the territory of the aggressor state.⁴⁴⁹ Over three million Ukrainians are fighting to survive in internal displacement. Another four million Ukrainians live in Russia-occupied Ukrainian territory.⁴⁵⁰ Under such conditions, it would be close to impossible to organize an inclusive and accessible voting apparatus. And that would put in doubt the legitimacy of any government elected under such conditions.

The question of legitimacy gains another wrinkle when citizens' fading trust in the government and democratic institutions is considered. After almost two years of life under martial law, Ukrainian society shows signs of stable trust in security institutions and declining trust in public organizations. Even though polls conducted under conditions of war have, as expected, a large margin of error, the results still deserve attention for the social dynamics and the relative ratios they reveal.

For example, according to a recent poll by the Razumkov Center, a nongovernmental think tank, the most trusted state bodies include military or war-related institutions and organizations: the armed forces (93 percent of respondents trust them), volunteer organizations (that support the army, 84 percent), the National Guard (81 percent), the State Border Service (76.5 percent), the president

---

447 Ukraine Releases 2024 Budget Plan, More Spending on Military, but Raising Enough Funding Will Be Tough. *Intellinews*, September 28, 2023, https://2cm.es/Oe8b.
448 Karakuts, A., Schedrin, Y., Davymuka, O. (2023). Future of Ukraine Workforce. *Center for Applied Research*, May 2023, https://cpd.com.ua/future-of-ukraine-workforce.pdf.
449 Ibid.; Report on Ukraine Refugees. *UNHCR*, n.d., https://data.unhcr.org/en/situations/ukraine.
450 Libanova, E. (2023). Ukraine's Demography in the Second Year of the Full-Fledged War. *Focus Ukraine*, June 27, 2023, https://www.wilsoncenter.org/blog-post/ukraines-demography-second-year-full-fledged-war.

(who is commander in chief, 72 percent), the Ministry of Defense (71 percent), and the Security Service (66 percent).[451] But trust in democracy-related institutions is falling. The majority of respondents expressed distrust in political parties (74 percent), public officials (72 percent), the courts (70 percent), parliament (64 percent), the National Anti-Corruption Bureau (53 percent), and the National Agency for the Prevention of Corruption (52 percent).

Despite being dissatisfied with the civil part of government, the population remaining within Ukraine's borders is opposed to the prospect of elections in 2024. According to the same Razumkov Center poll, only 15 percent of respondents support holding national elections before the end of the war, with almost two-thirds (64 percent) rejecting such a proposal and 21 percent of respondents undecided. Election supporters argue that elections are necessary to support democracy in the country (6 percent) and to show the world that Ukraine is a democratic state (5 percent); another 5 percent see the need to change the government or at least to renew President Zelensky's mandate (5 percent). Election opponents argue that elections are too expensive for the current state budget (36 percent), that the legislation does not allow them (32 percent), that voting would be insecure (31 percent), and that, under martial law, it is impossible to observe democratic standards (29 percent).

These data are supported by many other polls (such as ones conducted by KIIS and the IRI/SGR).[452] Altogether they show that Ukraine's wartime society has greater trust in the army than in civil authorities and values elections only if they are conducted as a genuine democratic process. More generally, even if a political system were to develop some adaptive legal-political flexibility, war is not conducive to democracy-reinforcing elections.

---

451 Citizens' Assessment of the Situation in the Country. *Razumkov Center*, October 15, 2023, https://2cm.es/LT3A.
452 National Survey of Ukraine: October 2023. *IRI/SGR*, October 27, 2023, https://2cm.es/LT3J; When Elections Should Be Held, Attitudes Towards Online Voting and Possible Restrictions on Citizens Rights. *KIIS*, October 30, 2023, https://www.kiis.com.ua/?lang=eng&cat=reports&id=1309&page=1.

Let's wait on elections and focus on core issues

I want to stress that the vox populi as represented, with all caveats, in the above polls and in experts' analysis is aligned, for one good reason: under current military conditions in Ukraine, it would be hugely risky to conduct elections. All available resources must be poured into defense and achieving victory. Elections would most likely not respond to the legitimate expectations of citizens and would not comply with OSCE standards. Even if the wartime restrictions on the political rights and freedoms of citizens and on the operations of the mass media were canceled, it would arguably take another year to return to the pre-2022 mode of operations. Public debate has long been absent, and Ukrainian society is fragmented, with new cleavages. It will take time for political parties to address both issues and restart meaningful competition for the voters' sympathies in Ukraine.

Without such careful preparation of society, elections would be a senseless formality that would only intensify the population's dissatisfaction with the government and negative reactions to those Western nations pushing for elections to be held. Even if some European politicians might not insist on the proper democratic quality to any election, the Ukrainian citizenry would be quite unlikely to tolerate electoral incongruencies.[453] And Zelensky needs real, essential democratic legitimacy in 2024.

I believe that the Zelensky administration should resist all pressures and postpone elections. Instead, it should address legitimate dissatisfaction with the public administration and the lack of access to trusted mass media, and focus on the major security needs of Ukraine.

---

453 Sdorenko, S., Kox, T. (2023). Nobody Will Blame Ukraine If Post-War Elections Are Not Perfect. Interview with PACE President. *Ukrainska Pravda*, May 16, 2023, https://www.eurointegration.com.ua/eng/interview/2023/05/16/7161793/.

Ukrainian society on the anniversary of twin tragedies

February 2024[454]

The last week of February 2024 marks the anniversary of two tragedies for Ukrainian society: the start of Russia's occupation of Crimea, in 2014, and the launch of Russia's large-scale invasion of Ukraine, in 2022.

Ten years ago, in 2014, this terrible week included the massacre on the Maidan, the flight of disgraced President Yanukovych to Russia, the appointment of an interim president and government, Russia's takeover of Crimea, and the start of the Russia-backed secessionist/irridentist movements in southeastern Ukraine.

Two years ago, this was the first week of the Russian full-scale invasion, marked by the bombing of cities and the precipitous departure of the first wave of refugees to Ukraine's western regions and Europe. This week two years ago also saw the start of Ukraine's ongoing resistance.

Both events—despite being separated by eight years—were part of a single historical process that has had a critical impact on the lives and security of the Ukrainian people. How are things with Ukrainians after ten years of Russia's growing aggression? How do they see the current situation, and their own and the country's future?

The sociopolitical context

In 2022, with the start of the Russian invasion, Ukrainian leadership and society entered into a specific state of public consciousness characterized by rallying around the flag, firm solidarity on the imperative of national resistance, and an outspoken faith in victory over the aggressor. Despite the existential threat, over 75 percent of

---

[454] A shorter version of this column has previously been published as: Minakov, M. (2024). Ukrainian Society on the Anniversary of Twin Tragedies. Focus Ukraine, February 23, https://www.wilsoncenter.org/blog-post/ukrainian-society-anniversary-twin-tragedies.

the population expressed optimism about the state of affairs in Ukraine and the country's future—an unusually high figure for Ukrainians (and for Eastern Europeans at large).

But with the passage of time, and as a result of military, demographic, and political challenges, society—and its opinion—began reverting to a more rational, sober state.

As happens in many societies at war, part of Ukraine's population looked for a safer life abroad. According to most recent data, over six million refugees are currently in Europe, between 1.2 million and five million Ukrainians are in Russia (many of whom were deported unwillingly or are being kept in Russia by force), and more than 400,000 Ukrainians have migrated to Canada and the United States. As well, more than 3.5 million Ukrainians have moved from dangerous areas to resettle in safer regions in central and western Ukraine.[455]

These migrations have radically changed the social structure and human geography of Ukraine. About a quarter of Ukraine's former population has left the country, and an additional 10 percent have changed their place of residence within the country. Formerly large urban centers from Kharkiv to Odesa in southeastern Ukraine are now depopulated. The regions close to the front line are inhabited by elderly people who do not want to leave their homes and by military staff. Cities and towns in the central and western regions have gained some younger people. Also, Kyiv has witnessed waves of leaving and returning citizens. Today, Ukrainian society has fewer people, skews much older than before, and has adapted to life in a state of constant war and destruction.

Ukraine's political class is adapting to the war as well. The sociopolitical role of military and security leaders and institutions has grown, as has trust in them. The conflict between President Zelensky and General Zaluzhny, as well as recent changes in the army's leadership, exemplify two major political trends wrought by the

---

455 Ukrainian Refugee Crisis: The Current Situation. *ReliefWeb*, January 25, 2024, https://reliefweb.int/report/ukraine/ukrainian-refugee-crisis-current-situation-encs; Registered IDP Area Baseline Assessment: Ukraine - Round 32 (January 2024). *ReliefWeb*, February 15, 2024, https://2cm.es/Oe8G.

ongoing war.[456] First, the politicians and the generals have started competing with each other for the public's trust, which can potentially evolve into a political struggle. Second, the civil government controls the generals. However, a Zaluzhny faction is taking shape in parliament—at least as far as can be discerned from voting patterns—and in wider society, suggesting leadership of the ex-commander.[457]

Behind the fractious relations between Zelensky's team and supporters of Zaluzhny, there is a deeper societal cleavage. As the public controversies over the draft law on mobilization demonstrate, Ukrainians are currently divided between those families whose members are in the army for two years with an unclear prospect of returning home and those families that don't want to send their sons and brothers to fight.[458] These two large factions are united in wanting victory over Russia but divided in their willingness to invest blood in achieving that victory.

Public opinion of Ukraine's development and leadership

In advance of the twin anniversaries, several polling organizations, including the Sociological Group "Rating" (SGR), the Kyiv International Institute of Sociology (KIIS), and the Razumkov Center, have published the results of surveys regarding what Ukrainians think about the current state of affairs in the country, the war, and the nation's leadership.

Probably the most important result is what can be called the sobering of Ukrainian society. Both KIIS and SGR polls

---

[456] The Feud between Ukraine's President and Army Chief Boils Over. *The Economist*, January 30, 2024, http://tiny.cc/xcanzz; Starting Today, a New Management Team Takes over the Leadership of the Armed Forces of Ukraine – Address by President Volodymyr Zelenskyy. *The President of Ukraine Official Website*, February 8, 2024, https://2cm.es/LT4c.

[457] Політичний потенціал Залужного (from Ukrainian: Political Potential of Zaluzhny). *Zaxidnet*, February 8, 2024, https://zaxid.net/statti_tag50974/.

[458] Short on Soldiers, Ukraine Debates How to Find the Next Wave of Troops. *The New York Times*, February 11, 2024, https://www.nytimes.com/2024/02/11/world/europe/ukraine-soldier-draft.html.

demonstrate that pessimistic assessments of Ukraine's development prevail again over the optimism of the first years of the war.[459] Ukrainians' inherent pessimism was challenged ten years ago by the Euromaidan, the annexation of Crimea, and the start of the Donbas war, all leading to a coalescing of a strong sense of nationhood and a desire to create and own the nation's future. The optimistic sentiment increased with the electoral victory of Zelensky in 2019 and prospects of peace and nonoligarchic development. And for the next two years, levels of optimism remained high, between 67 and 73 percent.

The war of attrition has exhausted the populace's optimism but not the will to victory, as the same polls show. The proportion of citizens who are absolutely confident that Ukraine will be able to win a war with Russia is 42 percent, and another 43 percent are rather sure. The proportion with greatest confidence is smaller than in October 2022 (74 percent and 22 percent, respectively), but it also demonstrates that even a "soberer" society does not experience a decrement in the will to resist. A rational explanation for this new state of public opinion emerges from the widespread understanding that Ukraine's victory is possible only if the West continues its support, an idea supported by 79 percent of respondents.

The public trust in the military and security leadership grows. According to the same KIIS poll, the most trustworthy leader in Ukraine is Valeriy Zaluzhny, whose trust level stands at 94 percent (5 percent distrust) and has only grown in the recent three months. Public trust has also increased in Kyrylo Budanov (chief of Defense Intelligence, 66 percent trust versus 19 percent distrust) and Oleksandr Syrsky (since February 8 the new commander in chief of the Armed Forces of Ukraine, 40 percent versus 35 percent). Political leaders are also among the most trusted persons, but their trust level has declined: Volodymyr Zelensky enjoys the trust of 60

---

[459] Direction of Affairs in the Country and Trust in Political, Military and Public Figures. *KIIS*, February 15, 2024, https://www.kiis.com.ua/?lang=eng&cat=reports&id=1368&page=1; Рейтинг Моніторинг, 26-та хвиля: Суспільно-політичні настрої населення (10–11 лютого 2024) (from Ukrainian: Rating Monitoring, 26th wave: Socio-Political Attitudes of the Ukrainian Population). *SGR*, February 10–11, 2024, https://2cm.es/LT4i.

percent of respondents (with a 40 percent level of distrust; a thirteen percentage point drop in his trust rating in three months) and Serhiy Prytula is trusted by 61 percent (with 33 percent distrusting; an eight percentage point drop in trust rating in three months). As KIIS data show, the dispute between the president and Zaluzhny, and the dismissal of the popular commander without open explanation to the people, have cost Volodymyr Zelensky some public support as well as some bitterness among army personnel.

Despite changes in the ratings of individual leaders, public support for government remains high. As the Razumkov Center's survey reveals, the Ukrainian government's performance receives high ratings on restoring energy facilities to working condition after missile strikes (78.5 percent of respondents gave high marks for this), ensuring the proper functioning of communal utilities, transport, and availability of food supplies despite the war (78 percent), cooperating with Western partners (68 percent), helping refugees (63 percent), and ensuring the nation's defense capability (62 percent).[460] Mid-range marks are given to the government on fighting crime (45 percent) and helping vulnerable groups (44.5 percent). Ukrainians are dissatisfied with the government for being unable to sustain social justice (especially with respect to the draft regulations; 51 percent), a functional economy (46 percent), and restoration of the housing stock (40 percent).

Support and trust levels for different governmental institutions vary. Among the most trusted are the military and security organizations (from 68 to 95 percent), the institution of the presidency (64 percent), the police service (58 percent), and Ukraine's National Bank (53 percent). But the public does not trust public officials (75 percent distrust), political parties (72 percent), the parliament (70 percent), the courts (68 percent), the cabinet (64 percent), and the anti-corruption organizations (51–52 percent).

---

460 Citizens' Assessment of the Situation in the Country and the Actions of the Authorities. Trust in Social Institutions, Politicians, Officials and Public Figures (January 2024) (in Ukrainian). *Razumkov Center*, February 7, 2024, https://ukraine-elections.com.ua/en/socopros/opinion_poll_show/2150.

Ten years of conflict with Russia have strongly affected Ukrainians. But despite all the shocks, challenges, and ills, Ukrainian society remains rational and keeps a critical eye on its leaders and its future. It sees problems, their causes, and possible solutions. And despite these tragic anniversaries, Ukrainians are still able to envision a bright future for themselves: today, 73 percent believe that in ten years' time, Ukraine will be a peaceful and prosperous country once again.[461]

The Ukrainian military assistance is finally approved by the US Congress

April 2024[462]

The mood in Ukraine before the US House of Representatives approved the Ukraine Security Supplemental Appropriations Act on April 20 had become increasingly somber. President Zelensky pinpointed the underlying problem when he said that without American support, the Ukrainian Armed Forces (UAF) could not win the war and would be forced to retreat, while Ukraine itself might not survive as a sovereign nation. The delay in US support for Ukraine did not change Ukrainians' belief in victory but did add a certain fatalism to this conviction.[463] Now that the debates in Washington on providing aid to Ukraine are mostly over, the situation on the ground in Ukraine should change for the better.

---

461 How do Ukrainians See the Future of Ukraine in 10 Years. *KIIS*, December 29, 2023, https://www.kiis.com.ua/?lang=eng&cat=reports&id=1348&page=1.
462 A shorter version of this column has previously been published as: Minakov, M. (2024). The Ukrainian Military Assistance Act Will Change the Situation on the Ground in Ukraine for the Better. *Focus Ukraine*, April 22, https://www.wilsoncenter.org/blog-post/ukrainian-military-assistance-act-will-change-situation-n-ground-ukraine-better.
463 IRI Ukraine Poll: Strong Majorities Believe in Victory over Russia, Support European Union and NATO Membership. *IRI*, April 4, 2024, https://www.iri.org/news/iri-ukraine-poll-strong-majorities-believe-in-victory-over-russia/.

The West's debates on supporting Ukraine

The US Congress started debating the provision of military and financial assistance in September 2023. That month, President Zelensky visited Congress with a message on the importance of American aid to UAF success in defending against Russian attacks. With Hamas's October 7 attack on Israel and the start of the Gaza war, military assistance packages for Ukraine and for Israel were tied together in a single bill. That bill was later expanded to include aid for Taiwan and proposed changes to immigration policy on the US-Mexico border. By January 2024, crafting an assistance bill that would satisfy both parties in Congress and many factions in D.C. looked nigh impossible.

With the ongoing debates in Washington seemingly yielding no solution and with Ukraine's defense in jeopardy, the EU member states approved a $54 billion aid package in February 2024. In March the EU added an additional $5 billion in military assistance for Ukraine.

Ukrainian aid in early 2024

In total, from January to early April 2024, Ukraine received financial aid in the form of both grants and loans in excess of US $13 billion. That sum included loans from the EU ($4.9 billion), Canada ($1.5 billion), and Japan ($1.1 billion), and an $880 million IMF loan tranche.[464] In the winter of 2023–2024 and the spring of 2024, Berlin considerably increased its military support for Ukraine, becoming Kyiv's second-largest defense partner. Japan, Norway, and the UK are also among Ukraine's biggest supporters.[465] Although these many packages of support have allowed Ukraine to stand strong in the war over the past six months, they could not fully substitute for the delayed US military and financial aid.

---

464 Samoiliuk, M. (2024). Ukraine War Economy Tracker. *Center for Economic Strategy*, September 13, https://ces.org.ua/en/tracker-economy-during-the-war/.
465 The Arms and Military Equipment Germany Is Sending to Ukraine. *The Federal Government of Germany Website*, September 19, 2024, https://n9.cl/vzs7bg.

Last week, the factions in the US Congress finally hit on a compromise: military and financial assistance to Ukraine is to be provided in the form of a "forgivable loan." President Zelensky has agreed to such a compromise solution. The ever-increasing hits on Ukraine's energy sector and critical infrastructure in the recent past have meant that further delays in US military support could not be tolerated.

Details of the Ukraine Security Supplemental Appropriations Act

The approved bill allocates funds from the US federal budget for fiscal year 2024 in the form of "supplemental appropriations for federal departments and agencies to respond to the conflict in Ukraine." According to the official document, the act provides resources for supporting US military operations in Europe, funding the Ukraine Security Assistance Initiative, and funding the Foreign Military Financing Program. It also covers "replacing defense articles that were provided to Ukraine" in recent months and reimburses the Department of Defense "for defense services and training provided to Ukraine." The act also provides a certain amount of economic support for the Ukrainian state budget.

The funding under this act includes:

> Over $23 billion for replenishing US weapons, stocks and facilities;
> Over $11 billion for US training of UAF servicemen and women;
> Almost $14 billion for the purchase of advanced weapons systems for Ukraine; and
> $9 billion in repayable economic assistance (which cannot be used for social payments in Ukraine).

After the Senate approves the bill and President Biden signs it, this act will add over $60 billion in funding to the previous $75 billion in US commitments.[466] The total US investment in Ukraine's defense and economic survival will then exceed $130 billion.

---

466 Masters, J., Merrow, W. (2024). How Much US Aid Is Going to Ukraine? *Council on Foreign Relations*, May 9, 2024, https://www.cfr.org/article/how-much-us-aid-going-ukraine.

The approved bill has some specific requirements. For example, it requires the US president to transfer long-range Army Tactical Missile Systems (ATACMS) to the UAF. And it expects other partners of Ukraine—from the EU, NATO, or the G7 countries—to match some of the US funding. It requests the US administration to develop and impose better "oversight and reporting requirements for assistance provided to Ukraine." Finally, the bill requires the US government to ensure that Ukraine repays the funds provided by the United States under this act.

The Act improves Ukraine's security and sociopolitical situation

As the United States resumes its robust support of Ukraine's defense of that country's existence, independence, and freedom, the situation on the ground will definitely improve. The Pentagon has already prepared a new military aid package for the UAF.[467] With an enhanced arsenal, Ukraine will be able to increase its defensive military operations on the front line and attempt to reverse the Russian Armed Forces' steady progress in the Donbas.

Most important, the US aid package shores up the ability of the Ukrainian leadership to plan its defense operations and economic steps for the next ten to twelve months. The strengthened US-Ukraine partnership is a critically important factor in bettering the security and sociopolitical situation of this country at war.

Five years of Zelensky's presidency

May 2024[468]

May 20, 2024, marked the end of President Volodymyr Zelensky's fifth year in office. Until the next election, which, deferred for now, may occur once martial law is lifted or new special electoral acts are

---

[467] Horton, A. (2024). Ukraine Weapons Package "Ready to Go" Once Aid Bill Clears Congress. *The Washington Post*, April 19, https://2cm.es/LT4Y.
[468] A shorter version of this column has previously been published as: Minakov, M. (2024). Five Years of Zelensky's Presidency. *Focus Ukraine*, May 21, https://www.wilsoncenter.org/blog-post/five-years-zelenskys-presidency.

approved, Zelensky will continue to serve as Ukraine's president. This anniversary of his inauguration offers an opportune moment to step back and consider the path he, his team, and all of Ukraine have traveled together so far.

Ukraine's post-Soviet history was full of both glorious and tragic events. But even against this rich background, Zelensky's term in office stands out. It started with an unusual electoral unity of Ukrainians around the young leader and his come-out-of-nowhere party, which promised to end the war, the oligarchs' rule, and poverty.[469] It continued under growing pressures from outside, mainly from Russia and separatists, and inside, especially from a multitude of opposition factions and pandemic-related social issues. The thirtieth anniversary of Ukraine's independence was celebrated on his watch. And after Russia's large-scale invasion of Ukraine, this presidency turned into a wartime leadership that started with a bang, with the unifying and unprecedented "Zelensky effect," leavened only by some recent disenchantment with him.[470]

During his enormously difficult five-year term, Volodymyr Zelensky reinvented himself and his program several times. What can be said about his presidency's achievement so far, and how might his legacy be seen in future?

Have Zelensky's electoral promises been fulfilled by 2024?

Candidate Zelensky made three major promises to voters, who gave him 73 percent of the vote in the 2019 presidential elections. In those days, as I described in the beginning of this book,

---

[469] Hosa, J., Wilson, A. (2019). Zelensky Unchained: What Ukraine's New Political Order Means for Its Future. *ECFR*, September 25, 2019, https://2cm.es/LT55; Chaisty, P., & Whitefield, S. (2022). How Challenger Parties Can Win Big With Frozen Cleavages: Explaining the Landslide Victory of the Servant of the People Party in the 2019 Ukrainian Parliamentary Elections. *Party Politics*, 28(1), 115-126.

[470] Yurcaba, N. (2023). More than Just a Joke: A Review of Olga Onuch & Henry E. Hale's The Zelensky Effect. *The New Eastern Europe*, November 3, 2023, https://2cm.es/Oe9S; d'Istria, T. (2024). Ukrainian Opposition Is Increasingly Critical of the Zelensky Administration. *Le Monde*, March 19, https://2cm.es/LT5b.

Zelensky's voters expected him to achieve peace with Russia in the Donbas, put in place good governance after the disappointing presidency of his predecessor, Petro Poroshenko, and improve the wellbeing of ordinary Ukrainian families.

The first expectation was not fulfilled. Initially President Zelensky managed to achieve a cease-fire in the Donbas. But the Minsk Process did not advance after the Paris Summit in December 2019. And on February 24, 2022, the Russian Federation invaded Ukraine, turning the military conflict in the Donbas into a full-fledged war. The current peace plan Zelensky has proposed envisages a cessation of hostilities and the withdrawal of Russian troops from all Ukrainian territories. Today, however, despite broad international support, the plan seems to be far from realization.

The path to installing the good governance Ukraine wanted would entail a decrease in oligarchic control and the end of corruption in the public sector. It is safe to say that the political influence of the established oligarchs on Ukrainian politics is minimal these days. However, this reduced influence has not yet translated into stable good governance practices or an effective anti-corruption system. Despite all efforts of the government and the wartime need for resources to be concentrated on national defense, corruption still undermines public sector efficacy.[471]

When Volodymyr Zelensky entered office, the Ukrainian GDP per capita, when adjusted by purchasing power parity (GDP PPP), was recorded at approximately $12,800.[472] Despite the pandemic's negative influence on economic development, in 2021 the GDP PPP had almost returned to the pre-Euromaidan level of $13,000. With the ongoing war against Ukraine, this index fell below $11,000 (projected) in 2023 — which is nonetheless an extraordinary achievement when compared with the GD PPP of other countries in the second year of a war of attrition.

---

471 Karatnycky, A. (2024). How Deep Does Corruption Run in Ukraine? *Foreign Policy*, March 6, https://foreignpolicy.com/2024/03/06/ukraine-corruption-reforms-russia-war/.
472 See data at: World Bank's Trading Economics on Ukraine, n.d., https://tradingeconomics.com/ukraine/gdp-per-capita-ppp.

Graph 1. Ukraine's GDP per capita PPP (real and projected, 2012-2023)[473]

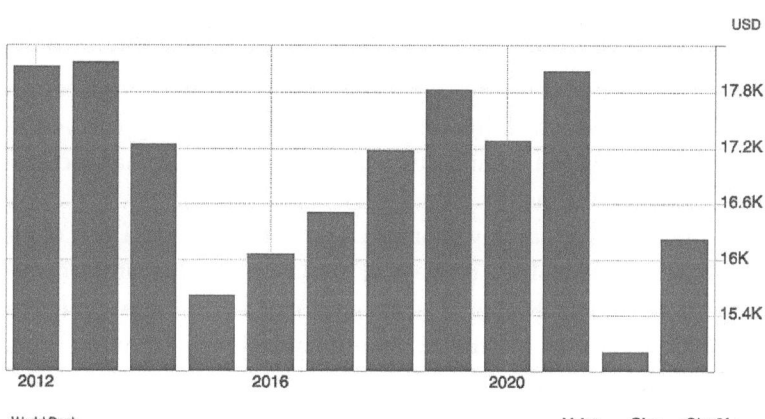

In sum, Zelensky was not able to deliver fully on his campaign promises, given the unexpected curves of history since 2019. However, there is evidence that he has adhered to his electoral program.

The bigger picture

Another way to evaluate Zelensky's presidency is to look at how his achievements fit into a bigger picture of Ukraine's historical path.

Zelensky is the sixth Ukrainian president since independence — and the fifth president to have to deal with Russia's Putin. Their first and final personal encounter in Paris in December 2019 started a long duel. After an attempt to find a solution to the Donbas and Crimea issues, their relations turned into open hostility in 2020-2021. In 2022, Zelensky stood up to the challenge of Putin's full-scale invasion, comparing himself to David fighting Goliath. Since then, and right up to Putin's recent remarks challenging Zelensky's legitimacy, this personal combat between two heads of state has raised the stakes almost on a daily basis.[474]

---

473 Ibid.
474 Putin Queries Political Legitimacy of Ukrainian President Zelenskiy in Absence of Elections. *Reuters*, May 17, 2024, https://2cm.es/LT5q.

From a Hegelian perspective, however, these two leaders represent a more general struggle of principles in Eastern Europe and northern Eurasia: a free republic versus tyranny. This philosophical framework is hugely important for all European and Eurasian nations' free future. And this construal of current events places an equally huge responsibility on President Zelensky to preserve liberties and rights in Ukraine during the war, a task he has increasingly much problems.

Once the Russian invasion of Ukraine turned into a war of attrition, it ceased to be a battle that could be couched in terms of armies and leaders. Rather, it is an existential conflict, the end result of which depends on the economy and demography of both Ukraine and Russia.

With respect to the economy, Ukraine is in dire straits. Its GDP was worth almost $200 billion in 2021. In 2022, it fell to $160.50 billion; for 2023, World Bank experts expect it to rise to only $163.71 billion. Simultaneously the Russian economy, after some drop in 2022 as the Western sanctions took effect, continued to grow: Russia's GDP for 2023 is projected to be $2.250 billion.[475] Even though IMF experts anticipate hardships and very problematic growth for Russia's economy in the near future, the Kremlin's ability to resist (and circumvent) sanctions and to use ramped-up military production to buttress the economy is worrisome. Ukraine's and Russia's GDP growth is one of the key dimensions of the ongoing war.

The "generals" leading the Ukrainian and Russian economies are among the key figures in this war, just as the economic alliances both sides nurture have become critically important to the outcome of the war. So far, Zelensky's administration has not achieved a military alliance with Western states but has managed to bring Western economies into Ukraine's industrial rear. Furthermore, the Ukrainian government tries to use Western support to develop its own military-industrial capacity.[476] Despite many opposing

---

[475] See data at: World Bank's Trading Economics on Russia, n.d., https://tradingeconomics.com/russia/gdp.
[476] Barigazzi, J. (2024). Ukraine Wants to Use EU Money to Grow Its Military-Industrial Complex. *Politico*, May 6, https://2cm.es/Oead.

currents, Zelensky is attempting to prepare the Ukrainian economy for long-term resilience.

Finally, this war is the dramatic fight of two, unequal in size peoples. Ukraine, whose current population is probably four to five times smaller than Russia's, needs an extremely carefully thought-out and smart demographic policy.

The government uses every means at its disposal to engage the male population in the ranks of the active-duty army. For this reason, despite the political risks involved, President Zelensky signed a controversial act on mobilization.[477] The decision to overstretch the "demographic forces" of Ukraine shows the president's dedication to winning this war, and to risk not only his political future but also the fate of the national population.

Ukrainian history and the history of the broader Eastern European region did not stop on May 20, 2024. Volodymyr Zelensky is one of those who personally participate in weaving its fabric. And in time, there will be a moment when his legacy can be assessed clear-sightedly and with greater understanding of how decisions and events played out.

Ukrainian politics reacts to the US electoral drama

July 2024[478]

On the surface, Ukrainian politics has mainly been on hold since February 2022. With President Zelensky's declaration of martial law on February 24, 2022, many constitutional freedoms were limited, the mass media came under strong government control, and political competition was rather restricted. National unity and solidarity of the power elites were the answer to the existential threat posed by the Russian invasion of Ukraine.

---

477 Ukraine's Controversial New Mobilisation Law Takes Effect. *Euronews*, May 19, 2024, https://2cm.es/LT5A.
478 A shorter version of this column has previously been published as: Minakov, M. (2024). Winds of Change: Ukrainian Politics Reacts to the US Electoral Drama. Focus Ukraine, July 23, https://www.wilsoncenter.org/blog-post/winds-of-change-ukrainian-politics-reacts-us-electoral-drama.

Beneath the surface, as I wrote above, various political factions have still continued to compete for some influence over society's sympathies, state budget spending, and projects connected to the nation's future. Out of reach for these factions were international politics and relations with the West. This domain was Volodymyr Zelensky's. A telling example of the enforcement of such a monopoly is the repeated ban on trips abroad for Petro Poroshenko. He and his supporters were prohibited from attending important meetings in the United States and the EU in 2022, 2023, and 2024. In the sixth year of Zelensky's presidency, international recognition and Western support are critically important to the stability of both the presidency and the presidential administration.

The current political turmoil in the United States creates new challenges for President Zelensky and new opportunities for the opposition. Ukrainian politicians of all camps have attentively observed the cautious language on Ukraine in the NATO summit declaration, the assassination attempt on Donald Trump, and the subsequent uptick in the likelihood of his winning the November election; with the same degree of attention they now watch the Democrats' debates over their new candidate after President Biden decided to withdraw from the race. These events have provoked multiple reactions and point to changes in Ukrainian politics in the upcoming months.

President Zelensky's team's reactions

President Zelensky returned from the Washington NATO summit with the understanding that Western leaders are preparing for a change in the White House and in the policies related to support for Ukraine. The turmoil in US politics is the likely cause of a change in Zelensky's plan to end the war. For the first time in two years, he has hinted at the possibility of a negotiated end to the war.[479]

Zelensky has also made an uneasy attempt to restart communication with former US president Donald Trump. Back in 2019,

---

[479] Kottasová, I. (2024). Facing Difficult Frontline Rreality and the Prospect of Trump in the White House, Zelensky Hints at Negotiations with Russia. *CNN*, July 20, https://2cm.es/Oegn.

both politicians had many disagreements.[480] On July 19, 2024, Zelensky's team initiated a phone call with the GOP candidate. Zelensky's team reported that in this conversation, the Ukrainian president congratulated Trump "on his nomination as the candidate of the Republican Party," "condemned the attempted assassination," and "emphasized the decisive role of bipartisan and bicameral support in the US Congress for the protection of our country from the Russian invasion."[481] For his part, Trump described it as "a very good phone call."[482] Later, however, Zelensky admitted it would be "hard work" to deal with Trump in the future.

Relations between the teams of President Biden and President Zelensky appear to be good. The proof is in the tone of Zelensky's message regarding Biden's withdrawal from the elections on X:

> Many strong decisions have been made in recent years and they will be remembered as bold steps taken by President Biden in response to challenging times. And we respect today's tough but strong decision.[483]

Kyiv definitely wants to continue a partnership with the White House, independent of who is in the Oval Office.

Since Washington is now increasingly focused on its own political agenda, Kyiv is diversifying its international contacts. President Zelensky's team is apparently looking for dialogue with other, non-Western influential players in international politics. On July 22, 2024, the Chinese foreign minister announced that China had organized a visit of Dmytro Kuleba, Ukraine's foreign minister, to Beijing, a visit few in Ukraine had anticipated. This is Kuleba's first visit to China's capital since the start of the Russian invasion, and

---

480 Sargent, G. (2022). Five Vile Things Trump Did to Zelensky and Ukraine That You Forgot About. *The Washington Post*, March 1, https://www.washingtonpost.com/opinions/2022/03/01/vindman-zelensky-ukraine-putin/.
481 Volodymyr Zelenskyy Had a Phone Conversation with Donald Trump. *The President of Ukraine Official Website*, July 20, 2024, https://2cm.es/Oegu.
482 Holmes, K. (2024). Trump Says He Had 'A Very Good Phone Call' With Zelensky, Discussed Russia-Ukraine War. *CNN*, July 19, https://edition.cnn.com/2024/07/19/politics/donald-trump-zelensky-phone-call-2024/index.html.
483 See the message at https://x.com/zelenskyyua/status/1815144292182348062?t=GsMOwID-2MzYTk-2E0jWmw.

some observers have already tied this trip to President Biden's announcement.[484]

Reactions of diverse opposition groups to President Biden's announcement

While preparing this material, I spoke with six MPs, mainly from opposition factions (which today include Yulia Tymoshenko's Batkivshchyna, Poroshenko's European Solidarity, and Holos/Voice, as well as several smaller MP groups formally totaling up to approximately 100 votes). Despite their different personal and party positions, they agreed on three issues.

First, the Zelensky team's informal focus on ties with Democrats could now create a backlash in the form of much cooler relations with Republicans. This would undermine the Zelensky administration's once undisputed dominance of internal politics.

Second, President Zelensky will probably try accelerating indirect diplomatic processes to freeze the war. Kyiv may be in a stronger position during such negotiations while the Democrats are still in control of the White House and Senate.

Third, the role of ex-president Poroshenko in Ukrainian politics is expected to increase. After five years on the margins of power, Poroshenko is slowly moving back to the center. He had rather productive relations with both Joe Biden and Donald Trump during their respective presidencies. Poroshenko's party ideology is close to the current GOP's in some matters. And Poroshenko, who has recently declared his intent to participate in presidential elections whenever announced, may find the global ideological turn to the right working in his favor.[485]

---

[484] Lau, S., Melkozerova, V. (2024). Ukraine's Kuleba to Visit China for First Time Since Start of War. *Politico*, July 22, https://www.politico.eu/article/ukraines-kuleba-to-visit-china-for-first-time-since-start-of-war/.

[485] Zelenskiy's Predecessor Poroshenko Says He Plans to Run For President. *RFE/RL*, April 3, 2024, https://www.rferl.org/a/ukraine-poroshenko-run-for-president-zelenskiy-war/32889626.html.

A shift in power flows: ramifications for Ukraine

Basically, the members of the Verkhovna Rada sense a change in the power flows and are trying to capitalize on it. The same phenomenon is shaping up outside parliament's halls.

The extraparliamentary opposition politicians and groups are less sensitive to changes in the United States. Ukraine's former commander of the Armed Forces of Ukraine and current ambassador to London, Valeriy Zaluzhny, remains silent. During Zelensky's recent visit to the UK, Zaluzhny appeared in photos greeting the president as a loyal diplomat.[486] After five months of silence and a return to the public eye as just another official in Zelensky's entourage, Ambassador Zaluzhny, once a promising new politician, seems to have accepted the loss of his political prospects.

But Olexiy Arestovych, once the voice of Zelensky's administration in the first months of the war and now in self-exile, and others in opposition are more outspoken on and reactive to American politics. They seem to think that the changes in Washington could lead to a freeze in the war and an end to martial law, which would clear the way for presidential and parliamentary elections to occur, as well as open up opportunities for new political forces in postwar Ukraine. They are preparing for a revival of political life and have started collecting the necessary resources for future competition.

The winds of change blowing from Washington are warming up Ukraine's frozen democracy. So far these winds are a light breeze, not a hurricane. The future will reveal how the political climate in Ukraine shifts under the stream of news coming out of the US capital.

---

486 Court, E. (2024). Zelensky Arrives in UK, Meets Zaluzhnyi. *The Kyiv Independent*, July 18, https://kyivindependent.com/zelensky-arrives-in-uk/.

Zelensky's six Independence Day speeches as milestones of his presidency

August 2024[487]

On August 24, 2024, Ukrainians marked their thirty-third Independence Day. Political tradition dictates that on that day, the president delivers a special speech, a message, that takes its cue from Taras Shevchenko's poem, "To the Dead, the Living, and the Unborn."

These speeches are usually short but include the president's personal take on the current situation, linking it to the country's history, and an inspiring look into the nation's future prospects as seen from the presidential chair atop the Pechersk Hills (the Kyiv area where most of the power institutes are headquartered). Typically, the presidents and their speechwriters try to spice up these speeches with hints at the nation's destiny.

For all these reasons, each such speech is an ideological performance and a milestone that allows tracing the arc of each presidency.

This year, Volodymyr Zelensky delivered his sixth Independence Day presidential speech, a rare achievement in Ukraine's history. It was a remarkable performance that shed light on his presidential path. Here I look back at all of Zelensky's presidential speeches and show how his presidency and Ukraine have evolved over the past five years.

2019

A young, lonely, and somewhat insecure-looking Volodymyr Zelensky starts his speech thanking the soldiers on the Donbas front.[488] He confesses that his daily routine starts with "an SMS

---

[487] A shorter version of this column has previously been published as: Minakov, M. (2024). Zelensky's Sixth Independence Day Speech. *Focus Ukraine*, September 3, https://www.wilsoncenter.org/blog-post/zelenskys-sixth-independence-day-speech.

[488] Speech by the President of Ukraine During the Independence Day Festivities. *The President of Ukraine Official Website*, August 24, 2019, https://www.presiden

from General Staff" on the frontline situation and losses. Then he recalls the thousand years of Ukraine's existence, from Kyivan Rus' to the Cossacks to the UN founding to Sergei Korolev's space projects to the activities of Ukrainian anti-Soviet dissidents, "who paved the path to independence."

He addresses the young generation born in independent Ukraine. He voices his expectation that youth will be the champion of the country's democracy and European future.

He recalls prewar Ukraine, when people came together around achievements in sports, business, pop culture, and space travel.

Then he turns to the Euromaidan and the start of the war. The need to defend the country has taught Ukrainians a new meaning of unity, he says.

His address ends with intimate words of love for Ukraine and pain for the losses the country and its people have sustained during the five-year-long war. He looks forward to peacetime, when his daily SMS report might bring news of how many kids are being born in Ukraine.

2020

A serious, self-assured man standing near his team on Sophia Square on August 29 starts his Independence Day speech for "the citizens of Ukraine" with the statement that his daily SMS report included zero losses in the Donbas.[489]

He mentions the historical significance of the square, where Yaroslav the Wise won over the Pechenegs in 1036, where Ukraine's Unity Act was announced in 1919, and from where the Nazis were kicked out in 1943. Speaking in this notable site, he continues the tradition of celebrating Ukraine's independence, together with 65 million ethnic Ukrainians around the globe.

---

t.gov.ua/en/news/vistup-prezidenta-ukrayini-pid-chas-urochistostej-z-nagodi-d-56937.

489 Speech of the President on the Occasion of the Independence Day of Ukraine. *The President of Ukraine Official Website*, August 24, 2020, https://www.president.gov.ua/en/news/promova-prezidenta-z-nagodi-dnya-nezalezhnosti-ukrayini-62953.

The COVID-19 pandemic has hit Ukraine hard, and the president refers to the need to care about the health of all Ukrainians.

Then he urges unity in the face of growing political tensions. He calls on his audience to "love Ukraine together" and stop competing over "who loves her more." He extends this call to those living in Donetsk and Crimea in the hope that these communities will rejoin Ukraine in future.

He promises to build a Ukraine for all—for those who live in and outside the country, in each region, and in each profession.

He ends his speech with a strong call for national unity around the project of Ukraine's dream.

2021

A wiser, almost smiling man starts his address with unusual pomp.[490] To an audience of "ladies and gentlemen, brothers, partners, and friends," he recalls that the day marks the thirtieth anniversary of Ukraine's independence, of the "renewal of its statehood" and the establishment of the Ukrainian Armed Forces. It is also the twenty-fifth anniversary of the Ukrainian currency and constitution, he notes. He concludes this part of his speech with the words:

> We are a young country with a thousand-year history. We are building our home on the land where our ancestors lived and created... We are the descendants of a powerful country that was the center of Europe.

Then he turns to his new ideology, and to memory politics. Kyiv is the city of origin of Orthodox Christianity, the Church Slavonic tongue, and the Ukrainian language. He promises to repatriate to Ukraine the remains of the historical Ukrainian heroes who were not buried on its territory. He promises to fight for each piece of history and each historical person, and not to allow "anyone to annex them ever again."

He reports that Ukraine is building a new army and naval fleet, new bases and weapons stockpiles, new roads and new digital

---

490 Speech by President Volodymyr Zelenskyy on the Occasion of the 30th Anniversary of Ukraine's Independence. *The President of Ukraine Official Website*, August 24, 2021, https://www.president.gov.ua/en/news/promova-prezidenta-volodimira-zelenskogo-z-nagodi-30-yi-rich-70333.

services. He also reports on taking away MPs' immunity, hinting on his readiness to punish corruption and treason in the parliament.

Then he promises to lead Ukraine to membership in NATO and the EU, and to return Donbas and the Crimea to Ukrainian control in the foreseeable future.

He ends by describing the Ukrainian populace as a multiethnic "national team" and bilingual "family" that can defend its country. And he calls for a moment of silence in memory of the fallen soldiers.

2022

An aged and tired man in a military t-shirt standing among Russian broken-down armored vehicles speaks to "the free people of independent Ukraine."[491] He states that after six months of the big war, Ukrainians remain resilient and strong people.

He assures his listeners that now every Ukrainian knows who is who: who is an enemy, a friend, a partner. And the world knows who Ukrainians are: they are people that none would ever again refer to as "living near Russia." He believes that Ukrainians "have given humanity a new hope that justice has not left our cynical world for good," and that this humanity has forced politicians around the world to support Ukraine.

He explains that the Ukrainian resistance to Russian invaders is a "new referendum" affirming independence. And the votes in this referendum are divided between those who "left for Monaco" and those who "stayed to defend Mariupol."

He explains his change of strategy: "We used to say peace. Now we say victory." He promises no more talks, only a struggle for final victory.

He ends by stating that now the national unity in Ukraine is around the fight, the independence, and the victory.

---

491 Speech by President Volodymyr Zelenskyy on Independence Day of Ukraine. *The President of Ukraine Official Website*, August 24, 2022, https://www.presiden t.gov.ua/en/news/privitannya-prezidenta-volodimira-zelenskogo-z-nagodi-dnya-n-77265.

2023

An even more aged and tired-looking man in a military *vyshyvanka*, flanked by a patriotic poster, looks directly into the eyes of the viewer. This man speaks to the "entire Ukrainian people."[492]

The struggle goes on the battlefield and in each small act of resistance, he says. He thanks each warrior, each warrior's family, each teacher and doctor, each volunteer, each supporter of Ukraine. He urges remembering each person who has given his or her life for the cause of independent Ukraine.

He ends his short address by thanking each victim of the war and everyone who continues in the resistance.

2024

An aged but energetic man in uniform standing among the dunes on the border of Russia's Kursk oblast speaks to "the dear people."[493]

Ukrainians "always pay their debts," he says. And: "Those who want to sow evil on our land will reap its fruits on their own territory." Russia that marched on Ukraine across this very border now sees the war brought home to its own territory. He refers to Vladimir Putin as a "sick old man" with "faded eyes" who brought down war on his "orcs" from "the swamps."

He promises that Ukraine will surprise the world with victory. And he thanks each person who has stood with Ukraine during all 913 days of fighting.

Every Ukrainian now knows what independence is, he says. He predicts that Ukraine will be free and the enemy will be punished soon.

---

492 Congratulations by President Volodymyr Zelenskyy on Independence Day of Ukraine. *The President of Ukraine Official Website*, August 24, 2023, https://www.president.gov.ua/en/news/privitannya-prezidenta-volodimira-zelenskogo-z-nagodi-dnya-n-85145.

493 Address by Volodymyr Zelenskyy on the Independence Day of Ukraine. *The President of Ukraine Official Website*, August 24, 2024, https://www.president.gov.ua/en/news/zvernennya-volodimira-zelenskogo-z-nagodi-dnya-nezalezhnosti-92805.

Zelensky's presidency has indeed seen different periods during his tenure. But these speeches demonstrate well how all those different periods mesh in a forward-looking account of destiny, his and the Ukrainians'.

Epilogue
The Three Ages of Zelensky's Presidency

June 2022, October 2024[494]

Since starting his presidency, Volodymyr Zelensky has presented himself as three rather different leaders of Ukraine in three distinctive ages. The first Zelensky was dedicated to his electoral program and the expectations of his voters and ended with endless Behemoth politics. The second Zelensky demonstrated the will to power and succeeded in suppressing formal and informal opposition, promising to establish a Ukrainian Leviathan. The third age demanded a leader able to steer the country at war, and Zelensky changed accordingly, to supply artistic talent on the global scene and startling military vigor on the battlefield. Even as his presidency continues, it is already possible to sum up his political path and possible legacy.

Servant, winner, and reformer: 2019–2020

Zelensky came to power in the spring of 2019 with a mandate from 73 percent of voters—rich and poor, urban and rural, speakers of Ukrainian and Russian—across all regions of Ukraine who were all equally tired of the endless conflicts in post-Maidan Ukraine. The older generation of Ukrainian politicians, as well as the Western and Eastern political establishments, regarded him with some concern and even suspicion. He was a comedian with no prior experience in public administration, what Zelensky might do once in office was unpredictable. Since the new president was not a professional politician, his team included no known diplomats and activists, and his platform was vague and heavily populist.

During his first 100 days, however, the political newcomer won early parliamentary elections and established a one-party

---

[494] A shorter and older version of this column has previously been published as: Minakov, M. (2022). The Three Ages of Zelensky's Presidency. *Focus Ukraine*, June 9, https://www.wilsoncenter.org/blog-post/three-ages-zelenskys-presidency.

majority in the Verkhovna Rada—something none of Ukraine's previous presidents had enjoyed. It is perhaps a mark of Ukrainian voters' intense desire for change that they gave Zelensky and his party, Servant of the People, a generous mandate, amounting almost to carte blanche, to fix some intractable problems and set Ukraine firmly on an orientation toward the West.

Zelensky and his team's program was perhaps deliberately nonspecific, leaving it up to the voters, who were frustrated by the divisive rule of former president Petro Poroshenko (2014–2019) and its taint of corruption, to vest their hopes for the future in a person who had no connection to the Ukrainian political class.

Zelensky and his team of new faces—politicians of the generation that had grown up during the era of independence and who were not connected to the old ways of getting things done, which too often involved cronyism and dealmaking—were tasked by voters to achieve peace in the Donbas, economic betterment for ordinary Ukrainians, and a noncorrupt and responsive government.

Between 2019 and 2020, Zelensky's team put forth an enormous effort to address the first and most important requisite, resolving the situation in the Donbas. The December 9, 2019, Paris meeting of President Zelensky and his counterparts from Germany, France, and Russia offered some prospects for peace. By August 2020, the level of shelling on the front lines of the temporarily occupied territories had fallen considerably, several POW swaps with Russians and the separatists controlling those territories had taken place, and a partial pullback of troops had some circumscribed success. Zelensky's team in the presidential office and his supporters in parliament and the first Cabinet of Ministers launched a number of reforms aimed at economic growth, good governance, and responsive politics.

However, lack of experience, public scandals, relentless conflicts with older politicians and oligarchs, and the COVID-19 pandemic forced Zelensky to change his policies and slow the pace of reforms.

Ruler: 2020–2021

The temptations of Ukrainian realpolitik; weak parliamentary opposition (which provided almost unlimited opportunities for the president to get his way); snowballing socioeconomic problems, worsened by the COVID-19 pandemic; and the never-ending conflict in the Donbas led to changes in the administration's policies and behavior in the fall of 2020. A new President Zelensky, very different from the 2019 version—more strategic in dealing with political forces, firmer in decision-making, and clearer in his drive for power—began to emerge.

Strategic maneuvering now aimed at new projects that had little connection with Zelensky's hazy electoral promises. Informally, the principal decision-making role moved to the National Security and Defense Council of Ukraine, beginning in October. President Zelensky and the senior members of his team began running major decisions on issues of domestic politics, international relations, and security matters through this body in lieu of trying to get resolutions passed by parliament, and then legally enforcing those decisions through presidential decree. Even though Ukraine formally remained a parliamentary-presidential republic, the real role of the Verkhovna Rada and the Cabinet of Ministers was informally redefined as supporting the presidential core.

Thus freed from the need to gain consensus in the Rada and the cabinet, Zelensky's administration, with its reshaped powers, could focus more on countering the harsh socioeconomic consequences of the COVID-19 pandemic, which the opposition was using to lambast the president and try to sink his popularity ratings.

The "Big Construction" project was designed to rebuild aging public infrastructure and prepare Ukraine for a fast post-COVID recovery. New and daring counter-oligarchic laws were passed, and policies were put in place that were intended to ensure that the recovery would increase the president's and the Security Council's authority and not be diverted by the clans for their own purposes. The president's powers were constantly increasing, and, despite an expected decline in his popularity rating, Zelensky remained the most popular among Ukraine's most prominent politicians, especially those with presidential ambitions. At that time, the prospect of creating a Leviathan-style politics loomed in Ukraine.

President Zelensky and his team also redefined their foreign policy, returning to and even honing former president Poroshenko's pro-Western policies. In 2021, Zelensky's administration had three priorities. First, as conflict with Russia was increasing, the administration restored the annexed Crimea to the center of Ukraine's foreign policy. The Crimean Platform, a new international forum launched in August 2021 to counter Russia's claims to Crimea and insist on the rule of law, has partially fulfilled this task. There was a notable uptick in Western democracies' public support for Ukraine in the conflict with Russia.

The second and third tasks were to ensure Ukraine's rapid integration with the EU and with NATO. However, neither organization opened its doors to Ukraine's membership in 2021, which led to more direct criticism on Zelensky's part of the "hypocritical West" and an equally unpromising response from the organizations' chiefs. Still, the West and Ukraine were able to ensure the development of the Ukrainian army in anticipation of the Russian attack.

All of these domestic and foreign policy efforts were conducted in the face of an increasing threat from Russia to launch a new and much more severe attack on Ukraine.

Wartime leader: 2022–2024

The Russian-Ukrainian war actually started in 2014, when Crimea was annexed and the Russian Federation militarily, politically, and economically supported the Donbas separatists and irredentists. On February 24, 2022, Russian and separatist army units attacked Ukraine on a larger scale, from the north, east, and south. Since that day, we have seen a new, third version of President Zelensky – and the third version of his administration.

With this invasion, Zelensky's number one priority became the defense of Ukraine by all possible – and seemingly impossible – means. Zelensky demonstrated courage and dedication to Ukraine's resistance during the worst initial days of the war. His presence in Ukraine and his guidance of the defense campaign encouraged Ukrainians in all regions and in all walks of life to come together in national unity and in the practice of resilience. His digital omnipresence in Ukrainian homes and in Western public spaces created the effect of international confidence in himself and an unprecedented solidarity with Ukraine.

In the spring of 2022, the Zelensky administration sought to distribute arms to as many fighters as possible. Economic policies were recalibrated to help households and companies survive while the government's social obligations were upheld. The government worked around the clock to stave off Russian advances, cement international support for Ukraine, and help the population survive, all of which resulted in Ukrainian forces winning the battles for Kyiv and northern Ukraine.

By April 2022, however, the Zelensky administration had adapted to the war situation and endorsed a multidimensional approach, simultaneously pursuing many tasks, some more politically focused than others. And the president himself made a historical choice: to deny the almost finalized "Istanbul Peace" and to accept the "Ramstein offer," to continue resisting with Western aid "for as long as it takes."

For the next two years, the president's team continued working on immediate war-related issues, in particular gaining increased military, political, humanitarian, and financial support from the United States, the EU, the G7, and NATO.

His administration has also started preparing for a longer war of attrition and for the reconstruction of Ukraine in the future, which led to victorious results, at least in the beginning. In 2022, the Ukrainian Armed Forces freed northern Ukraine, Kharkiv oblast, and the left-bank Kherson region. But then the military situation changed, and after the unsuccessful UAF counterattack of 2023 and a series of military failures in the Donbas in 2024, the Zelensky administration faced increasing challenges, both on the defensive and political fronts.

The fall of 2024 saw growing fatigue from the war inside Ukraine and from her Western partners. The 25th Ramstein high-level meeting, scheduled for October 12, 2024, was delayed, provoking rumors of disturbing differences between Kyiv and Washington, DC. A variety of political, military, and civil society opposition groups increased pressure on the Zelensky administration, demanding long-overdue elections.

Zelensky remains the nationally and internationally recognized leader of Ukraine. But he has entered a moment that might require another transformation. Will the phoenix genius of Zelensky help him again, as he accepts a new role? This remains to be seen. But his presidency has definitely entered into the fourth fatal moment, and the way he reacts may be decisive for his future and the destiny of Ukraine.

Key Literature and Sources

Address by Volodymyr Zelenskyy on the Independence Day of Ukraine. *The President of Ukraine Official Website*, August 24, 2024, https://www.president.gov.ua/en/news/zvernennya-volodimira-zelenskogo-z-nagodi-dnya-nezalezhnosti-92805.

Amicus Curiae brief on the limits of subsequent (a posteriori) review of constitutional amendments by the Constitutional Court. *The Venice Commission*, June 17-18, 2022, https://www.venice.coe.int/webforms/documents/?pdf=CDL-AD(2022)012-e.

Belarus' Role in the Russian Military Aggression of Ukraine. *European Council*, March 2, 2022, https://n9.cl/9ngad.

Ben, B. (2020). Ukraine's New Government: More Oligarchic, More Pro-Russian. *Euromaidan Press*, March 6, https://euromaidanpress.com/2020/03/06/ukraines-new-government-more-oligarchic-more-pro-russian/.

Bennetts, M. (2018). Ukraine's National Militia: "We're not neo-Nazis, we just want to make our country better". *The Guardian*, March 13, https://2cm.es/LR-0.

Bezruk, T. (2021). Ukraine's All-Powerful Interior Minister Resigns – and Leaves a Legacy of Impunity Behind. *OpenDemocracy*, July 16, https://www.opendemocracy.net/en/odr/ukraine-avakov-resignation-impunity/.

Biden - Harris Administration's National Security Strategy. *White House*, October 2022, https://2cm.es/LT1O.

Bikus, Z. (2019). World-Low 9% of Ukrainians Confident in Government. *Gallup*, March 21, 2019, https://news.gallup.com/poll/247976/world-low-ukrainians-confident-government.aspx.

Bobasu, A., De Santis, R.A. (2022). The Impact of the Russian Invasion of Ukraine on Euro Area Activity via the Uncertainty Channel. *European Central Bank*, Issue 4/2022, https://2cm.es/LS-0.

Borrell, J. (2022). The War in Ukraine and Its Implications for the EU. *EU External Action*, March 14, https://www.eeas.europa.eu/eeas/war-ukraine-and-its-implications-eu_en.

Chaisty, P., & Whitefield, S. (2022). How Challenger Parties Can Win Big with Frozen Cleavages: Explaining the Landslide Victory of the Servant of the People Party in the 2019 Ukrainian Parliamentary Elections. *Party Politics*, 28(1), 115-126.

Commission Opinion on Ukraine's Application for Membership of the European Union. *European Commission*, June 17, 2022, p. 5, https://2cm.es/Oe5s.

Congratulations by President Volodymyr Zelenskyy on Independence Day of Ukraine. *The President of Ukraine Official Website*, August 24, 2023, https://www.president.gov.ua/en/news/privitannya-prezidenta-volodimira-zelenskogo-z-nagodi-dnya-n-85145.

Decision on Ukraine's Admission to the EU Largely Depends on Its Members' Political Will — Dmytro Kuleba. *Yalta European Summit*, September 11, 2021, https://2cm.es/LSjq.

Diamantopoulou, A. (2022). The Three Challenges for the West in the New Cold War. *ECFR*, September 20, 2022, https://ecfr.eu/article/the-three-challenges-for-the-west-in-the-new-cold-war/.

Dutsyk, D., Dyczok, M. (2020). Ukraine's New Media Laws: Fighting Disinformation or Targeting Freedom of Speech? *Focus Ukraine*, February 10, 2020, https://2cm.es/LR-O.

Early Parliamentary Elections, 21 July 2019. *OSCE*, July 2019, https://www.osce.org/odihr/elections/ukraine/422585.

ECA (2021). Reducing Grand Corruption in Ukraine: Several EU Initiatives, But Still Insufficient Results. *European Court of Auditors*, March, https://op.europa.eu/webpub/eca/special-reports/ukraine-23-2021/en/.

Engelhart, K. (2014). Putin's Legalism. *Foreign Policy*, March 24, https://foreignpolicy.com/2014/03/24/putins-legalism/.

European Council Conclusions on Ukraine. *European Council*, December 15, 2016, https://www.consilium.europa.eu/media/24151/15-euco-conclusions-ukraine.pdf.

Evaluation of the judicial systems (2018 – 2020). *Council of Europe*, September 24, 2020, https://rm.coe.int/en-ukraine-2018/16809fe0cb.

Fisun, O. (2012). Rethinking post-Soviet politics from a neopatrimonial perspective.*Demokratizatsiya. The Journal of Post-Soviet Democratization*, 1, 87-96.

Formuszewicz, R., Łoskot-Strachota, A. (2021). Deal between Germany and the US on Nord Stream 2. *Center for Eastern Studies*, July 2, https://2cm.es/LSjx.

Full Text of Volodymyr Zelenskyy's First Speech as President of Ukraine. *Hromadske*, May 20, 2019, https://hromadske.ua/en/posts/full-text-of-volodymyr-zelenskyys-first-speech-as-president-of-ukraine.

Gic, A. (2019). Yulia Tymoshenko: A Ghost of Ukraine's Past. *New Eastern Europe*, January 21, https://neweasterneurope.eu/2019/01/21/yulia-tymoshenko-a-ghost-of-ukraines-past/.

Hale, H. E. (2017). Russian patronal politics beyond Putin. *Daedalus*, 146(2), 30-40.

Hale, H. E., & Orttung, R. W. (eds.). (2016). *Beyond the Euromaidan: Comparative Perspectives on Advancing Reform in Ukraine*. Stanford University Press.

Hirsh, M. (2022). Why Russia's Economy Is Holding On. *Foreign Policy*, April 22, 2022, https://foreignpolicy.com/2022/04/22/russia-war-economy-sanctions-ruble/.

Hosa, J., Wilson, A. (2019). Zelensky Unchained: What Ukraine's New Political Order Means for Its Future. *ECFR*, September 25, 2019, https://2cm.es/LT55.

Istrate, D. (2019). Ukraine's shadow economy nearly half of GDP. *Emerging Europe*, October 16, https://emerging-europe.com/analysis/study-ukraines-shadow-economy-nearly-half-of-gdp/.

Jacobsen, K. (2016). How a Fictional President Is Helping Ukrainians Rethink Their Absurd Politics. *Foreign Policy*, December 13, 2016, https://2cm.es/LR-U.

Jarábik, B. (2019). Ukraine's Joke of an Election. *Politico*, February 5, https://www.politico.eu/article/ukraine-joke-election-vladimir-Zelensky/.

Jarábik, B., & Bila, Y. (2015). And Then There Were Five: The Plight of Ukraine's Oligarchs. *Carnegie Endowment for International Peace*, June 15, https://n9.cl/md11t.

Joint Statement of the G7 and the World Bank on Constitutional Court Decision on Illicit Enrichment. *The EU Diplomatic Service*, March 7, 2019, https://www.eeas.europa.eu/node/59235_en.

Karakuts, A., Schedrin, Y., Davymuka, O. (2023). Future of Ukraine Workforce. *Center for Applied Research*, May 2023, https://cpd.com.ua/future-of-ukraine-workforce.pdf.

Karatnycky, A. (2024). How Deep Does Corruption Run in Ukraine? *Foreign Policy*, March 6, https://foreignpolicy.com/2024/03/06/ukraine-corruption-reforms-russia-war/.

Konończuk, W. (2015). Oligarchs after the Maidan: the Old System in a "New" Ukraine. *Center for Eastern Studies*, February 16, https://2cm.es/OdmW.

Kusa, I., Minakov, M. (2022). Ukraine-Russia Negotiations: What's Possible? *Focus Ukraine*, April 11, 2022 https://www.wilsoncenter.org/blog-post/ukraine-russia-negotiations-whats-possible.

Libanova, E. (2023). Ukraine's Demography in the Second Year of the Full-Fledged War. *Focus Ukraine*, June 27, 2023, https://www.wilsoncenter.org/blog-post/ukraines-demography-second-year-full-fledged-war.

Loginova, E. (2021). Pandora Papers Reveal Offshore Holdings of Ukrainian President and his Inner Circle. *Organized Crime and Corruption Reporting Project*, October 3, https://2cm.es/Odn3.

Ludewig, A. (2021). Westlessness? Challenges for the EU's Soft Power Approach. *Australian and New Zealand Journal of European Studies*, 13(1), 23-33.

Magyar, B., & Madlovics, B. (2020). *The Anatomy of Post-Communist Regimes*. Budapest: CEU Press.

Masters, J., Merrow, W. (2024). How Much US Aid Is Going to Ukraine? *Council on Foreign Relations*, May 9, 2024, https://www.cfr.org/article/how-much-us-aid-going-ukraine.

Matuszak, S., Żochowski, P. (2021). Growing importance of the Security Council in Ukraine. *Center for Eastern Studies*, April 1, https://www.osw.waw.pl/en/publikacje/analyses/2021-04-01/growing-importance-security-council-ukraine.

Minakov, M. (2017). Reconstructing the Power Vertical: The Authoritarian Threat in Ukraine. *OpenDemocracy*, June 29, https://www.opendemocracy.net/en/odr/reconstructing-power-vertical-authoritarian-threat-in-ukraine/.

Minakov, M. (2018). *Development and dystopia*. Stuttgart: ibidem Verlag.

Minakov, M. (2019). Democratisation and Europeanisation in 21st century Ukraine. *The Struggle for Good Governance in Eastern Europe. Second Edition*. Brussels: CEPS, 83-121, https://3dcftas.eu/publications/democratisation-and-europeanisation-in-21st-century-ukraine.

Minakov, M. (2019). Hot Summer in Kyiv: President Zelensky and The Rada. *Focus Ukraine*, June 6, https://www.wilsoncenter.org/blog-post/hot-summer-kyiv-president-Zelensky-and-the-rada.

Minakov, M. (2019). One-Party Majority: Just Another Victory for Zelensky. *Focus Ukraine*, July 24, https://www.wilsoncenter.org/blog-post/one-party-majority-just-another-victory-for-Zelensky.

Minakov, M. (2019). Presidential Elections in Ukraine: Candidates and Chances. *Focus Ukraine*, February 12, https://www.wilsoncenter.org/blog-post/presidential-elections-ukraine-candidates-and-chances.

Minakov, M. (2019). Rearranging the Elite Landscape: Parliamentary Elections and New Political Cleavages in Ukraine. *Focus Ukraine*, July 17, https://www.wilsoncenter.org/blog-post/rearranging-the-elite-landscape-parliamentary-elections-and-new-political-cleavages.

Minakov, M. (2019). Republic of clans: The evolution of the Ukrainian political system. Magyar, B. (ed.). *Stubborn structures: reconceptualizing post-communist regimes*. Budapest: Central European University Press, 217-245.

Minakov, M. (2019). Results of the Normandy Format Talks for Ukraine: Hope, with Reservations. *Focus Ukraine*, December 11, https://www.wilsoncenter.org/blog-post/results-the-normandy-format-talks-for-ukraine-hope-reservations.

Minakov, M. (2019). Ukraine's Presidential Elections: New Cycle, Same Names. *Focus Ukraine*, April 3, https://www.wilsoncenter.org/blog-post/ukraines-presidential-elections-new-cycle-same-names.

Minakov, M. (2019). War and Peace in Ukraine's Presidential Race. *Focus Ukraine*, March 14, https://www.wilsoncenter.org/blog-post/war-and-peace-ukraines-presidential-race.

Minakov, M. (2019). Zelensky's Government and the Challenge for Checks and Balances. *Focus Ukraine*, September 9, https://www.wilsoncenter.org/blog-post/Zelenskys-government-and-the-challenge-for-checks-and-balances.

Minakov, M. (2020). Ukraine's Current Political Agenda. *Focus Ukraine*, August 31, https://www.wilsoncenter.org/blog-post/ukraines-current-political-agenda.

Minakov, M. (2020). Zelensky Relaunches His Administration with a Fresh Cohort. *Focus Ukraine*, March 5, https://www.wilsoncenter.org/blog-post/Zelensky-relaunches-his-administration-fresh-cohort.

Minakov, M. (2020). Zelensky's Version of Perestroika and the Role of the Oligarchs. *Focus Ukraine*, March 19, 2020, https://www.wilsoncenter.org/blog-post/Zelenskys-version-perestroika-and-role-oligarchs.

Minakov, M. (2021). Fighting Oligarchy or the Oligarchs? *Focus Ukraine*, June 10, https://www.wilsoncenter.org/blog-post/fighting-oligarchy-or-oligarchs.

Minakov, M. (2021). Just Like All the Others: The End of the Zelensky Alternative? *Focus Ukraine*, November 2, 2021, https://www.wilsoncenter.org/blog-post/just-all-others-end-zelensky-alternative.

Minakov, M. (2021). Post-Soviet Sovereignty and Ukraine's Political Development. *Ukraine Analytica*, 2 (24): 26-34, https://ukraine-analytica.org/post-soviet-sovereignty-and-ukraines-political-development/.

Minakov, M. (2021). The Afghanistan Syndrome and US–Ukraine Relations. *Focus Ukraine*, September 27, 2021, https://www.wilsoncenter.org/blog-post/afghanistan-syndrome-and-us-ukraine-relations.

Minakov, M. (2021). Three Decades of Ukraine's Independence. *Focus Ukraine*, September 13, 2021, https://www.wilsoncenter.org/blog-post/three-decades-ukraines-independence.

Minakov, M. (2021). Ukraine's Political Agenda for 2022. *Focus Ukraine*, January 25, 2022 https://www.wilsoncenter.org/blog-post/ukraines-political-agenda-2022-european-integration-deoligarchization-and-economic-growth.

Minakov, M. (2021). Ukraine's Political Agenda for the First Half of 2021. *Focus Ukraine*, January 22, https://www.wilsoncenter.org/blog-post/ukraines-political-agenda-first-half-2021.

Minakov, M. (2021). Waiting for the Storm? Ukraine's Political Situation before the Autumn of 2021. *Focus Ukraine*, September 2, https://www.wilsoncenter.org/blog-post/waiting-storm-ukraines-political-situation-autumn-2021.

Minakov, M. (2021). Zelensky's Presidency at the Two-Year Mark. *Focus Ukraine*, June 3, https://www.wilsoncenter.org/blog-post/zelenskys-presidency-two-year-mark.

Minakov, M. (2022). LPR and DPR Threaten Ukrainian Sovereignty as Russia Tries to Broaden Its Union State. *Focus Ukraine*, February 17, https://www.wilsoncenter.org/blog-post/lpr-and-dpr-threaten-ukrainian-sovereignty-russia-tries-broaden-its-union-state.

Minakov, M. (2022). Referendum as Violence and Humiliation in Southeastern Ukraine. *Focus Ukraine*, September 29, 2022 https://www.wilsoncenter.org/blog-post/referendum-violence-and-humiliation-southeastern-ukraine.

Minakov, M. (2022). Russia's War on Ukraine: The First Two Months. *Focus Ukraine*, April 27, 2022, https://www.wilsoncenter.org/blog-post/russias-war-ukraine-first-two-months.

Minakov, M. (2022). The Kremlin's Plans to Annex Southeastern Ukraine Go into Effect. *Focus Ukraine*, July 26, https://www.wilsoncenter.org/blog-post/kremlins-plans-annex-southeastern-ukraine-go-effect.

Minakov, M. (2022). The Militarist Remapping of Europe and Northern Eurasia. *Focus Ukraine*, November 3, 2022 https://www.wilsoncenter.org/blog-post/militarist-remapping-europe-and-northern-eurasia.

Minakov, M. (2022). The Three Ages of Zelensky's Presidency. *Focus Ukraine*, June 9, https://www.wilsoncenter.org/blog-post/three-ages-zelenskys-presidency.

Minakov, M. (2022). The War and the Future of Ukraine's Oligarchy. *Focus Ukraine*, August 3, https://www.wilsoncenter.org/blog-post/war-and-future-ukraines-oligarchy.

Minakov, M. (2022). The War Has Helped Ukraine Rein in the Oligarchs. *Focus Ukraine*, November 15, 2022 https://www.wilsoncenter.org/blog-post/war-has-helped-ukraine-rein-oligarchs.

Minakov, M. (2022). The War on Ukraine: The Beginning of the End of Putin's Russia. *Focus Ukraine*, February 28, https://www.wilsoncenter.org/blog-post/war-ukraine-beginning-end-putins-russia.

Minakov, M. (2022). Ukraine, EU Member Candidate. *Focus Ukraine*, June 28, https://www.wilsoncenter.org/blog-post/ukraine-eu-member-candidate.

Minakov, M. (2022). Ukraine's Wartime Governance Dilemma: Balancing Military and Socioeconomic Needs. Focus Ukraine, May 26, 2022, https://www.wilsoncenter.org/blog-post/ukraines-wartime-governance-dilemma-balancing-military-and-socioeconomic-needs.

Minakov, M. (2022). Ukraine's Wartime Politics Takes a New Turn. *Focus Ukraine*, July 19, https://www.wilsoncenter.org/blog-post/ukraines-wartime-politics-takes-new-turn.

Minakov, M. (2022). Ukrainian Statehood at Risk: The Kremlin's Secessionist Plans. *Focus Ukraine*, April 19, 2022 https://www.wilsoncenter.org/blog-post/ukrainian-statehood-risk-kremlins-secessionist-plans.

Minakov, M. (2022). Zelensky Versus Putin: The Personality Factor in Russia's War on Ukraine. *Focus Ukraine*, April 13, 2022 https://www.wilsoncenter.org/blog-post/zelensky-versus-putin-personality-factor-russias-war-ukraine.

Minakov, M. (2023). Fighting Corruption in Wartime Ukraine. *Focus Ukraine*, February 13, https://www.wilsoncenter.org/blog-post/fighting-corruption-wartime-ukraine.

Minakov, M. (2023). Local "Elections" in the Occupied Ukrainian Territories. Focus Ukraine, September 18, https://www.wilsoncenter.org/blog-post/local-elections-occupied-ukrainian-territories.

Minakov, M. (2023). Political Competition in Wartime Ukraine. *Focus Ukraine*, March 27, https://www.wilsoncenter.org/blog-post/political-competition-wartime-ukraine.

Minakov, M. (2023). Political Will or Procedure? Assessing Ukraine's EU Membership Goals in 2023. *Focus Ukraine*, February 13, https://www.wilsoncenter.org/blog-post/political-will-or-procedure-assessing-ukraines-eu-membership-goals-2023.

Minakov, M. (2023). The Constitutional Process in Wartime Ukraine. *Focus Ukraine*, March 14, https://www.wilsoncenter.org/blog-post/constitutional-process-wartime-ukraine.

Minakov, M. (2023). The Paradox of De-oligarchization. Focus Ukraine, June 27, https://www.wilsoncenter.org/blog-post/paradox-de-oligarchization.

Minakov, M. (2023). Ukraine and the Rise of the Middle Powers. Focus Ukraine, July 31, https://www.wilsoncenter.org/blog-post/ukraine-and-rise-middle-powers.

Minakov, M. (2023). Ukraine's Historical Moment. *Focus Ukraine*, February 21, 2023 https://www.wilsoncenter.org/blog-post/ukraines-historical-moment.

Minakov, M. (2023). War, De-Oligarchization, and the Possibility of Anti-Patronal Transformation in Ukraine. In Madlovics, B., Magyar, B. (eds.). *Ukraine's Patronal Democracy and the Russian Invasion: The Russia-Ukraine War, Volume One* (. Central European University Press, 141–166.

Minakov, M. (2024). Elections in Wartime Ukraine Would Test Ukraine's Legal-Political Flexibility. *Kennan Cable*, January 2024 https://www.wilsoncenter.org/publication/kennan-cable-no-85-elections-wartime-ukraine-would-test-ukraines-legal-political.

Minakov, M. (2024). Five Years of Zelensky's Presidency. *Focus Ukraine*, May 21, https://www.wilsoncenter.org/blog-post/five-years-zelenskys-presidency.

Minakov, M. (2024). *Post-Soviet Human*. Stuttgart: ibidem Verlag.

Minakov, M. (2024). The Ukrainian Military Assistance Act Will Change the Situation on the Ground in Ukraine for the Better. *Focus Ukraine*, April 22, https://www.wilsoncenter.org/blog-post/ukrainian-military-assistance-act-will-change-situation-ground-ukraine-better.

Minakov, M. (2024). Ukrainian Society on the Anniversary of Twin Tragedies. Focus Ukraine, February 23, https://www.wilsoncenter.org/blog-post/ukrainian-society-anniversary-twin-tragedies.

Minakov, M. (2024). Winds of Change: Ukrainian Politics Reacts to the US Electoral Drama. Focus Ukraine, July 23, https://www.wilsoncenter.org/blog-post/winds-change-ukrainian-politics-reacts-us-electoral-drama.

Minakov, M. (2024). Zelensky's Sixth Independence Day Speech. *Focus Ukraine*, September 3, https://www.wilsoncenter.org/blog-post/zelenskys-sixth-independence-day-speech.

Minakov, M. & Rojansky, M. (2019). What to Expect from Ukraine's Next President. *Focus Ukraine*, April 25, https://www.wilsoncenter.org/blog-post/what-to-expect-ukraines-next-president.

Minakov, M., Mylovanov, T. (2016). Why the Post-Soviet Presidential Institution Is Flawed. *Vox Ukraine*, June 14, https://voxukraine.org/en/why-is-the-post-soviet-presidential-institution-flawed-en/.

Minakov, M., Prokip, A. (2019). Ukraine's Democratic Leakocracy. *Focus Ukraine*, February 27, 2020, https://www.wilsoncenter.org/blog-post/ukraines-democratic-leakocracy.

Minakov, M., Prokip, A. (2020). President Zelensky's Personnel Problem. *Focus Ukraine*, September 18, https://www.wilsoncenter.org/blog-post/president-zelenskys-personnel-problem.

Minakov, M., Rojansky, M. (2019). The First Six Months: An Assessment of Zelensky's Achievements. *Focus Ukraine*, November 13, https://www.wilsoncenter.org/blog-post/the-first-six-months-assessment-Zelenskys-achievements.

Mylovanov, T., Sologoub, I. (2021). The Development of Ukraine's Private Sector. In: Minakov, M. et al. (eds.). *From "The Ukraine" to Ukraine: A Contemporary History, 1991–2021.* Stuttgart: ibidem Verlag, 53–94.

Nikolov, Y. (2023). Тилові пацюки Міноборони під час війни «пиляють» на харчах для ЗСУ більше, ніж за мирного життя (from Ukrainian: Rear Rats of the Ministry of Defence 'Cut' More on Food for the Armed Forces During the War Than in Peaceful Life). *Dzerkalo Tyzhnya*, January 21, https://2cm.es/LS-n.

Oligarchs. *The Ukrainian Week*, November 11, https://ukrainianweek.com/twilight-of-the-oligarchs/; Grytsenko, O., Sorokin, O. (2019). Media Grab: Oligarchs, Pro-Russian Forces Use TV to Push Political Agenda. *Kyiv Post*, June 21, https://www.kyivpost.com/post/10260.

Onuch, O., & Hale, H. E. (2022). *The Zelensky Effect*. London: Hurst.

Opinion on the draft law "On Amendments to Certain Legislative Acts of Ukraine on improving the procedure for the selection of candidates for the position of judge of the Constitutional Court of Ukraine on a Competitive Basis". *The Venice Commission*, December 16-17, 2022, https://www.venice.coe.int/webforms/documents/?pdf=CDL-AD(2022)054-e.

Opinion on the Law on the Prevention of Threats to National Security, Associated with Excessive Influence of Persons Having Significant Economic or Political Weight in Public Life (Oligarchs). *The Venice Commission*, June 9-10, 2023, https://www.venice.coe.int/webforms/documents/?pdf=CDL-AD(2023)018-e.

Plokhy, S. (2015). *The last empire: The final days of the Soviet Union*. London: Hachette UK.

Presidential Election, 31 March and 21 April 2019. *OSCE*, April 2019, https://www.osce.org/odihr/elections/ukraine/407660.

Putin, V. (2022). On the Historical Unity of Russians and Ukrainians. *President of Russia Official Website*, https://www.prlib.ru/en/article-vladimir-putin-historical-unity-russians-and-ukrainians.

Sakwa, R. (2021). Sad Delusions: The Decline and Rise of Greater Europe. *Journal of Eurasian Studies*, 12(1), 5-18.

Skorkin, K. (2021). Merge and Rule: What's in Store for the Donetsk and Luhansk Republics. *Carnegie Endowment for International Peace (CEIP)*, March 16, https://n9.cl/99qmm.

Slunkin, P. (2022). Putin's Last Ally: Why the Belarusian Army Cannot Help Russia in Ukraine. *ECFR*, October 27, https://ecfr.eu/article/putins-last-ally-why-the-belarusian-army-cannot-help-russia-in-ukraine/.

Speech by President Volodymyr Zelenskyy on Independence Day of Ukraine. *The President of Ukraine Official Website*, August 24, 2022, https://www.president.gov.ua/en/news/privitannya-prezidenta-volodimira-zelenskogo-z-nagodi-dnya-n-77265.

Speech by President Volodymyr Zelenskyy on the Occasion of the 30th Anniversary of Ukraine's Independence. *The President of Ukraine Official Website*, August 24, 2021, https://www.president.gov.ua/en/news/promova-prezidenta-volodimira-zelenskogo-z-nagodi-30-yi-rich-70333.

Speech by the President of Ukraine During the Independence Day Festivities. *The President of Ukraine Official Website*, August 24, 2019, https://www.president.gov.ua/en/news/vistup-prezidenta-ukrayini-pid-chas-urochistostej-z-nagodi-d-56937.

Speech of the President on the Occasion of the Independence Day of Ukraine. *The President of Ukraine Official Website*, August 24, 2020, https://www.president.gov.ua/en/news/promova-prezidenta-z-nagodi-dnya-nezalezhnosti-ukrayini-62953.

Tarasov, S. (2023). The Role of Civil-Military Cooperation in the Protection of Civilians: The Ukraine Experience. *Center for Civilians in Conflict*, October 2023, https://2cm.es/LT2S.

The Effects of the War in Ukraine on the Western Balkans. *The International Institute for Strategic Studies*, August 2022, https://2cm.es/Oe3h.

The European Commission Recommends to Council Confirming Ukraine, Moldova and Georgia's Perspective to Become Members of the EU and Provides Its Opinion on Granting Them Candidate Status. *The European Commission*, June 17, 2022, https://ec.europa.eu/commission/presscorner/detail/en/IP_22_3790.

The future of the Ukrainian oligarchs (report). *Ukrainian Institute of Future*, June 13, 2019, https://uifuture.org/en/news-en/reportmaybutnieukrainskycholigarchiv/.

The War in Ukraine and Its Wider Impact on the Eurasia Region. *The International Institute for Strategic Studies*, May 19, 2022, https://2cm.es/LS-2.

Ukraine, Early Parliamentary Elections, 26 October 2014: Final Report. *OSCE*, December 19, 2014, https://www.osce.org/odihr/elections/ukraine/13255.

Urgent Joint Opinion of the Venice Commission and the Directorate General of Human Rights and Rule of Law (DGI) of the Council of Europe on the Legislative Situation Regarding Anti-Corruption Mechanisms Following Decision No. 13-R/2020 of the Constitutional Court Of Ukraine - CDL-PI(2020)018. *The Venice Commission*, pp. 18-20, https://www.venice.coe.int/webforms/documents/default.aspx?pdffile=CDL-PI(2020)018-e.

Urgent Opinion on the draft law "On Amendments to Certain Legislative Acts of Ukraine on improving the procedure for the selection of candidates for the position of judge of the Constitutional Court of Ukraine on a Competitive Basis". *The Venice Commission*, November 23, 2022, https://www.venice.coe.int/webforms/documents/?pdf=CDL-PI(2022)046-e.

Vitkine, B. (2022). Putin Changes Course With Mobilization of 300,000 Reservists and Nuclear Blackmail. *Le Monde*, September 21, https://n9.cl/iifb2.

Volkov, D. (2015). How Authentic is Putin's Approval Rating? *Carnegie Endowment for International Peace*, July 27, https://2cm.es/LSP3.

Weder di Mauro, B. et al. (2022). A Blueprint for the Reconstruction of Ukraine. *CEPR Office*, April 7, https://cepr.org/voxeu/columns/blueprint-reconstruction-ukraine.

Wilson, A. (2021). Faltering Fightback: Zelensky's Piecemeal Campaign Against Ukraine's Oligarchs. *European Council on Foreign Relations*, July 6, https://ecfr.eu/publication/faltering-fightback-zelenskys-piecemeal-campaign-against-ukraines-oligarchs/.

UKRAINIAN VOICES

Collected by Andreas Umland

1. *Mychailo Wynnyckyj*
   Ukraine's Maidan, Russia's War
   A Chronicle and Analysis of the Revolution of Dignity
   With a foreword by Serhii Plokhy
   ISBN 978-3-8382-1327-9

2. *Olexander Hryb*
   Understanding Contemporary Ukrainian and Russian Nationalism
   The Post-Soviet Cossack Revival and Ukraine's National Security
   With a foreword by Vitali Vitaliev
   ISBN 978-3-8382-1377-4

3. *Marko Bojcun*
   Towards a Political Economy of Ukraine
   Selected Essays 1990–2015
   With a foreword by John-Paul Himka
   ISBN 978-3-8382-1368-2

4. *Volodymyr Yermolenko (ed.)*
   Ukraine in Histories and Stories
   Essays by Ukrainian Intellectuals
   With a preface by Peter Pomerantsev
   ISBN 978-3-8382-1456-6

5. *Mykola Riabchuk*
   At the Fence of Metternich's Garden
   Essays on Europe, Ukraine, and Europeanization
   ISBN 978-3-8382-1484-9

6. *Marta Dyczok*
   Ukraine Calling
   A Kaleidoscope from Hromadske Radio 2016–2019
   With a foreword by Andriy Kulykov
   ISBN 978-3-8382-1472-6

7. *Olexander Scherba*
   Ukraine vs. Darkness
   Undiplomatic Thoughts
   With a foreword by Adrian Karatnycky
   ISBN 978-3-8382-1501-3

8. *Olesya Yaremchuk*
   Our Others
   Stories of Ukrainian Diversity
   With a foreword by Ostap Slyvynsky
   Translated from the Ukrainian by Zenia Tompkins and Hanna Leliv
   ISBN 978-3-8382-1475-7

9. *Nataliya Gumenyuk*
   Die verlorene Insel
   Geschichten von der besetzten Krim
   Mit einem Vorwort von Alice Bota
   Aus dem Ukrainischen übersetzt von Johann Zajaczkowski
   ISBN 978-3-8382-1499-3

10. *Olena Stiazhkina*
    Zero Point Ukraine
    Four Essays on World War II
    Translated from the Ukrainian by Svitlana Kulinska
    ISBN 978-3-8382-1550-1

11 Oleksii Sinchenko, Dmytro Stus, Leonid Finberg (compilers)
Ukrainian Dissidents
An Anthology of Texts
ISBN 978-3-8382-1551-8

12 John-Paul Himka
Ukrainian Nationalists and the Holocaust
OUN and UPA's Participation in the Destruction of Ukrainian Jewry, 1941–1944
ISBN 978-3-8382-1548-8

13 Andrey Demartino
False Mirrors
The Weaponization of Social Media in Russia's Operation to Annex Crimea
With a foreword by Oleksiy Danilov
ISBN 978-3-8382-1533-4

14 Svitlana Biedarieva (ed.)
Contemporary Ukrainian and Baltic Art
Political and Social Perspectives, 1991–2021
ISBN 978-3-8382-1526-6

15 Olesya Khromeychuk
A Loss
The Story of a Dead Soldier Told by His Sister
With a foreword by Andrey Kurkov
ISBN 978-3-8382-1570-9

16 Marieluise Beck (Hg.)
Ukraine verstehen
Auf den Spuren von Terror und Gewalt
Mit einem Vorwort von Dmytro Kuleba
ISBN 978-3-8382-1653-9

17 Stanislav Aseyev
Heller Weg
Geschichte eines Konzentrationslagers im Donbass 2017–2019
Aus dem Russischen übersetzt von Martina Steis und Charis Haska
ISBN 978-3-8382-1620-1

18 Mykola Davydiuk
Wie funktioniert Putins Propaganda?
Anmerkungen zum Informationskrieg des Kremls
Aus dem Ukrainischen übersetzt von Christian Weise
ISBN 978-3-8382-1628-7

19 Olesya Yaremchuk
Unsere Anderen
Geschichten ukrainischer Vielfalt
Aus dem Ukrainischen übersetzt von Christian Weise
ISBN 978-3-8382-1635-5

20 Oleksandr Mykhed
„Dein Blut wird die Kohle tränken"
Über die Ostukraine
Aus dem Ukrainischen übersetzt von Simon Muschick und Dario Planert
ISBN 978-3-8382-1648-5

21 Vakhtang Kipiani (Hg.)
Der Zweite Weltkrieg in der Ukraine
Geschichte und Lebensgeschichten
Aus dem Ukrainischen übersetzt von Margarita Grinko
ISBN 978-3-8382-1622-5

22 Vakhtang Kipiani (ed.)
World War II, Uncontrived and Unredacted
Testimonies from Ukraine
Translated from the Ukrainian by Zenia Tompkins and Daisy Gibbons
ISBN 978-3-8382-1621-8

23 Dmytro Stus
Vasyl Stus
Life in Creativity
Translated from the Ukrainian by
Ludmila Bachurina
ISBN 978-3-8382-1631-7

24 Vitalii Ogiienko (ed.)
The Holodomor and the
Origins of the Soviet Man
Reading the Testimony of
Anastasia Lysyvets
With forewords by Natalka
Bilotserkivets and Serhy
Yekelchyk
Translated from the Ukrainian by
Alla Parkhomenko and
Alexander J. Motyl
ISBN 978-3-8382-1616-4

25 Vladislav Davidzon
Jewish-Ukrainian Relations
and the Birth of a Political
Nation
Selected Writings 2013-2021
With a foreword by Bernard-
Henri Lévy
ISBN 978-3-8382-1509-9

26 Serhy Yekelchyk
Writing the Nation
The Ukrainian Historical
Profession in Independent
Ukraine and the Diaspora
ISBN 978-3-8382-1695-9

27 Ildi Eperjesi, Oleksandr
Kachura
Shreds of War
Fates from the Donbas Frontline
2014-2019
With a foreword by Olexiy
Haran
ISBN 978-3-8382-1680-5

28 Oleksandr Melnyk
World War II as an Identity
Project
Historicism, Legitimacy
Contests, and the (Re-)Con-
struction of Political Commu-
nities in Ukraine, 1939–1946
With a foreword by David R.
Marples
ISBN 978-3-8382-1704-8

29 Olesya Khromeychuk
Ein Verlust
Die Geschichte eines gefallenen
ukrainischen Soldaten, erzählt
von seiner Schwester
Mit einem Vorwort von Andrej
Kurkow
Aus dem Englischen übersetzt
von Lily Sophie
ISBN 978-3-8382-1770-3

30 Tamara Martsenyuk,
Tetiana Kostiuchenko (eds.)
Russia's War in Ukraine
During 2022
Personal Experiences of
Ukrainian Scholars
ISBN 978-3-8382-1757-4

31 Ildikó Eperjesi, Oleksandr
Kachura
Shreds of War. Vol. 2
Fates from Crimea 2015–2022
With an interview of Oleh
Sentsov
ISBN 978-3-8382-1780-2

32 Yuriy Lukanov
The Press
How Russia Destroyed Media
Freedom in Crimea
With a foreword by Taras Kuzio
ISBN 978-3-8382-1784-0

33 Megan Buskey
Ukraine Is Not Dead Yet
A Family Story of Exile and
Return
ISBN 978-3-8382-1691-1

34 *Vira Ageyeva*
Behind the Scenes of the Empire
Essays on Cultural Relationships between Ukraine and Russia
With a foreword by Oksana Zabuzhko
ISBN 978-3-8382-1748-2

35 *Marieluise Beck (ed.)*
Understanding Ukraine
Tracing the Roots of Terror and Violence
With a foreword by Dmytro Kuleba
ISBN 978-3-8382-1773-4

36 *Olesya Khromeychuk*
A Loss
The Story of a Dead Soldier Told by His Sister, 2nd edn.
With a foreword by Philippe Sands
With a preface by Andrii Kurkov
ISBN 978-3-8382-1870-0

37 *Taras Kuzio, Stefan Jajecznyk-Kelman*
Fascism and Genocide
Russia's War Against Ukrainians
ISBN 978-3-8382-1791-8

38 *Alina Nychyk*
Ukraine Vis-à-Vis Russia and the EU
Misperceptions of Foreign Challenges in Times of War, 2014–2015
With a foreword by Paul D'Anieri
ISBN 978-3-8382-1767-3

39 *Sasha Dovzhyk (ed.)*
Ukraine Lab
Global Security, Environment, and Disinformation Through the Prism of Ukraine
With a foreword by Rory Finnin
ISBN 978-3-8382-1805-2

40 *Serhiy Kvit*
Media, History, and Education
Three Ways to Ukrainian Independence
With a preface by Diane Francis
ISBN 978-3-8382-1807-6

41 *Anna Romandash*
Women of Ukraine
Reportages from the War and Beyond
ISBN 978-3-8382-1819-9

42 *Dominika Rank*
Matzewe in meinem Garten
Abenteuer eines jüdischen Heritage-Touristen in der Ukraine
ISBN 978-3-8382-1810-6

43 *Myroslaw Marynowytsch*
Das Universum hinter dem Stacheldraht
Memoiren eines sowjetukrainischen Dissidenten
Mit einem Vorwort von Timothy Snyder und einem Nachwort von Max Hartmann
ISBN 978-3-8382-1806-9

44 *Konstantin Sigow*
Für Deine und meine Freiheit
Europäische Revolutions- und Kriegserfahrungen im heutigen Kyjiw
Mit einem Vorwort von Karl Schlögel
Herausgegeben von Regula M. Zwahlen
ISBN 978-3-8382-1755-0

45 *Kateryna Pylypchuk*
The War that Changed Us
Ukrainian Novellas, Poems, and Essays from 2022
With a foreword by Victor Yushchenko
Paperback
ISBN 978-3-8382-1859-5
Hardcover
ISBN 978-3-8382-1860-1

46 Kyrylo Tkachenko
   Rechte Tür Links
   Radikale Linke in Deutschland,
   die Revolution und der Krieg in
   der Ukraine, 2013-2018
   ISBN 978-3-8382-1711-6

47 Alexander Strashny
   The Ukrainian Mentality
   An Ethno-Psychological,
   Historical and Comparative
   Exploration
   With a foreword by Antonina
   Lovochkina
   Translated from the Ukrainian
   by Michael M. Naydan and
   Olha Tytarenko
   ISBN 978-3-8382-1886-1

48 Alona Shestopalova
   From Screens to Battlefields
   Tracing the Construction of
   Enemies on Russian Television
   With a foreword by Nina
   Jankowicz
   ISBN 978-3-8382-1884-7

49 Iaroslav Petik
   **Politics and Society in the
   Ukrainian People's Republic
   (1917–1921) and
   Contemporary Ukraine
   (2013–2022)**
   A Comparative Analysis
   With a foreword by Mykola
   Doroshko
   ISBN 978-3-8382-1817-5

50 Serhii Plokhy
   **Der Mann mit der
   Giftpistole**
   Eine Spionagegeschichte aus dem
   Kalten Krieg
   ISBN 978-3-8382-1789-5

51 Vakhtang Kipiani
   **Ukrainische Dissidenten
   unter der Sowjetmacht**
   Im Kampf um Wahrheit und
   Freiheit
   Aus dem Ukrainischen übersetzt
   von Christian Weise
   ISBN 978-3-8382-1890-8

52 Dmytro Shestakov
   **When Businesses Test
   Hypotheses**
   A Four-Step Approach to Risk
   Management for Innovative
   Startups
   With a foreword by Anthony J.
   Tether
   ISBN 978-3-8382-1883-0

53 Larissa Babij
   A Kind of Refugee
   The Story of an American Who
   Refused to Leave Ukraine
   With a foreword by Vladislav
   Davidzon
   ISBN 978-3-8382-1898-4

54 Julia Davis
   In Their Own Words
   How Russian Propagandists
   Reveal Putin's Intentions
   With a foreword by Timothy
   Snyder
   ISBN 978-3-8382-1909-7

55 Sonya Atlantova, Oleksandr
   Klymenko
   Icons on Ammo Boxes
   Painting Life on the Remnants of
   Russia's War in Donbas, 2014-21
   Translated from the Ukrainian by
   Anastasya Knyazhytska
   ISBN 978-3-8382-1892-2

56 Leonid Ushkalov
   Catching an Elusive Bird
   The Life of Hryhorii Skovoroda
   Translated from the Ukrainian
   by Natalia Komarova
   ISBN 978-3-8382-1894-6

57 Vakhtang Kipiani
   **Ein Land weiblichen
   Geschlechts**
   Ukrainische Frauenschicksale
   im 20. und 21. Jahrhundert
   Aus dem Ukrainischen übersetzt
   von Christian Weise
   ISBN 978-3-8382-1891-5

58 Petro Rychlo
„Zerrissne Saiten einer überlauten Harfe ..."
Deutschjüdische Dichter der Bukowina
ISBN 978-3-8382-1893-9

59 Volodymyr Paniotto
Sociology in Jokes
An Entertaining Introduction
ISBN 978-3-8382-1857-1

60 Josef Wallmannsberger (ed.)
Executing Renaissances
The Poetological Nation of Ukraine
ISBN 978-3-8382-1741-3

61 Pavlo Kazarin
The Wild West of Eastern Europe
A Ukrainian Guide on Breaking Free from Empire
Translated from the Ukrainian by Dominique Hoffman
ISBN 978-3-8382-1842-7

62 Ernest Gyidel
Ukrainian Public Nationalism in the General Government
The Case of Krakivski Visti, 1940–1944
With a foreword by David R. Marples
ISBN 978-3-8382-1865-6

63 Olexander Hryb
Understanding Contemporary Russian Militarism
From Revolutionary to New Generation Warfare
With a foreword by Mark Laity
ISBN 978-3-8382-1927-1

64 Orysia Hrudka, Bohdan Ben
Dark Days, Determined People
Stories from Ukraine under Siege
With a foreword by Myroslav Marynovych
ISBN 978-3-8382-1958-5

65 Oleksandr Pankieiev (ed.)
Narratives of the Russo-Ukrainian War
A Look Within and Without
With a foreword by Natalia Khanenko-Friesen
ISBN 978-3-8382-1964-6

66 Roman Sohn, Ariana Gic (eds.)
Unrecognized War
The Fight for Truth about Russia's War on Ukraine
With a foreword by Viktor Yushchenko
ISBN 978-3-8382-1947-9

67 Paul Robert Magocsi
Ukraina Redux
Schon wieder die Ukraine ...
ISBN 978-3-8382-1942-4

68 Paul Robert Magocsi
L'Ucraina Ritrovata
Sullo Stato e l'Identità Nazionale
ISBN 978-3-8382-1982-0

69 Max Hartmann
Ein Schrei der Verzweiflung
Aquarelle von Danylo Movchan zu Russlands Krieg in der Ukraine
Mit einem Vorwort von Mateusz Sora
Paperback
ISBN 978-3-8382-2011-6
Hardcover
ISBN 978-3-8382-2012-3

70 Vakhtang Kebuladze (Hg.)
Die Zukunft, die wir uns wünschen
Essays aus der Ukraine
ISBN 978-3-8382-1531-0

71 Marieluise Beck, Jan Claas Behrends, Gelinada Grinchenko und Oksana Mikheieva (Hgg.)
   Deutsch-ukrainische Geschichten
   Bruchstücke aus einer gemeinsamen Vergangenheit
   ISBN 978-3-8382-2053-6

72 Pavlo Kazarin
   Der Wilde Westen Ost-Europas
   Der ukrainische Weg aus dem Imperium
   Aus dem Ukrainischen übersetzt von Christian Weise
   ISBN 978-3-8382-1843-4

73 Radomyr Mokryk
   Die ukrainischen »Sechziger«
   Chronologie einer Revolte
   ISBN 978-3-8382-1873-1

74 Leonid Finberg
   My Ukraine
   Rethinking the Past, Building the Present
   ISBN 978-3-8382-1974-5

75 Joseph Zissels
   Consider My Inmost Thoughts
   Essays, Lectures, and Interviews on Ukrainian Matters at the Turn of the Century
   ISBN 978-3-8382-1975-2

76 Margarita Yehorchenko, Iryna Berlyand, Ihor Vinokurov (eds.)
   Jewish Addresses in Ukraine
   A Guide-Book
   With a foreword by Leonid Finberg
   ISB 978-3-8382-1976-9

77 Viktoriia Grivina
   Kharkiv—A War City
   A Collection of Essays from 2022–23
   ISBN 978-3-8382-1988-2

78 Hjørdis Clemmensen, Viktoriia Grivina, Vasylysa Shchogoleva
   Kharkiv Is a Dream
   Public Art and Activism 2013–2023
   With a foreword by Bohdan Volynskyi
   ISBN 978-3-8382-2005-5

79 Olga Khomenko
   The Faraway Sky of Kyiv
   Ukrainians in the War
   With a foreword by Hiroaki Kuromiya
   ISBN 978-3-8382-2006-2

80 Daria Mattingly, Jonathon Vsetecka (eds.)
   The Holodomor in Global Perspective
   How the Famine in Ukraine Shaped the World
   With a foreword by Anne Applebaum
   ISBN 978-3-8382-1953-0

81 Olga Khomenko
   Ukrainians beyond Borders
   Nine Life Journeys Through the History of Eastern Europe
   With a foreword by Zbigniew Wojnowski
   ISBN 978-3-8382-2007-9

82 Mykhailo Minakov
   From Servant to Leader
   Chronicles of Ukraine under the Zelensky Presidency, 2019–2024
   With a foreword by John Lloyd
   ISBN 978-3-8382-2002-4

83 Volodymyr Hromov (ed.)
   A Ruined Home
   Sketches of War, 2022–2023
   ISBN 978-3-8382-2008-6

84 *Olha Tatokhina (ed.)*
 Why Do They Kill Our People?
 Russia's War Against Ukraine as
 Told by Ukrainians
 With a foreword by Volodymyr
 Yermolenko
 ISBN 978-3-8382-2056-7

Book series "Ukrainian Voices"

Coordinator
Andreas Umland, National University of Kyiv-Mohyla Academy

Editorial Board
Lesia Bidochko, National University of Kyiv-Mohyla Academy
Svitlana Biedarieva, George Washington University, DC, USA
Ivan Gomza, Kyiv School of Economics, Ukraine
Natalie Jaresko, Aspen Institute, Kyiv/Washington
Olena Lennon, University of New Haven, West Haven, USA
Kateryna Yushchenko, First Lady of Ukraine 2005-2010, Kyiv
Oleksandr Zabirko, University of Regensburg, Germany

Advisory Board
Iuliia Bentia, National Academy of Arts of Ukraine, Kyiv
Natalya Belitser, Pylyp Orlyk Institute for Democracy, Kyiv
Oleksandra Bienert, Humboldt University of Berlin, Germany
Sergiy Bilenky, Canadian Institute of Ukrainian Studies, Toronto
Tymofii Brik, Kyiv School of Economics, Ukraine
Olga Brusylovska, Mechnikov National University, Odesa
Mariana Budjeryn, Harvard University, Cambridge, USA
Volodymyr Bugrov, Shevchenko National University, Kyiv
Olga Burlyuk, University of Amsterdam, The Netherlands
Yevhen Bystrytsky, NAS Institute of Philosophy, Kyiv
Andrii Danylenko, Pace University, New York, USA
Vladislav Davidzon, Atlantic Council, Washington/Paris
Mykola Davydiuk, Think Tank "Polityka," Kyiv
Andrii Demartino, National Security and Defense Council, Kyiv
Vadym Denisenko, Ukrainian Institute for the Future, Kyiv
Oleksandr Donii, Center for Political Values Studies, Kyiv
Volodymyr Dubovyk, Mechnikov National University, Odesa
Volodymyr Dubrovskiy, CASE Ukraine, Kyiv
Diana Dutsyk, National University of Kyiv-Mohyla Academy
Marta Dyczok, Western University, Ontario, Canada
Yevhen Fedchenko, National University of Kyiv-Mohyla Academy
Sofiya Filonenko, State Pedagogical University of Berdyansk
Oleksandr Fisun, Karazin National University, Kharkiv
Oksana Forostyna, Webjournal "Ukraina Moderna," Kyiv
Roman Goncharenko, Broadcaster "Deutsche Welle," Bonn
George Grabowicz, Harvard University, Cambridge, USA
Gelinada Grinchenko, Karazin National University, Kharkiv
Kateryna Härtel, Federal Union of European Nationalities, Brussels
Nataliia Hendel, University of Geneva, Switzerland
Anton Herashchenko, Kyiv School of Public Administration
John-Paul Himka, University of Alberta, Edmonton
Ola Hnatiuk, National University of Kyiv-Mohyla Academy
Oleksandr Holubov, Broadcaster "Deutsche Welle," Bonn
Yaroslav Hrytsak, Ukrainian Catholic University, Lviv
Oleksandra Humenna, National University of Kyiv-Mohyla Academy
Tamara Hundorova, NAS Institute of Literature, Kyiv
Oksana Huss, University of Bologna, Italy
Oleksandra Iwaniuk, University of Warsaw, Poland
Mykola Kapitonenko, Shevchenko National University, Kyiv
Georgiy Kasianov, Marie Curie-Skłodowska University, Lublin
Vakhtang Kebuladze, Shevchenko National University, Kyiv
Natalia Khanenko-Friesen, University of Alberta, Edmonton
Victoria Khiterer, Millersville University of Pennsylvania, USA
Oksana Kis, NAS Institute of Ethnology, Lviv
Pavlo Klimkin, Center for National Resilience and Development, Kyiv
Oleksandra Kolomiiets, Center for Economic Strategy, Kyiv

Sergiy Korsunsky, Kobe Gakuin University, Japan
Nadiia Koval, Kyiv School of Economics, Ukraine
Volodymyr Kravchenko, University of Alberta, Edmonton
Oleksiy Kresin, NAS Koretskiy Institute of State and Law, Kyiv
Anatoliy Kruglashov, Fedkovych National University, Chernivtsi
Andrey Kurkov, PEN Ukraine, Kyiv
Ostap Kushnir, Lazarski University, Warsaw
Taras Kuzio, National University of Kyiv-Mohyla Academy
Serhii Kvit, National University of Kyiv-Mohyla Academy
Yuliya Ladygina, The Pennsylvania State University, USA
Yevhen Mahda, Institute of World Policy, Kyiv
Victoria Malko, California State University, Fresno, USA
Yulia Marushevska, Security and Defense Center (SAND), Kyiv
Myroslav Marynovych, Ukrainian Catholic University, Lviv
Oleksandra Matviichuk, Center for Civil Liberties, Kyiv
Mykhailo Minakov, Kennan Institute, Washington, USA
Anton Moiseienko, The Australian National University, Canberra
Alexander Motyl, Rutgers University-Newark, USA
Vlad Mykhnenko, University of Oxford, United Kingdom
Vitalii Ogiienko, Ukrainian Institute of National Remembrance, Kyiv
Olga Onuch, University of Manchester, United Kingdom
Olesya Ostrovska, Museum "Mystetskyi Arsenal," Kyiv
Anna Osypchuk, National University of Kyiv-Mohyla Academy
Oleksandr Pankieiev, University of Alberta, Edmonton
Oleksiy Panych, Publishing House "Dukh i Litera," Kyiv
Valerii Pekar, Kyiv-Mohyla Business School, Ukraine
Yohanan Petrovsky-Shtern, Northwestern University, Chicago
Serhii Plokhy, Harvard University, Cambridge, USA
Andrii Portnov, Viadrina University, Frankfurt-Oder, Germany
Maryna Rabinovych, Kyiv School of Economics, Ukraine
Valentyna Romanova, Institute of Developing Economies, Tokyo
Natalya Ryabinska, Collegium Civitas, Warsaw, Poland
Darya Tsymbalyk, University of Oxford, United Kingdom
Vsevolod Samokhvalov, University of Liege, Belgium
Orest Semotiuk, Franko National University, Lviv
Viktoriya Sereda, NAS Institute of Ethnology, Lviv
Anton Shekhovtsov, University of Vienna, Austria
Andriy Shevchenko, Media Center Ukraine, Kyiv
Oxana Shevel, Tufts University, Medford, USA
Pavlo Shopin, National Pedagogical Dragomanov University, Kyiv
Karina Shyrokykh, Stockholm University, Sweden
Nadja Simon, freelance interpreter, Cologne, Germany
Olena Snigova, NAS Institute for Economics and Forecasting, Kyiv
Ilona Solohub, Analytical Platform "VoxUkraine," Kyiv
Iryna Solonenko, LibMod - Center for Liberal Modernity, Berlin
Galyna Solovei, National University of Kyiv-Mohyla Academy
Sergiy Stelmakh, NAS Institute of World History, Kyiv
Olena Stiazhkina, NAS Institute of the History of Ukraine, Kyiv
Dmitri Stratievski, Osteuropa Zentrum (OEZB), Berlin
Dmytro Stus, National Taras Shevchenko Museum, Kyiv
Frank Sysyn, University of Toronto, Canada
Olha Tokariuk, Center for European Policy Analysis, Washington
Olena Tregub, Independent Anti-Corruption Commission, Kyiv
Hlib Vyshlinsky, Centre for Economic Strategy, Kyiv
Mychailo Wynnyckyj, National University of Kyiv-Mohyla Academy
Yelyzaveta Yasko, NGO "Yellow Blue Strategy," Kyiv
Serhy Yekelchyk, University of Victoria, Canada
Victor Yushchenko, President of Ukraine 2005-2010, Kyiv
Oleksandr Zaitsev, Ukrainian Catholic University, Lviv
Kateryna Zarembo, National University of Kyiv-Mohyla Academy
Yaroslav Zhalilo, National Institute for Strategic Studies, Kyiv
Sergei Zhuk, Ball State University at Muncie, USA
Alina Zubkovych, Nordic Ukraine Forum, Stockholm
Liudmyla Zubrytska, National University of Kyiv-Mohyla Academy

Friends of the Series

Ana Maria Abulescu, University of Bucharest, Romania
Łukasz Adamski, Centrum Mieroszewskiego, Warsaw
Marieluise Beck, LibMod—Center for Liberal Modernity, Berlin
Marc Berensen, King's College London, United Kingdom
Johannes Bohnen, BOHNEN Public Affairs, Berlin
Karsten Brüggemann, University of Tallinn, Estonia
Ulf Brunnbauer, Leibniz Institute (IOS), Regensburg
Martin Dietze, German-Ukrainian Culture Society, Hamburg
Gergana Dimova, Florida State University, Tallahassee/London
Caroline von Gall, Goethe University, Frankfurt-Main
Zaur Gasimov, Rhenish Friedrich Wilhelm University, Bonn
Armand Gosu, University of Bucharest, Romania
Thomas Grant, University of Cambridge, United Kingdom
Gustav Gressel, European Council on Foreign Relations, Berlin
Rebecca Harms, European Centre for Press & Media Freedom, Leipzig
André Härtel, Stiftung Wissenschaft und Politik, Berlin/Brussels
Marcel Van Herpen, The Cicero Foundation, Maastricht
Richard Herzinger, freelance analyst, Berlin
Mieste Hotopp-Riecke, ICATAT, Magdeburg
Nico Lange, Munich Security Conference, Berlin
Martin Malek, freelance analyst, Vienna
Ingo Mannteufel, Broadcaster "Deutsche Welle," Bonn
Carlo Masala, Bundeswehr University, Munich
Wolfgang Mueller, University of Vienna, Austria
Dietmar Neutatz, Albert Ludwigs University, Freiburg
Torsten Oppelland, Friedrich Schiller University, Jena
Niccolò Pianciola, University of Padua, Italy
Gerald Praschl, German-Ukrainian Forum (DUF), Berlin
Felix Riefer, Think Tank Ideenagentur-Ost, Düsseldorf
Stefan Rohdewald, University of Leipzig, Germany
Sebastian Schäffer, Institute for the Danube Region (IDM), Vienna
Felix Schimansky-Geier, Friedrich Schiller University, Jena
Ulrich Schneckener, University of Osnabrück, Germany
Winfried Schneider-Deters, freelance analyst, Heidelberg/Kyiv
Gerhard Simon, University of Cologne, Germany
Kai Struve, Martin Luther University, Halle/Wittenberg
David Stulik, European Values Center for Security Policy, Prague
Andrzej Szeptycki, University of Warsaw, Poland
Philipp Ther, University of Vienna, Austria
Stefan Troebst, University of Leipzig, Germany

[Please send requests for changes in, corrections of, and additions to, this list to andreas.umland@stanforalumni.org.]

ibidem.eu